D1001855

THE SAGA OF THEMISTOCLES

ASPECTS OF GREEK AND ROMAN LIFE

General Editor: H. H. Scullard

THE SAGA
OF
THEMISTOCLES

Robert J. Lenardon

with 35 illustrations and 4 maps

THAMES AND HUDSON

Library of Congress Catalog card number 77-83213

PRINTED IN GREAT BRITAIN BY
LATIMER TREND & COMPANY LTD
PLYMOUTH

CONTENTS

LIST OF ILLUSTRATIONS

Dedicated to my mother
and the memory of my father

PREFACE

I owe so much to so many people over the years – teachers, colleagues, students and friends – without whom it would have been impossible to write this biography of Themistocles; and, although I cannot list them all by name, my heartfelt gratitude is none the less sincere. Colleagues in the Department of Classics at the Ohio State University have been particularly helpful: Professor Charles L. Babcock has been willing to offer advice during numerous discussions concerning problems of every sort, and he has been generous enough to read the manuscript carefully and suggest many improvements. Professor Stephen V. Tracy has been helpful in my selection of photographs of the *ostraka*; and Professor Kenneth M. Abbott has provided valuable information by consulting on my behalf the expert opinion of Dr Emmerich von Haam. Professor Mark P. O. Morford, as chairman, has continually offered sympathetic understanding and support, and has been most cooperative, along with Dean Arthur E. Adams and the College of Humanities, in the assignment of a quarter of research duty.

Others too have contributed. Professor A. Geoffrey Woodhead has always been most encouraging, and was also kind enough to read the manuscript in its entirety. In particular he has made significant corrections in my translation of the Epistles; and concerning difficulties in their manuscript, Professor Mervin R. Dilts has answered many questions. Mr Charles A. McCloud has made various suggestions for stylistic improvements. Miss Cathy Reid has been extremely patient in typing more than one draft of the manuscript; and an equally patient Mrs Colette Armstrong has shared in the task. Mr Roland F. Haag has been very helpful in the preparation of the Indexes.

I am also grateful to the Fellows of Corpus Christi College, Cambridge University (and once again to Geoffrey Woodhead) for the honour of being invited to spend a term with them in the spring of 1971. Among the plethora of enrichments and rewards was an unforgettable trip to Wellingborough for a gathering of ancient historians and a most pleasurable meeting with Professor H. H. Scullard; and thus, eventually, plans for this biography were initiated. Professor Scullard and Thames and Hudson have been more understanding than I deserve; for this I am very thankful.

Finally I should like to express my gratitude to my friend and mentor, Professor Malcolm F. McGregor, whose kindly guidance and inspired teaching first led me to the study of Themistocles. I am also grateful for the many corrections that he has made in both the content and style of this book.

The Ohio State University
Columbus, 1976

CHAPTER I

INTRODUCTION

Many years ago when I first began a serious study of Themistocles, my ultimate goal was to write a biography of this great Athenian statesman and general. But faced with the overwhelming problems (not least of all chronological), which soon became only too apparent, I thought that definitive solutions had to be found before any lucid interpretation of his life could be attempted. I have now come to realize that my youthful and optimistic belief in the possibility of establishing firm answers was naïve and unwarranted. Our extant sources, by their very nature, are just not adequate for dogmatic conclusions about many issues, some most crucial; and until new evidence appears we must frequently be content with possibilities and probabilities and forego the comforting reassurance of irrefutable fact. Discoveries such as the Decree of Themistocles and new *ostraka* reaffirm one's hope that fresh evidence can on occasion come to light. Unfortunately, however, the debate that continues about the authenticity of this decree in particular may very well enhance, rather than alleviate, our dilemmas.

I have often been asked the disturbing question: 'Is it really possible to write a biography of Themistocles at all?'[1] An immediate, irresponsible and unfair retort leaps readily to mind: 'Plutarch, at any rate, thought that he could.' But serious reflection reveals that the question is well-intended and important, with many searching implications. Is our evidence for Themistocles too meagre for a substantial recreation of his career that will be satisfactorily meaningful and complete? To what degree do we possess information that will prove historically gratifying and factually reliable? At the mercy of his sources, can the biographer, at best, merely highlight stages in Themistocles' life, the actual details of which have already long ago become irrevocably distorted through the colouring and invention of literary and political bias and the exaggeration of heroic legend?

Yes, these limitations are very real. But they exist in one degree or another for virtually every significant figure in the ancient as well as in the modern world. Yet, undeterred, writers justifiably compose biographies – of various kinds, to be sure, in length, quality, purpose and nature. Can we ever really know (or would we ever want actually to reproduce) any man's life in its entirety? How soon, even before his death, will imagination have obscured reality, not only in the multiple reconstructions and evaluations of events themselves but also in the more insubstantial elucidations and judgments concerning character, emotions and psychology?

Many stories (too often blatant in their contradictions) were embedded in the tradition that grew up about Themistocles, apparently from the very beginning; and even a Thucydides is wary of pronouncing upon the veracity of much that he sees fit to consider. It would then be presumptuous and foolhardy for us today to imagine that we are able confidently to reconstruct the hidden issues and circumstances surrounding, for example, Themistocles' role in connection with Salamis, or his condemnations and flight. The historian of antiquity need only contemplate the pitfalls in the quest for truth about events contemporary with himself to feel even more deeply the pangs of doubt and dismay. The brutal assassination of President Kennedy – to mention only one outstanding and tragic example – has been and continues to be voluminously investigated and reported; and the terrifying moment of the murder itself was actually caught and preserved for posterity by the lens of more than one camera. Yet the essential questions remain unanswered, perhaps forever, although conjecture and debate will continue.

The hazards in the writing of history are deceptive and treacherous; and many of the immense and innumerable difficulties that it inevitably imposes defy resolution. Aristotle in a famous passage in his *Poetics*, which attempts to define the fundamental differences between the poet and the historian, strikes at the very heart of the matter:[2]

The work of the poet is not to relate what has happened but the kinds of things that may happen [or have happened] and are possible according to probability or necessity. For the distinction between the historian and the poet does not lie in the composition of verse or prose, since the books of Herodotus would be no less a species of history, with or without metre. Rather the essential difference is defined by the fact that the historian records what has happened, the poet, the sorts of things that may happen [or have happened]. Therefore poetry is more philosophical and serious than history; for poetry is more concerned with the universal, whereas the historian deals with the particular. The universal involves the types of things that a type of person happens to say or to do according to likelihood or necessity; and poetry attaches its identifications with the universal as its aim. But the particular deals with what Alcibiades actually did or experienced.

The fascinating and perplexing difficulties in the translation and interpretation of this controversial pronouncement cannot be given their full due, but in this context a few basic observations are very much in order. Both generic and poetic characteristics are inherent in the conception and execution of the universal masterpieces of both Herodotus and Thucydides; and, although Aristotle is surely right in insisting that history must be primarily concerned with the truth about the past, nevertheless he presents us, by implication, with a frustrating paradox. The historian, by the very nature of things, cannot always know with certainty and report what actually was; instead, more often than not, he is compelled to decide what was possible and very well might have happened, according to probability and necessity on the basis of the available evidence, and, by the same token, to attempt to establish not only what a Themistocles said or did, but also what he is likely to have said and done. It is fundamental, albeit disconcerting, to realize that the realms of the poet and the historian are not mutually exclusive. What has happened, to be sure, is a fact. What may happen or might have happened has the potential of truth or falsehood, until some absolute criterion for judgment (in itself a problematical concept) is forthcoming. When the past is seen through the perceptions of an artist, historical fact, conjecture and interpretation are transformed by his genius into a dramatic recreation embodying the most profound truths of poetic composition.

Our primary goal, as Aristotle observes, is to establish as well as we can the facts about Themistocles. Of fundamental importance, therefore, is an evaluation of the ancient literary evidence, in the light of which not only epigraphical and archaeological finds but also the theories of modern scholarship must be assessed. Historians, however, are by no means agreed about many of their attitudes and methods in the treatment of our sources; and indeed only a few very obvious criteria involving the rejection of the utterly incredible or ridiculous appear, in any degree, to possess ultimate validity. Most judgments of necessity remain personal and subjective mainly because of the very nature and character of ancient historiography in general (with its novelistic techniques in the depiction of incidents, scenes and characters) and the haphazard fate of its survival. Some rely heavily on the fifth-century testimony of Herodotus and Thucydides and view later unique information with serious reservations; yet, at the same time, it will be readily admitted that the art and theology of Herodotean epic history pose their own special problems, coupled with an alleged bias against Themistocles as a result of hostile Alcmaeonid sources. Thucydides, too, is not above suspicion, since his narrative centring upon Themistocles' flight to Persia is coloured by the supposedly uncharacteristic inclusion of intimate, dramatic details. What then are we to make of the additions and embellishments in the later tradition?

It must be remembered that many writers, earlier than or contemporary with Herodotus or Thucydides, and of some quality as far as we can ascertain, wrote about the Persian Wars and Themistocles (Charon of Lampsacus or Hellanicus of Lesbos, for example); their works, surviving today only in fragments, were available to ancient authors, along with other types of non-literary evidence now lost. Late accounts are likely to preserve authentic material and in addition actually do provide credible interpretations that cannot be ignored, even though their sources may or may not be identified. Thus any item of information that is not demonstrably false, beyond a shadow of a doubt, must receive respectful consideration; and perhaps in the last analysis all that we can do, for better or worse, is to attempt to fit together all the pieces, even those of dubious legitimacy, in the creation of a portrait, however flawed.[3] Of course the most careful and analytical evaluation of any evidence may display a relentless logic that is compelling and attractive, but it does not necessarily follow that the ensuing reconstruction of events must be historically accurate. We should be wary of being seduced by a brilliant hypothesis into believing that it represents anything more than a probable likelihood. I need only refer again to a contemporary example. If the incredible revelations of Watergate had never been made public, a logical and credible history of the Nixon administration would inevitably be not only incomplete but inaccurate. The platitude that truth is stranger than fiction is most disturbing to any serious historian.

We have, transmitted to us from antiquity, a cumulative tradition about Themistocles that has never really remained static; over the centuries it has been continually enlarged and often enriched by the discoveries and theories of modern scholars. In the writing of this book I have taken for granted that primary among my many responsibilities is to communicate the ancient tradition, in particular, as completely and faithfully as possible. At times I have been overwhelmed by the extent to which we are literally at the mercy of our sources. The one thing that we do know for certain is what Herodotus, Thucydides, Plutarch and the others have said about Themistocles or, at least, what their edited texts, as we know them, tell us that they said.

Thus I have taken great pains to place before the reader all the essential ancient testimony, either in close paraphrase, or, as is more often the case, in direct translations of my own. My emphasis, therefore, had to be upon the texts of the most crucial importance both in substance and quantity – those of Aeschylus, Herodotus, Thucydides, Diodorus, Plutarch and the spurious Epistles that have come down to us under Themistocles' name. Scholars differ in their appraisals of the worth of these letters; but I should be hard pressed to decide whether they contain a greater proportion of fiction than either Diodorus or

Plutarch. At any rate they are interesting and entertaining, and most certainly controversial; and I am pleased to have the opportunity to offer them for the first time in a complete English translation.

My method of presentation is designed to allow the reader to appreciate and evaluate the literary and historical qualities of the original sources albeit in translation; thus, he is placed in a position where he can make decisions for himself that would otherwise be impossible, not only about the testimony itself but also about many of the hypotheses that it has inspired. To read the evidence and observe at first hand its inherent and sometimes insuperable problems is a far different and, I believe, more rewarding experience than merely to be submitted to even a judicious interpretation. It can be sobering, indeed, to turn from the elaborate reconstructions of Themistocles' activities in the period from 500 to 480 to the actual meagre and ambiguous testimony out of which these reconstructions have been made. In the reporting of the same episode by several authors duplication of material is both inevitable and desirable; for the awareness of subtle differences in method, detail and style is not only pleasurable in itself but often essential for historical judgment.

I have entitled this biography *The Saga of Themistocles* with full awareness of all that this implies. The headings of the various chapters have also been deliberately chosen to underline the realization that the ancient tradition for his life has obviously been embellished from the very outset with recurrent elements and themes of various kinds to be found in mythology, folk-tale and legend.[4] Aeschylus in *The Persians* sheds an inspiring aura of tragic and fatalistic grandeur in his poetic treatment of the battle of Salamis. Herodotus' account is replete with divine intervention and heroic characterization; for Themistocles he composes speeches and provides psychological motivation in the manner of epic. Thucydides can 'quote' Themistocles' letter to Artaxerxes and in his narration of the flight from Argos to Persia he scrupulously preserves a wealth of dramatic detail that smacks suspiciously of both oral invention and literary artifice. Later accounts are flagrant in their exaggerated additions to the journey. A moral Plutarch writes of the extraordinary childhood of Themistocles and his youthful struggle for recognition in such a way as to suggest the hero rather than the man; and in his account of conflicting versions of various stages in Themistocles' career he reveals the multi-faceted and dubious accretions. The meeting with Xerxes and the suicide are each in their own way designed to mete out poetic justice on a heroic and dramatic scale. Each reader will rightfully make his own judgments about the extent of legendary distortion in the tradition, and I shall not even attempt here to list all the numerous examples. But the thirty-seven anecdotes collected in the last chapter are very much a case in point.

Of course it is true that specific facts in the real life of any great man like Themistocles will inevitably duplicate to some extent the thematic material of saga; but as his legend becomes generic, invention increasingly blurs the thin lines between history and fiction.

My purpose has not been to write another history of the Persian Wars; rather I have allowed the sources for Themistocles himself to determine the form and emphasis of my investigation. Thus his role at Salamis and the events of his later career, which are more fully documented, receive the more lengthy treatment that they deserve.

For the most part I have used Romanized forms for proper names; but I have tried to choose commonly accepted spellings rather than to be absolutely consistent. Also I employ the following designations: Hellas and Hellenes, not Greece and Greeks; Spartans, not Lacedaemonians; Persians, not Medes, although I keep the term Medism for collusion with the Persians; and Suidas, not the *Suda*. Specialized bibliography is incorporated into the notes; usually I refer to the most recent studies or to those that will afford easy access to the voluminous literature. In general I have used the Greek and Roman texts of the *Loeb Classical Library* for my references, although the translations are my own. There is a special index isolating the ancient authors quoted or mentioned. All dates are BC unless otherwise indicated.

CHAPTER II

ORIGINS OF A HERO

PARENTS AND FAMILY

Our text of Plutarch's *Life of Themistocles* begins as follows (an opening sentence or sentences may be lost):

As for Themistocles, his family background was too obscure to insure political recognition, for he was the son of Neocles (of the deme Phrearrhioi and the tribe Leontis), who was not among those who were very conspicuous at Athens.[5]

Although Themistocles' family was politically obscure we are not to assume automatically that his father Neocles or his ancestors in general were financially or even socially insignificant.[6] For Themistocles belonged in all likelihood to the family of the Lycomidae, a clan of substance and nobility. Plutarch infers as much:

It is evident that Themistocles belonged to the family of the Lycomidae for, when the chapel (*telesterion*) at Phlya, which belonged to the Lycomidae, was burned by the Persians, he himself had it rebuilt and adorned with paintings at his own expense, as Simonides has stated.[7]

This chapel was dedicated to the worship of Demeter and Persephone among other deities and the Lycomid clan had connections with the celebration of the mysteries at Eleusis.[8] Themistocles' deme (parish) Phrearrhioi was situated in southern Attica near the mining district of Laurium, the silver from which was later to play such an important role in his life. The deme of Phlya, the site of the Lycomid chapel, was probably to the northeast of Athens. Themistocles' residence in Athens itself belonged in the deme of Melite, southwest of the Potters' Quarter (Ceramicus).[9] There is little of worth to be interpreted from these meagre facts in terms of Themistocles himself or his family – their sources of income, prestige and the like – although hypotheses have not been lacking.[10] We know little about Neocles, Themistocles' father. Epistle

1 tells us that he had spent some time in Argos and had friends there, and Nepos confirms what we have already deduced, namely that he was a man of high birth (*generosus*).[11]

We possess more information about Themistocles' mother, most of which is extremely dubious. Plutarch maintains that Themistocles was of mixed parentage (*νόθος*) and quotes as proof the following epitaph, which is obviously a late invention:

> I am Abrotonon, a Thracian woman;
> but I say that I gave birth to Themistocles
> the Great for the Hellenes.

Phanias, however, writes that the mother of Themistocles was not Thracian but Carian, and her name was not Abrotonon but Euterpe, and Neanthes even gives her a city in Caria as well, Halicarnassus.[12]

Nepos, on the other hand, tells us: 'Neocles married an Acarnanian woman, a citizen [of Athens], who bore Themistocles.'[13]

It is impossible to decide which, if any, of these versions is correct; and we become even more suspicious upon being explicitly told elsewhere that Themistocles' mother was a prostitute or slave (*hetaira*), since Abrotonon (or Habrotonon) appears as a stock name for the harlot in New Comedy.[14]

Thus one might well wonder how Nepos knows that the mother of Themistocles was an Athenian citizen or that Neocles ever married her at all. For there is an inherent ambiguity in the word *νόθος* itself. It means 'of mixed parentage', or 'alien' (i.e. having a non-Athenian mother), but also 'bastard'.

Plutarch tells an anecdote that is of no help whatsoever, since it seems to be patently contrived primarily to establish the clever and liberal spirit expected of a young Themistocles:

Those of mixed parentage (*νόθοι*) used to frequent Cynosarges, a gymnasium of Heracles outside the gates; for he also was not legitimate (*γνήσιος*) among the gods but there was something alien about him because his mother was mortal. And so Themistocles persuaded some of the youths who were well born to go to Cynosarges and work out with him. It is thought that by this clever manoeuvre he removed the distinction between those of mixed parentage (*νόθοι*) and pure Athenians (*γνήσιοι*).[15]

All that we can conclude is that Themistocles' mother was probably of foreign extraction. This coupled with later exaggeration contributed to the depiction of Themistocles as somewhat less than a true aristocrat, despite the probability of his sterling Lycomid connections. There can be no doubt, however, about the fact that Themistocles himself, like his father, was a full-fledged Athenian citizen. Therefore it is misleading to call him an alien.

Much discussion has centred about the propriety of the Roman designation 'new man' (*novus homo*) that has been applied to Themistocles. In my view it is most apt, if we are clear in understanding it to mean that he had very much to make his own way in politics and nothing more, i.e., his family generally was politically obscure and his father Neocles in particular had never pursued a career in politics. This, at any rate, is the impression given by the sources.

IMMEDIATE RELATIVES

Other immediate relatives of Themistocles are named as follows: An uncle, also called Themistocles, mentioned in Epistle 8, whom some scholars believe to be invented; others suggest he was eponymous archon in 493/2.[16]

A brother, Agesilaus, who also is considered to be fictitious. Plutarch records the following heroic tale about him, on the authority of an Agatharchides of Samos: When Xerxes was anchored near Artemisium, the Athenians in their consternation sent Agesilaus, Themistocles' brother, to act as a spy, even though Neocles, his father, dreamed that his son lost both his hands. Agesilaus, disguised as a Persian, killed Mardonius, one of the King's bodyguards, thinking that he was the King himself. He was arrested and brought in bonds before Xerxes who was about to sacrifice to the god of the Sun. Thereupon Agesilaus put his right hand on the altar and without a cry endured the amputation. When released from his bonds he exclaimed: 'We Athenians are all men of this sort; and if you don't believe me, I shall also offer my left hand for sacrifice.'

Xerxes was exceedingly taken aback and ordered that he be put under guard.[17]

A nephew Phrasicles, whom we shall mention again shortly, is also known. Since *he* at least seems to be real, Themistocles must have had a brother or a sister.

Thus we may draw up the following stemma:

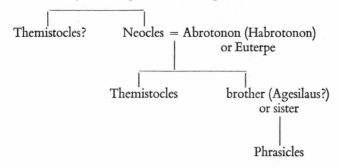

YOUTH AND CHARACTER

Plutarch has much to say about Themistocles' boyhood, education and character.[18] As a youth he was impetuous, naturally clever, and by choice drawn to a life of political renown. Unlike the other boys he spent his leisure time not in idleness or play but in composing or rehearsing to himself mock speeches in accusation or defence of one or another of his colleagues. As a result his teacher was inclined to remark ominously: 'My boy, there is going to be nothing insignificant about you; somehow or other you will become a great man, either for good or evil.'

Plutarch also informs us of Themistocles' reluctance to study lessons of an ethical nature or those intended to cultivate character and the graceful pleasures of the liberal arts. He remained unskilled in music but was instead intent upon practical and political subjects. Plutarch rightly rejects, on chronological grounds, Stesimbrotus' assertion that Themistocles was a pupil of Anaxagoras or the physicist Melissus, although it is not impossible that he knew these men in his maturity. Plutarch prefers rather to believe those who say that Themistocles studied with Mnesiphilus, who was from the same deme, Phrearrhioi – a man described as neither a rhetorician nor a physical philosopher, but one devoted to the study of wisdom (σοφία), in the sense of cleverness in politics and practical intelligence. It has been conjectured that this designation of Mnesiphilus as Themistocles' teacher is merely an elaborative invention based upon Herodotus' account of how the Athenian Mnesiphilus advised Themistocles at Salamis.[19] But several *ostraka* bearing Mnesiphilus' name have been found belonging to the 480s, possibly to be linked to the very year of Megacles' ostracism, 487/6, when Themistocles may also have been a candidate; and Plutarch records that Mnesiphilus helped and encouraged Themistocles when he was at first disliked for his rashness and lack of restraint. Thus Mnesiphilus seems to be very real indeed, a politically active influence upon the career of his younger fellow demesman, Themistocles.[20]

Plutarch comments upon the impetuous and erratic nature of Themistocles in his youth before he became tempered by training and experience. But Plutarch does not believe (nor can we, for obvious reasons) the exaggerated claims that his father Neocles disinherited him and his mother committed suicide because of his disgrace. In this context Plutarch relates the story of an opposite tenor that had Themistocles' father attempt to keep him from politics by pointing out old triremes wrecked and abandoned on the seashore to remind him of how the people treated their leaders once they were of no further use.

Conflicting too are accounts of Themistocles' nature upon reaching maturity. Some maintained, according to Plutarch, that he was eager to make money because he needed a generous income to indulge his fondness for lavish entertaining. Others instead accused him of great stinginess and avarice, saying that he would even sell provisions sent to him as gifts.[21]

These traditions, amply elaborated in the many anecdotes about Themistocles, are typical inventions for any hero, fictitious or otherwise; consequently one is hard put, if not foolish, to sift them for any kind of specific truth. The consensus that he was ambitious and vehement in his rivalries is a likely guess; and it is easy to believe (although not inevitable) that a Themistocles would be a practical politician rather than a sensitive man. Certainly he was a persuasive speaker, as events throughout his career amply attest. He could win over an individual or a state to his point of view, often with telling consequences in a crisis. Although he may never have learned to play the lyre himself, he was apparently very much alive to the power of the arts, particularly for political purposes; as we shall see, he is to be associated (however ambiguously) with the playwrights Phrynichus and Aeschylus and the poets Simonides and Timocreon. The spirit of the following anecdote, then, is perhaps not inappropriate: Themistocles while still young and obscure invited Epicles of Hermione, a lyre-player who was very much admired by the Athenians, to practise at his house, so that many would come to see him often.[22]

WIVES

We do not know when Themistocles married but the name of his first wife was Archippe, daughter of Lysander of the deme Alopeke, who was, as we can tell from the meagre information, an aristocrat.[23] To what extent the marriage was a political one can only be conjectured. Since he was a Lycomid should we not expect him to marry well?

Themistocles later married a second time; whether before or after he fled from Greece is impossible to determine. It is generally assumed (rightly or wrongly) that this second wife is not the woman who, Diodorus claims, was given to him by the King of Persia.[24] On the basis of Plutarch's untidy information, his various children may be divided between his two wives as follows:

Sons by Archippe:

Neocles: he and his brother Diocles were the eldest. Neocles died from a horse-bite while still a boy.

Diocles: adopted by his grandfather Lysander.

Archeptolis: married his half-sister Mnesiptolema (see below).

Polyeuctus: about whom nothing is known.

Cleophantus: Plutarch refers to Plato's mention of him in the *Meno* (93 B-E) as an excellent horseman but not good for anything else. As we shall see later, Cleophantus was given special privileges in Lampsacus.[25]

Demopolis: probably an invented son. He is linked with Neocles (above, who was supposed to have died young) in stories that smack of fiction. We are told, for example, that Neocles and Demopolis, not being recognized as the sons of Themistocles, took part in funeral games at Athens. They won and were crowned, but when they became known after the contest they almost were stoned to death by the enemies of Themistocles, who reminded the Athenians of the laws concerning fugitives;[26] for Themistocles was an exile.

Daughters by Themistocles' Second Wife:
Themistocles had several daughters; two at least, Mnesiptolema and Asia, are by his second wife. We cannot be sure whether the others came from his first or second marriages.

Mnesiptolema: married her half-brother Archeptolis. She was said to be a priestess in Asia Minor.[27]

Italia: married Panthoides, the Chian.

Sybaris: married Nicomedes, the Athenian.

Nicomache: married Themistocles' nephew Phrasicles, who after the death of his uncle sailed to Magnesia to receive her from her brothers.[28]

Asia: the youngest of all the children; Phrasicles took charge of her when he married Nicomache.[29]

THE DATE OF THEMISTOCLES' BIRTH

We do not know the exact year of Themistocles' birth and in general the chronological problems for his entire career are immense. But if one believes that he held the eponymous archonship in 493/2 and thus must have been at least thirty years old then, he will have been born c. 524.[30]

DESCENDANTS OF THEMISTOCLES

Among the descendants of Themistocles who may be identified, two deserve special mention:

A Themistocles of the second century who by issuing coins with a trophy on the prow of a trireme seems to claim relationship to his famous ancestor, the victorious general of the sea-battle at Salamis.[31]

Plutarch concludes his *Life of Themistocles* by mentioning a Themistocles, descendant of the great statesman, who was his friend and fellow-student in the school of Ammonius the philosopher. This same Themistocles (the Stoic) appears as a speaker in one of Plutarch's philosophical dialogues.[32]

SOME GENERAL CONCLUSIONS

Themistocles was probably born *c.* 524; he was the son of Neocles and belonged to the aristocratic family of the Lycomidae. His mother, whose name and origins are uncertain, was probably of foreign extraction. We cannot be sure if she was an Athenian citizen or whether Neocles ever married her at all. Whatever the case, a shadow was cast upon Themistocles' genuine Athenian credentials and derogatory stories about his mother became exaggerated.

Themistocles had at least two wives and many children. The fact that all his sons seem to be attributed to one wife and all his daughters to another is at least suspicious. At any rate among his sons, Neocles, Diocles and Archeptolis (is his name, 'Magistrate of the City', meant to reflect a particular office held by Themistocles?) may be real but Cleophantus is the only one to emerge later with any significant historical identity. His daughters, although perhaps genuine enough, all bear names which apparently reflect stages and interests in Themistocles' career. Mnesiptolema and Nicomache ('Reminder of Battle' and 'Victory in Battle') suggest Themistocles' achievement at Salamis; and Italia and Sybaris perhaps are so named to indicate Themistocles' apparent interest in the West; and Asia of course recalls his travels and sojourn with the Persians. Yet each is given a specific identity by Plutarch and for all we know his information may be accurate; if he did have access to any family archives in the possession of his Stoic friend, Themistocles, we may very well wish that they had been put to better use. In any event, Plutarch's characterization of the young Themistocles is coloured by his conception of a hero, although some of his generic observations are in themselves credible enough; and his identification of Mnesiphilus as Themistocles' teacher and associate is probably to be taken seriously.

CHAPTER III

THE BEGINNINGS OF A HERO'S CAREER

PRE-THEMISTOCLEAN ATHENS

I can attempt only the briefest survey of Athenian history before the fifth century, with the sole purpose in mind of providing essential background for Themistocles' career.[33] One of the most important of post-Mycenaean developments was the amalgamation of the entire area of Attica into the single city-state of Athens. In this early period monarchy prevailed but, through gradual encroachments upon the power and the title of the king, by the mid-seventh century the chief magistracy became the archonship, held by three officials called archons elected annually: the eponymous archon, who managed civil duties and gave his name to the year (thus, since assumption of office was in summer, archon-dates must be designated by two years, e.g. the first recorded eponymous archon held office in 682/1); a polemarch or war archon who was in charge of the military; and a king archon (*basileus*) who handled religious matters. Eventually six more archons (*thesmothetai*) were added to record the law – making in all a board of nine. An aristocratic Council, called the Areopagus (composed of ex-archons who became members for life), held firm and uncompromising control over the political and judicial administration of the state. The Assembly of the people, the *Ecclesia*, was at the beginning limited in its membership and virtually powerless. The subsequent development of the Athenian constitution culminating in the full democracy under Pericles had as its end result the curtailment of the authority of both the archons and the Areopagus and the assumption by the *Ecclesia* of final and sovereign power. But this democratic evolution, in which Themistocles was to play a role either directly or indirectly, was by no means rapid or continuous.

The inflexible and self-serving control of the aristocratic élite led to severe economic and judicial oppression of the people. The law was systematized and recorded for the first time by Draco in 621; but his legal code favoured the upper class and was particularly brutal in the punishment of certain minor offences. In 594/3 the wise statesman and poet Solon was elected archon with extraordinary powers to accomplish badly needed reforms, which, as it turned out, were far-reaching in their impact. But they were not effective enough immediately to cure the serious political problems and financial distress, and the threat of tyranny that had been temporarily postponed (Cylon failed to seize power in 632) finally became a reality when Peisistratus, backed by the oppressed populace and a military force, gained control of Athens in 561/0. It was not, however, until his third attempt, probably in 546/5, that he was able to secure his unconstitutional power, and he ruled from that time until his death in 528/7. Through his great gifts as an administrator Peisistratus established for the Athenians a standard of economic stability and artistic endeavour that was to provide a sound basis for the glorious achievements to follow in the next century.

Peisistratus was succeeded by his two sons, Hippias and Hipparchus, who, as far as we can tell from the ambiguous evidence, shared jointly in their rule; Hippias was dominant in the management of political affairs, while Hipparchus acted like a veritable Maecenas in his patronage of poets and sponsorship of the arts. But Hipparchus was assassinated in 514/3 by Harmodius and Aristogeiton. The immediate instigation of the murder was personal; yet it laid bare a more widespread discontent with authoritarian power, and the plot, supported by an anti-tyrannical faction, included the intended assassination of Hippias (and not only Hipparchus), which by a chance set of circumstances was inadvertently aborted. So Hippias continued as sole ruler and the Peisistratid tyranny had by no means been brought to an end, although later propaganda proclaimed Harmodius and Aristogeiton to be national heroes, the tyrannicides who had liberated Athens. Upon the murder of his brother, Hippias, because of insecurity and fear, assumed all the characteristics of a real 'tyrant', illustrating by his despotic and ruthless behaviour the later evil connotations inherent in the very word itself. And so he was expelled from Athens in 511/10 through the efforts of the Alcmaeonidae, one of the most influential and important aristocratic families of Athens, supported by the people and the intervention of a military force dispatched by Sparta, in this period the strongest city-state in all Hellas. Hippias fled to Persia (as Themistocles was to do later); in 490, even though by then an old man, he made a futile attempt, as we shall see, to be reinstated in Athens, relying upon the vain hope that Persian might would prevail and that he would receive a welcome reception from at least some of his fellow Athenians.

In the bitter political struggle caused by the expulsion of Hippias, it was an Alcmaeonid named Cleisthenes who won control in the very year, 508/7, when his rival Isagoras held the archonship. Spartan military interference proved of no avail against Cleisthenes with his sympathetic appeal to the democratic aspirations of the Athenian people (the *demos*). Through the genius of Cleisthenes basic reforms were undertaken as a result of which Athenian democracy became a reality. We do not know in what official capacity he initiated his programme nor how long it took for completion but certainly and most importantly it was all the citizens in the *Ecclesia* who in the last analysis voted their final approval.

Cleisthenes' reorganization of the Athenian state was many-faceted, thorough and complex. Today we cannot reconstruct or fully comprehend many of its intricacies, some of which appear, perhaps because of our ignorance, extremely artificial. Nevertheless, his major goals seem in general to be clear enough. For our purposes a few fundamental facts must be realized. The Athenian people were regrouped into ten tribes (previously there had been only four), and a new emphasis was placed upon individual registration for citizenship in a deme, one of many geographical units into which Attica was divided. Tribal division and demotic organization were both designed to cut through but not necessarily break the entrenched monopolies of the old and wealthy aristocratic families, particularly in their influence upon the outcome of a vote; and every Athenian was now encouraged to identify himself by the name of his deme rather than that of his father or his family, in an attempt to further a democratic spirit of equality among all citizens.

Extremely important was the emergence of the *strategia*, a board of ten generals (*strategoi*), elected annually one from each tribe. Our evidence for the early years of the democracy does not allow us to distinguish between the duties of the newly influential generals and the firmly established archonship; but it was not too long before the two offices were to vie for supreme power and eventually the ten generals emerged as the highest and most important officials in the administration of both political and military affairs. The ancient Council of the Areopagus still remained a potent force but some of its duties now inevitably had to be shared and its prestige began to be even further eroded as the importance of the archonship (from which its members were drawn) waned. Finally in 462/1 it was to be stripped of all its political power by a radical, Ephialtes; as I shall explain later, Themistocles was erroneously linked with Ephialtes in this democratic reform.[34] The blunder is in itself a sufficient reminder of Themistocles' influence upon the direction that Athenian democracy was subsequently to take. It remained for Pericles (another democrat and Alcmaeonid like Cleisthenes) to guide the development to some of its perhaps inevitable conclusions. But it is important to recognize that one of the initial basic strengths in the survival of Cleisthenes' reforms was the shrewd and diplomatic merger of the old with the new. When Themistocles first appears on the political scene, the stage has already been set for him by the vision of a new democratic ideal and reality, still deeply imbued with the old traditional values and rights of an aristocracy very much to be reckoned with. Yet the assembly of the people, the *Ecclesia*, now held control of the government; and it was rendered even more efficient in its power by the creation of a Council of five hundred (*Boule*), consisting of fifty members selected by lot from each of the ten

tribes. Primary among the duties of this *Boule* were the preparation and organization of the business that awaited the final
decision of the *Ecclesia*.

OSTRACISM

One of the important reforms attributed to Cleisthenes was a
law concerning ostracism that stipulated that any Athenian who
had become offensive because of suspected or overt dictatorial
and autocratic ambition could be sent into exile for a period of
ten years.[35] The motive for the device was, at least in the
beginning, to protect the new democracy from any possible
threat that hated tyranny might return once again. The first
ostracism actually effected (although it and others may have
previously been unsuccessfully attempted) was that of Hipparchus in 488/7, the son of Charmus and a relative of Peisistratus;
this was almost certainly the same man who had been archon in
496/5 and who, according to Aristotle, was the acknowledged
leader of those pro-tyrant sympathizers who still remained in
Athens. In fact, Aristotle claims that Cleisthenes originally
instituted the practice of ostracism because of his overwhelming
desire to get rid of this Hipparchus.[36]

The procedures for conducting an ostracism were as follows.
Every winter the general question was put to the *Ecclesia* in
regular session whether or not they wanted to hold an ostracism
that year. If they voted in the affirmative, a special meeting was
called in early spring to determine if there were enough votes
against any one individual to secure his removal from the city.
For this second meeting a section of the Agora (or Market-place)
was fenced off and each citizen cast his ballot, written side down
– his ballot being an *ostrakon*, e.g. a broken piece of pottery upon
which was inscribed the name of his candidate for removal from
the city (Plates 1–14). The voting was under the supervision of
the *Boule* and the archons. When all the *ostraka* had been counted,
whoever's name appeared the most often was thereupon
ostracized, provided that at least 6000 votes in all had been cast;
conflicting testimony, however, claims that 6000 votes had to

be cast for any one candidate for an ostracism to occur.

The procedure in subsequent years (the last ostracism took place in 416) was employed not only against a potential tyrant but as a weapon to be manipulated by an individual and his supporters in political rivalry of every sort. Thus the ostracism of an influential statesman often represented, as it were, a vote of confidence for his opposition.

It is of fundamental importance to realize that the exile imposed by ostracism was honourable and implied no disgrace, only political defeat. Any ostracized person could enjoy the revenues of his estate and could return to Athens after ten years, having lost neither his property nor his rights of citizenship, a far different experience, indeed, from that of a judicial indictment and the sentence of a fine or exile. Themistocles, as we shall see, was ostracized but while in ostracism criminal charges were formally brought against him. Rather than face trial, he fled and went into self-imposed exile, a fugitive from his homeland. These two episodes in his career are not in any way to be confused.

Archaeologists have already unearthed literally thousands of *ostraka*, the majority from the Agora and Ceramicus (Potter's Quarter), in Athens. Those bearing upon Themistocles' career, including of course those inscribed with his very name, will be considered later. But a few words about the nature and character of *ostraka* in general are necessary here.

The inscribed potsherds are of various kinds, depending upon the type of vessel of which they were originally a part. They appear in different shapes and sizes but each, as one would suspect, can be easily held in one's hand. There is no consistency in the way the names of the candidates were inscribed. An Athenian's full name would be given as follows: Themistocles, son of Neocles, of the deme Phrearrhioi. But we do not usually find all three designations; the name alone may sometimes appear; very often only the patronymic is added and sometimes only the demotic. There is great variation too in spelling; much depended upon the literacy of the voter. Although misspellings are frequent and amusing, a different rendering of the same name may not always be illegitimate. Thus we find Themistokles more often than not also inscribed as Themisthokles, and thus his name may very well have been correctly pronounced and spelled either way (Pls 6–13).

Writing is normally inscribed, or occasionally painted, from left to right and from the top line down; but the inscriptions on certain *ostraka* are retrograde (from right to left) or boustrophedon (over and back, like the turning of oxen in ploughing); some are even graced with additional graffiti: exclamations, verses, invectives, caricatures, and the like.

One might assume that each voter prepared his own *ostrakon*. This was not always the case; from the similarities among groups of *ostraka* and their numbers it seems that scribes set up booths to provide the lazy or illiterate with sherds, either blank or inscribed. Politicians and their supporters may very well have taken every opportunity for flooding the market-place with *ostraka* all prepared with a rival's name to foist upon uncertain or corruptible voters.

No discussion of ostracism would be complete without the inclusion of a popular anecdote recorded by Plutarch about the famous rival of Themistocles, Aristeides, who because of his righteousness was known as the Just (Pl. 1).[37] When the voters were preparing their *ostraka*, an illiterate peasant handed his sherd to Aristeides, without at all realizing who he was, and requested him to write the name Aristeides on it. Aristeides in his astonishment asked the fellow what harm Aristeides could possibly have ever done to him; and this was the reply: 'I don't even know the man, but I am sick and tired of hearing him called "The Just".'

THE PERSIAN THREAT AND THE IONIAN REVOLT

Outside of Hellas events were taking place in this early period that were to have momentous consequences for all Hellenes, not least the Athenians and Themistocles, during the first quarter of the fifth century. In the East the conqueror Cyrus the Great effected the amalgamation of the Persians with their kinsmen the Medes and expanded and consolidated a vast and powerful Persian Empire.[38] With the fall of Sardis in 546 and the capitulation of Croesus, King of Lydia, Cyrus and the Persians gained control over Asia Minor and their authority was extended to the very coast. Cyrus died in 529 and he was succeeded by his son Cambyses, whose most significant achievement was the acquisition of Egypt in 525. Darius, who was the successor of his father Cambyses in 521, undertook a thorough and systematic political and financial reorganization of the Persian Empire; and it was he who initially crossed over into Europe by campaigning successfully against the Thracians and even securing the allegiance of Macedonia; but his further attempt beyond the Danube against the Scythians was at most a dubious achievement. Most significant for us, however, was the fateful Ionian Revolt (499–494), which erupted under Darius' rule.

With the conquest of Lydia by Cyrus, Hellenes on the seaboard of Asia Minor now for the first time had been made subject to Persian authority – a fact that in retrospect can be seen as the real beginning of Hellenic woes. For the conquered city-states grew restless and finally their discontent with Darius' rule culminated in a revolution, the focal point of which was Ionia, a region on the western coast of Asia Minor. It must be realized that the Hellenes as a race distinguished among themselves three major divisions on the basis of dialect and geography: Ionians, Dorians, and Aeolians. The Spartans were the most significant Dorians in mainland Greece; the Athenians, the most prominent Ionians, and it was their Ionian 'kinsmen' in Asia Minor who were incited to revolt against the Persian Empire.

Aristagoras, an ambitious and devious tyrant of the city of Miletus, became the prime instigator of the rebellion; and in 499/8 he sailed to Hellas in the hope of eliciting support. At Sparta his appeals were rejected. But Athens dispatched twenty ships, and Eretria, a city on the island of Euboea, sent five; their decision to cooperate was ominous for the future course of events. Although the participation of both cities was ultimately ineffectual, they were irrevocably compromised. The Athenians and Eretrians joined Aristagoras in an unsuccessful occupation of Sardis; the city was devastated by fire but they failed to capture the citadel. After a defeat near Ephesus, the Athenians returned home. It has been suggested that the election in Athens of the Peisistratid, Hipparchus, to the eponymous archonship of 496/5 reflects a hostile reaction against the earlier anti-Persian policy responsible for Athenian involvement in Ionia.

The final suppression of the Ionian Revolt in 494 was signalled by the siege and capture of Miletus. The power and might of the Persian Empire had effectively quelled opposition in Asia Minor. What was to be done about those Hellenes across the Aegean who had dared to intervene?

THE ARCHONSHIP OF THEMISTOCLES

The reader at this point may very well be tempted to ask about Themistocles' role in all these momentous events of the late sixth and early fifth centuries. Other than the meagre information about his family, childhood, and early training discussed in Chapter II above, our sources record no specific event in Themistocles' life that we can identify with certainty earlier than his eponymous archonship in 493/2 – and even the fact of his archonship in this year has been seriously questioned by scholars.

As I have conjectured, Themistocles was probably born c. 524; thus it was during his impressionable early years that Hipparchus was murdered and Hippias ruled as tyrant until his expulsion in 511/10. Certainly Themistocles as a young man must have been very much aware of Cleisthenes' struggle and victory in the drafting of the new democracy, which was to have such a direct impact upon the course of his career; and there can be no doubt that the power of Persia and the ramifications of the Ionian Revolt were to influence profoundly his political attitudes. But any meaningful recreation of the life of a youthful Themistocles, in the absence of direct evidence, must remain elusive for the careful historian, although there is much that might fire the imagination of the conscientious historical novelist.

Dionysius of Halicarnassus tells us that Themistocles was

archon at Athens in 493/2,[39] and the chronographic tradition recorded by Eusebius lends particular support to the assumption encouraged by other evidence that it was as archon in that very year (rather than in any official capacity later) that he began the fortification of the Piraeus.[40]

All sorts of doubts have been cast upon these two facts attesting the beginning of Themistocles' career in the 490s. Some have suggested that it was his uncle – another Themistocles, and mentioned only once, in Epistle 8 – who was archon in 493/2, with or without the beginning of work at the Piraeus. Others believe in the great Themistocles' archonship for this year but claim that he did not begin the fortification of the Piraeus until some time later; for it was not actually resumed until after the battle of Salamis and the naval policy it seems to envisage might appear more credible in the context of Themistocles' success later (c. 483) in the building of a fleet. In fact, since we do not know the name of the eponymous archon for 482/1, Themistocles has been suggested as candidate for *that* year; not an extremely likely conjecture in itself, and as far as we can tell it was impossible for anyone to hold the archonship twice.

Is it really too difficult to imagine a Themistocles of such persistent vision, who would doggedly and consistently pursue a naval policy from as early as 493 until its final culmination after the second expulsion of the Persian invaders in 479? I can believe in Themistocles' archonship in 493/2, with the beginning of plans for the Piraeus in that very year. The concept of fortifying the three natural harbours of the Piraeus was brilliant in its logic and practicality, for it would assure a much more serviceable and secure naval base than the open and indefensible bay of Phalerum, which the Athenians up until that time had used as their major harbour. After the suppression of the Ionian Revolt in 494, the Persians presented Athens with a very real and imminent threat; and there was as well the hostility of the nearby island of Aegina, with which Athens was openly at war at various times between 505 and 481.[41] But we do not know to what extent Themistocles' plans for the Piraeus were originally fulfilled and why they were curtailed for so many years. Was it

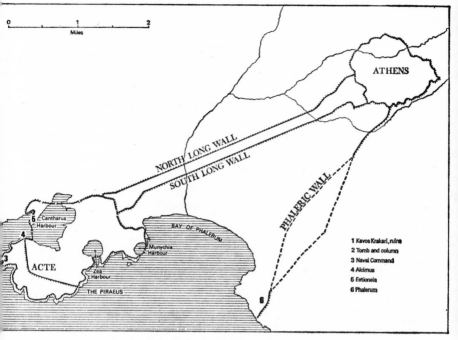

Map I   Athens and the Piraeus, showing the Themistoclean walls and pertinent sites

perhaps initially because Miltiades arrived upon the scene to promote policies that ran counter to those of Themistocles?

This Miltiades belonged to the aristocratic family of the Philaidae, which like that of the Alcmaeonidae (who were sometimes, if not continuously, rivals) was a potent force in Athenian society and politics. For many years he had been absolute ruler, under the authority of Persia, in the area of the Thracian Chersonese, where the Peisistratid tyranny had encouraged a policy of Athenian encroachment. But amidst the Persian retaliations after the Ionian Revolt, Miltiades barely escaped with his life during his flight home to Athens in 493, the very period of Themistocles' archonship. Upon his return, Miltiades was brought to trial by enemies, who are unnamed, on the curious charge of tyranny in the Chersonese, but he won acquittal and thereupon was elected general by the people.[42] We possess no direct evidence for the relationship between Themistocles and Miltiades in the 490s. But Plutarch in the context of describing Themistocles' success in his persuasion of the Athenians to build a fleet (c. 483) goes on to observe more generally that Themistocles by his policies transformed the Athenians from steadfast hoplites with spear and shield into sea-tossed mariners of the rowing-pad and oar; then, quoting Stesimbrotus, Plutarch says that Themistocles accomplished this despite the opposition of Miltiades. Now Miltiades was dead by 483; but perhaps his conflict with Themistocles actually did occur earlier, in 493/2 when the programme concerning the Piraeus was initiated?[43] At any rate, as far as we can ascertain, with Miltiades' election to the generalship, Themistocles' career after his archonship was eclipsed.

A much more tenuous association has been imagined between Themistocles as archon in 493/2 and the playwright Phrynichus. Conjecture has it that Phrynichus produced his play, *The Sack of Miletus*, at the dramatic festival of the Dionysia in 493 (or perhaps 492) at the instigation of Themistocles, who for political reasons wanted to arouse anti-Persian sentiment. Phrynichus was fined because of his emotional treatment of a very touchy subject and thus Themistocles, by implication, also became discredited. It is startling in itself that Phrynichus could or would so quickly have composed a tragedy upon events that had barely occurred; but, in any case, ancient testimony provides us with no fixed date for his play. I now feel that a much more cogent historical reconstruction would place Phrynichus' treatment of the fall of Miletus in 476; and so I shall postpone further discussion.[44]

A completely fanciful hypothesis attempts to link Themistocles' archonship with another playwright, this time the famous Aeschylus, who is supposed to have written his *Suppliants*, the setting of which is in Argos, to support a Themistoclean pro-Argive policy, but because of a subsequent triumph of an anti-Argive Miltiadean reaction, Aeschylus' play, although composed in 493/2, was not actually produced until 463.[45] The date of *The Suppliants* is still by no means secure, despite the discovery of a papyrus fragment that purports to give us some clues; and the dramatic text itself contains nothing historically precise enough for an interpretation of Themistocles' career at any time; yet it has also been construed in connection with Themistocles' sojourn at Argos while in ostracism.[46] Thus *The Suppliants* offers us no concrete evidence for Themistocles at all. Aeschylus' *Persians*, however, is of course quite another matter.

We hear about various duties and activities attributed to Themistocles but it is impossible to know whether they belong in the 490s and thus support the arguments for his rise to power and his archonship in that decade or are to be placed later.[47] Also our sources do not make it clear whether he acted as archon or general in the performance of certain functions or held some other special office or offices. Two anecdotes record that he was responsible for judicial decisions of one sort of another.[48] We are told that he was Water Commissioner and that he dedicated a bronze statue of a maiden called the Water-Carrier from the fines imposed upon those convicted of tapping and stealing the water supply.[49] At the time of the following two incidents, Themistocles need not have been in office at all; they do, however, indicate in varying degrees his influence and prestige. In a quarrel between the Corcyraeans and the Corinthians he settled the dispute and decided in favour of the Corcyraeans, who made him their benefactor; and he advised the Athenians to reject the appeal of Admetus, King of the Molossians in Epirus, for an alliance.[50]

THE BATTLE OF MARATHON

Darius, having settled affairs in Asia Minor after the Ionian Revolt, turned his attention to securing Persian authority in Thrace and Macedonia with the eventual intention, as it turned out, of punishing the Hellenes for their participation in the revolt; whether his ultimate goal was the absolute conquest of mainland Hellas or merely the imposition of allegiance is impossible to determine. At any rate, in 492 Mardonius, a son-in-law of Darius, crossed the Hellespont into Thrace. But his campaign on land proved to be a dubious success and his fleet was badly damaged by a storm as it was rounding Mount Athos, a headland on the eastern promontory of the Chalcidian peninsula.

Undaunted by these difficulties, Darius by a different strategy moved directly against Hellas itself. He dispatched envoys to various city-states who demanded earth and water as tokens of submission. Many acquiesced, including Aegina, whose hostility to nearby Athens throughout this period has already been mentioned; at both Athens and Sparta, however, the Persian ambassadors were put to death.[51] Darius also fitted out an expedition, under the command of Datis and Artaphernes, which set sail across the Aegean for retaliation against the Hellenes, not least of all Athens and Eretria, the two city-states who had sent ships in support of the rebellious Ionians. The extent of Persian forces is difficult to ascertain; Herodotus' figure of 600 triremes is generally considered to be exaggerated;[52] an estimate of about 100 ships with 20,000 fighters (including both infantry and cavalry) is certainly reasonable, if not conservative. With the Persian fleet was the aged Hippias, no doubt an excellent adviser, who hoped to secure power in Athens once again, under the aegis of the Persian King. The existence and the number of pro-Persian or pro-tyrant sympathizers among the Athenians are impossible to determine but nevertheless keenly debated by scholars.

After causing many of the islanders along the way to submit, the Persians landed on Euboea, where Carystus surrendered after a siege; thereupon Eretria was sacked and the people led away as captives. The fleet did not make directly for Athens but under the guidance of Hippias landed at the plain of Marathon on the east coast of Attica. Athens was now in dire peril, and what should be done to face the crisis was the subject of hot dispute in the city.

One of the ten generals in the year 490 was Miltiades (he was probably elected to this office continually from 492 to 489); and it was his genius that determined the course of events that followed. His brilliant strategy and his persistence in carrying it through, despite opposition, brought about victory against extraordinary odds. Miltiades, according to fourth-century tradition, initiated a decree by which the people resolved 'to take food and march'; an interesting foreshadowing of the disputed Decree of Themistocles in connection with the battle of Salamis a decade later.[53] When news arrived that the Persians had landed at Marathon, the Athenians marched out to face the enemy there.

The actual working of the Athenian command in connection with the battle remains in many respects a mystery. Herodotus' account is far from clear and perhaps anachronistic.[54] At any rate the generalship created by Cleisthenes had certainly by 490 become extremely important and among the ten elected for that year Miltiades assumed the role of a kind of commander-in-chief. But the archonship was still an office of influence and power; and the role of the polemarch, Callimachus, was apparently very significant in the implementation of Miltiades' tactics. Callimachus himself won eternal fame for distinguishing himself in the fighting and he died a glorious death. The size of the Hellenic army that faced the Persians at Marathon is disputed; probably there were about 9000 Athenians, who were joined by a force of about 1000 from Plataea in Boeotia, an ally of Athens. Miltiades employed his limited forces to the greatest advantage by weakening the centre of his army and keeping the wings strong; thus the vastly superior numbers of the enemy became their liability. Herodotus' figures for the dead, 192 Athenians as compared with 6400 Persians, are suspiciously chauvinistic;[55] but they emphatically confirm the unquestionable fact of an overwhelming and astounding Athenian victory.

The Persians took to their ships and sailed around the cape of Sunium at the southern tip of Attica and anchored off the shore in the bay of Phalerum. But the Athenian army valiantly hastened back to Athens and the Persians, realizing the hopelessness of their situation, returned home in defeat. A mysterious shield signal was reported to have been given to the Persians before their departure, supposedly at the instigation of sympathizers in Athens. One may very well wonder if it was intended to encourage the enemy to invade or warn them to go home. At any rate Herodotus, I believe justifiably, absolves the Alcmaeonidae from any subversive involvement.[56]

Upon the fall of Eretria and before they left Athens for Marathon, the Athenian generals sent as a herald to Sparta a trained runner named Pheidippides (or Philippides) to elicit their aid. The Spartans, however, said that because of their law they could not march out on the ninth day of the month but would have to wait until the moon was full. When the time was right they actually did dispatch a force of 2000 men who made their way as quickly as possible but arrived at Marathon too late for the battle. After congratulating the Athenians on a job well done, they returned home.

Yet what about Themistocles in connection with the glorious Athenian achievement at Marathon? The only direct evidence that we have comes from Plutarch, who in his *Life of Aristeides* says that in the battle the Persians held out longest against the Athenian centre, which was the hardest pressed; and there where the tribes Leontis and Antiochis were stationed Themistocles, a Leontid, and Aristeides, an Antiochid, fought brilliantly side by side.[57] Even without Plutarch, there could hardly be any doubt that Themistocles fought along with his fellow Athenians at Marathon. But does Plutarch's text warrant the assumption that Themistocles held an official position of any sort in 490? It is curious that Plutarch makes no mention of Themistocles at Marathon in his *Life of Themistocles*; all the more suspicious then is this dramatic juxtaposition of the pair, Themistocles and Aristeides, traditionally linked together, usually in subsequent years, more often as rivals than as friends. It is frustrating to realize how very few names of generals have survived for an office that involved the election of ten men every year. There were, we know, ten generals at Marathon; who, then, were the other nine along with Miltiades? Plutarch assures us that Aristeides was one of them when relating how he was most important in the determination of the outcome of the battle by his influential acquiescence in the authority of Miltiades.[58] Aristeides was not to become eponymous archon until after Marathon, probably in 489/8. If Themistocles already had held the archonship in 493/2 would he not be a logical and likely candidate as a fellow general, particularly since Plutarch's testimony emphasizes the tribal leadership of both Aristeides and Themistocles and the election of the generals was determined on a tribal basis? Unfortunately, no final answer as yet is possible.

We do know, however, that Marathon was very much Miltiades' victory with his expert command of a hoplite army. Except for the problematical mention of Themistocles' archonship in 493/2 and the emphasis upon his naval policy in the Piraeus, the virtual silence of the evidence suggests his eclipse, for which Miltiades may have been primarily responsible. Whatever the case, the ancient tradition is primarily concerned with Themistocles' (second?) rise to power in the 480s, focusing upon his creation of a fleet c. 483, and his subsequent achievement. As a result his earlier career, especially in the 490s, was almost hopelessly obscured or, in the view of the scholarly opposition, became the product of imaginary and hypothetical invention.

Miltiades' career, however, did not end in glory. Shortly after Marathon, he persuaded the Athenians to provide him with a squadron of seventy ships. He did this, according to Herodotus,[59] by promising to make them rich as a result of his intended expedition but without actually identifying the people whom he would attack. As it turned out, his designs were directed against the island of Paros, since the Parians had contributed one trireme to the Persians in their invasion of Hellas. Miltiades' venture was a dismal failure and he returned home in disgrace. He was brought to trial on the charge of deceiving the people by Xanthippus, the son of Ariphron, who married the niece of the Alcmaeonid Cleisthenes and who was to be ostracized (c. 485/4). Miltiades incurred a heavy fine of fifty talents, which was paid by his son Cimon, and he died soon thereafter from an injury to his thigh or his knee that he suffered during his ill-fated campaign against Paros.

The tragic ending of Miltiades' glorious career is ominous indeed when one considers the subsequent fate of Themistocles. For Miltiades' actions after his victory at Marathon closely parallel Themistocles' aggression against the islanders ten years later, after his own great victory against the Persians at Salamis;

and Themistocles too was impeached and discredited. Did Miltiades actually oppose Themistocles' plans for the Piraeus because of strategic reasons before Marathon, as I have conjectured above, although he realized the potential of the navy later under different circumstances? What lessons did Themistocles learn from Miltiades' diverse experiences and adventures? And what about the impressions of a young Cimon, who was eventually to emerge as Themistocles' enemy, and the leader of a naval confederacy of Hellenes under Athenian control? Our inadequate evidence will allow only insubstantial speculations concerning these intriguing questions.

CHAPTER IV

SALAMIS: A HERO'S GLORY

THEMISTOCLES' RISE TO POWER IN THE 480S

The only clear and direct literary evidence about Themistocles' activities in the 480s dwells upon his proposal in 483/2 by which he persuaded the Athenians to pay for the building of a fleet; and the unanimity of our sources makes this the earliest indisputable fact that we possess about Themistocles' career. But there are perhaps latent implications in Plutarch's description of Themistocles' ambitions after Marathon that at least suggest that his influence in politics might logically have begun to be felt earlier in the decade.

Although still a young man ($\nu\acute{\epsilon}o\varsigma$), Plutarch tells us, at the time of Marathon when the generalship of Miltiades was being acclaimed by all, Themistocles became introspective and thoughtful, sleepless at night and no longer willing to accept invitations to drinking parties. His explanation for the change in his character and habits was that Miltiades' trophy of victory would allow him no sleep. Most of the Athenians believed that the defeat of the Persians at Marathon meant the end of the war; but Themistocles realized it was only the beginning of greater struggles. Therefore, in anticipation of what was to come, he saw to it that his own city was prepared and ordained himself champion of all Hellas. But Plutarch goes on to state that first of all ($\pi\rho\tilde{\omega}\tau o\nu$) Themistocles was responsible for the construction of a fleet.[60]

Plutarch's text here seems to confine Themistocles' rise to power solely to the 480s and whatever hints he may give us elsewhere about earlier activities in the 490s appear inadvertent and obscure. Themistocles in the context above is said to be 'young' at the time of Marathon, whatever that may mean precisely, and his first step in politics was to initiate his naval programme. Yet it is not unreasonable to suspect that Themistocles did not suddenly burst upon the political scene in 483, whether or not one believes in his archonship in 493/2 or his generalship at Marathon in 490. Aristotle gives us a glimpse of several important events in the period of the 480s, which have been with some justification interpreted as suggesting a possible bid for recognition and power by Themistocles in the years from 489 to 483, although our literary sources are completely silent concerning any involvement on his part.

After mentioning the first ostracism, that of the Peisistratid Hipparchus, the acknowledged leader of the friends of the tyrants in Athens, Aristotle proceeds to introduce the following events:[61]

In the very next year [after the ostracism of Hipparchus] in the archonship of Telesinus [487/6], the Athenians now for the first time after the fall of the tyranny elected the nine archons by lot, out of five hundred candidates already selected by the demesmen; previously all the archons were elected; and Megacles, son of Hippocrates, of the deme Alopeke was ostracized. Then for three years they continued to ostracize the friends of the tyrants, on account of whom the law had specifically been enacted. Afterwards in the fourth year, they began to remove any other person as well, if he seemed to be too great; and the first one ostracized of those unassociated with tyranny was Xanthippus, son of Ariphron.

If we add to this testimony the evidence of a large number of *ostraka* identifying a Callias, son of Cratius, of the deme Alopeke, a few of which clearly designate him as a Persian (Μῆδος or ἐκ Μέδων), with one actually presenting a caricature of him dressed in Persian garb, we now perhaps know the third friend of the tyrants, who, Aristotle says, was ostracized though he leaves him unnamed.[62] Thus the following chronological list of ostracism for the 480s may be drawn up:[63]

488/7	Hipparchus, a Peisistratid	Friends of the tyrants, according to Aristotle
487/6	Megacles, an Alcmaeonid	
486/5	Callias (?), pro-Persian	
485/4	Xanthippus, an Alcmaeonid	

Now Megacles was an important Alcmaeonid and Xanthippus,

the father of Pericles, married into the family. And it has been conjectured by many, quite plausibly, that Themistocles as a political rival may have had a hand in the removal of his enemies, using against them the charge (whether true or false) of pro-tyrant and pro-Persian sympathies – as we have mentioned earlier, the Alcmaeonidae were allegedly held responsible for the shield signal that was given to the Persians after Marathon. The literary evidence does tell us that Themistocles was instru-mental in the removal of his opponent Aristeides, who was ostracized in 483/2; and as we shall see shortly, the most logical implication is that their opposition focused upon Themistocles' naval programme in that year. It is not unlikely, then, that Themistocles employed the weapon of ostracism earlier. Further corroboration for this hypothesis seems to be provided by *ostraka*.

We have already observed in the previous chapter that abundant finds of *ostraka*, especially from the Agora and the Ceramicus of Athens, provide significant evidence concerning the institution of ostracism in general, but they also offer important, albeit controversial, information about Athenian politics in the period of the 480s and Themistocles in particular.

First of all it must be borne in mind that we have a surprisingly large number of *ostraka* inscribed with Themistocles' name (sometimes written Themisthocles as we have noted), most of which on the basis of the archaeological evidence are dated before 480 rather than in the 470s and the time of his actual ostracism. It must be admitted, though, that the chronology for the *ostraka* themselves is not always easy to identify, particu-larly in their assignment to individual years. A few bearing Themistocles' name are of special interest: one is unusually large (6 in. long, 4 in. wide and 1 in. thick (Pl. 11); another is graced with the exclamatory command *ito* (Pl. 13) – 'Themis-tocles, son of Neocles, out with him'; yet another bears an inscription which Podlecki roughly translates as follows:[64]

> For Themistocles of Phrearrhioi
> This ostrakon – his reward [$\tau\iota\mu\tilde{\eta}s\ \dddot{\epsilon}\nu\epsilon\kappa\alpha$].

Typically some of his *ostraka* give all three designations, name, patronymic and deme, or just his name alone. Although many offer his name with patronymic, a surprising number designate only his name and his deme. Unfortunately we cannot be sure whether these latter might not reflect a conscientious attempt on Themistocles' part to be democratic and popularly known as the Phrearrhian.

Interesting too is a group of 191 *ostraka* (found in a well on the north slope of the Acropolis, Pls 12, 14) which, because of the similarity in pottery and the limited number of hands identifiable, are thought to have been deliberately prepared – probably for an ostracism in the late 480s perhaps in the very year of Aristeides' ostracism in 483/2. This attempt by the opposition to get rid of Themistocles turned out to be a failure. In fact, as far as can be ascertained, these prepared *ostraka* seem never to have been used at all; it may be that they were discards, an indication perhaps that over-optimism had prompted the inscribing of too many sherds ahead of time. Whatever may have been the case, many other Themistoclean *ostraka* that were obviously used also belong to the time when Aristeides was ostracized; but there are others that appear to be demonstrably earlier.

Another startling revelation afforded by the *ostraka* is the large proportion that bear the names of Alcmaeonids: Callixenus, son of Aristonymus of Xypete, heretofore unknown, received a surprising number of votes in the period before 480 (Pl. 3); several too went to another Alcmaeonid, Hippocrates, son of Alcmeonides of Alopeke (Pl. 2);[65] and Xanthippus, ostracized in 485/4, whom we have already identified, is also represented. But by far the largest number belong to the Alcmaeonid Megacles, son of Hippocrates and nephew of Cleisthenes, who was ostracized in 487/6 (Pl. 5).

Now it happens that many *ostraka* of Themistocles have been found in conjunction with those of Megacles; and three in particular bearing Megacles' name actually join three others inscribed with the name of Themistocles, indicating that the sherds come from the same source. Thus Themistocles may very well have been a candidate for ostracism as early as 486.

Furthermore, some of the large number of Themistoclean *ostraka* may be for the years 486–483 although many probably belong to the late 480s and the year of Aristeides' ostracism in particular. Also the proportionate numbers of *ostraka* assigned to various years in this period seem to indicate a shift in votes from the Alcmaeonids Callixenus and Hippocrates to Aristeides. In all likelihood, then, Themistocles was an active and known political force at least as early as 486.

A few sherds have appeared with the names of Athenians associated with Themistocles in one way or another. It would be rash, however, to press any hypothetical political ramification for Themistocles that might be suggested by these finds. At any rate, Mnesiphilus of Phrearrhioi, the reputed teacher of Themistocles and his adviser at Salamis, is now confirmed as historically real by a few *ostraka*. Habronichus, the Athenian who brought the news of the Hellenic defeat at Artemisium and became one of Themistocles' colleagues on the embassy to Sparta concerning the fortification of Athens after Salamis and to whom Epistles 4 and 10 are written, also is identified; and finally, Leager, son of Glaucon, to whom Epistle 8 is addressed, interestingly enough is proven by his *ostraka* not to be a mere invention of the letter-writer.[66]

The implications of the literary evidence and the testimony of the *ostraka* support the hypothesis that Themistocles was politically active before 483. He may have used ostracism as a political weapon against his enemies earlier in the decade, just as he did against Aristeides in 483/2; and it seems likely too that his enemies tried to employ the same tactics against him, but without success. In my view also greater support can be found by implication for his career in the 490s; i.e. it was not as a young unknown that he became a candidate for ostracism in 486. Perhaps he was even involved in the first ostracism in the previous year, that of the Peisistratid Hipparchus, son of Charmus, for whom *ostraka* have also been found. Yet once we try to be too specific about the issues and attempt to align individuals or their families into 'parties' of one kind or another, our efforts are doomed to failure because of the inadequacy of the evidence.

The Reform of the Archonship in 487/6

In the passage quoted above, Aristotle tells us that in the archonship of Telesinus (487/6) the nine archons were now elected by lot out of five hundred candidates already selected by the demesmen; previously all the archons were elected by vote. It is to be assumed that this brief item of information has been mentioned because it represents a step of some significance in the development of the Athenian constitution; and the standard interpretation maintaining that it did in fact mark an important stage in the evolution of power for both the archonship and the generalship represents, I believe, a reasonable assumption.[67] As we have seen, the reforms of Cleisthenes gave new importance to the office of the ten generals, who were elected annually, one from each tribe; but Aristotle informs us that the Polemarch was still the supreme commander of the whole army.[68] There is no reason, then, to believe that Cleisthenes intended to break the power of the archonship completely or that it had already become relatively unimportant in the 490s, although our sources do not make clear how the generalship was to function in relation to the long established prestige of the nine archons. At Marathon the Polemarch Callimachus continued to play a significant role, but as general Miltiades revealed the potential inherent in his position.[69] Miltiades, for example, because of the authority that he had won at Marathon, managed to fit out an expedition to Paros. The generals could be re-elected to office year after year; such continuous tenure was impossible for the archons. It is not difficult, then, to imagine that, when election to the archonship was determined ultimately by lot in 487/6, the power of the generalship was further enhanced. This does not mean that the eclipse of the archonship was immediate and final. Ex-archons still became life members of the Areopagus, a prestigious political body until the reform of Ephialtes in 462. Yet with Themistocles' achievement at Salamis as general in 480 and the influential role of Cimon as general in the subsequent years of the Delian Confederacy, it became only too clear in whom the greatest power had finally come to reside. The challenge and experience of the Persian Wars, perhaps more than any other factors, determined the gradual shift in authority that is marked by the legislation of 487/6. The military command became concentrated in the generalship and inevitably political and civil authority followed in its wake.

It may at first glance seem rash to associate Themistocles with this reform of the archonship in the face of the silence of our sources. Yet all we have is Aristotle's brief mention of the fact itself. If, as Plutarch maintains, Themistocles was particularly aware and envious of Miltiades' generalship at Marathon, would he not most likely be the one to see that his hopes for glory lay in that very office, particularly if he too had himself been one of the generals in that very same year? He was, according to my argument, eponymous archon in 493/2; where was he to turn for the re-establishment of a significant and long-lived political career? Others too, of course, must have been aware of the potential of the generalship; and if, per-chance, Themistocles was in no way involved in the legislation of 487/6, it nevertheless turned out to be fortunate both for his own advantage and that of Athens.

THEMISTOCLES' NAVAL BILL[70]

Herodotus first introduces Themistocles into his narrative at the point when Xerxes' invasion of Greece in 480 is imminent, explaining that he was the one who offered the best interpreta-tion of the oracle concerning the wooden walls, i.e. the Athen-ians should rely upon their ships:[71]

Now there was a certain man among the Athenians, who recently (νεωστί) had entered the ranks of those in first place; his name was Themistocles but he was called the son of Neocles.

Then Herodotus goes on to mention the proposal concerning the building of a fleet, which Themistocles had previously initiated:[72]

On a previous occasion another opinion of Themistocles proved to be best at a critical moment. At the time when the Athenians acquired in their treasury a great sum of money, which came to them from the mines at Laurium, they were going to distribute it individually, ten drachmas a man. On this occasion Themistocles persuaded the Athenians to stop this distribution of money and to build with it two hundred ships for the war, referring to the war against Aegina. The outbreak of this war saved Hellas at that time, since it compelled the Athenians to become interested in the sea. The ships were not used for the purpose for which they were built and thus turned out to be a boon for Hellas in her hour of need.

These previously built ships were available to the Athenians and others in addition that they felt had to be constructed. They decided, upon deliberation after the oracle, to face the enemy with their ships and in full force, along with those Hellenes who were willing, as he came against Hellas.

Thucydides, after completing his survey of navies worthy of note in Hellas before Xerxes' expedition, has this to say about Themistocles' naval bill:[73]

Indeed the Aeginetans and Athenians and whatever other naval powers there were had acquired few ships and most of them fifty-oared galleys (pentekonters); and later Themistocles persuaded the Athenians, while they were at war with the Aeginetans and when at the same time the Persian invasion was expected, to build ships – the very ones that they used in the sea-battle at Salamis. And these ships did not yet have decks throughout their length [i.e. they had only fore and aft decks that did not run the whole length of the ship].

Aristotle too offers important testimony about Themistocles' naval programme, with the addition of significant details:[74]

In the archonship of Nicomedes [483/2], when [the productivity of] the mines in Maroneia [i.e. in the district of Laurium] became clear and the state attained a surplus of a hundred talents because of work there, some advised that the money be distributed among the people but Themistocles prevented this. He did not say how he would use the money but proposed that one talent should be lent to each of a hundred Athenians who were most wealthy. Then, if the money was spent in a way that was acceptable, the state would be satisfied; if not, the money would have to be paid back by the borrowers. Once he had obtained the use of the money on these conditions, he had a hundred triremes built, each of the hundred borrowers providing for the construction of one ship; with this fleet they fought at Salamis against the Persians. And at this time Aristeides, the son of Lysimachus, was ostracized. But three

years later in the archonship of Hypsichides [481/0] all those in ostracism
were recalled because of Xerxes' invasion.

Finally Plutarch provides further information, not so far
encountered:[75]

First of all, when the Athenians were accustomed to distribute among
themselves the revenue from the silver mines at Laurium, Themistocles
alone dared to speak before the people and propose that they must
give up the distribution of this money and use it to construct triremes
for the war against the Aeginetans. For this war especially was at its
height in Hellas and these islanders were in control of the sea because
of the number of their ships. And so it was all the more easy for
Themistocles to persuade the citizens, since he did not employ the
threat of Darius[76] and the Persians (for they were far away and offered
no really imminent fear of certain invasion) but instead relied upon the
immediate and timely jealous rivalry that they felt against Aegina.
From this money, then, they constructed one hundred triremes, with
which they actually fought against Xerxes.

From the evidence[77] it appears certain that in the year 483/2
Themistocles made his successful proposal to build a fleet
of triremes (Pls 17–19). He very probably anticipated the real
possibility of a second Persian invasion and, although he surely
was not alone in his foresight, it was the immediate conflict
between Athens and Aegina that decided the question of
what to do with the funds. It seems certain, too, that the money
for the ships came from the silver mines of Laurium. Beyond
these major conclusions, the conflicts in the ancient evidence
pose certain problems, which in the last analysis must remain
insoluble. I present my own views, which admittedly are
vulnerable.

First of all, had the money from the mines been distributed
over the years as a kind of dole for the populace, which our
later sources clearly indicate?[78] I am inclined to think not,
although there can be little doubt that the revenues from the
silver and lead mines of Laurium had for many years provided
a source of income for the state. What seems more likely on the
basis of Herodotus and Aristotle is that a lucky strike in the
particular area or village called Maroneia suddenly created a

surplus of funds; hence the debate about how this surplus should be spent. How much earlier than 483/2 the find was discovered is impossible to determine.

Another serious problem concerns the number of ships built as a result of the decision of the *Ecclesia*. Our sources are divided. Was it one or two hundred triremes? Is a reconciliation between the two figures possible? Aristotle may be right in indicating that the original proposal of Themistocles resulted in the construction of one hundred ships, whatever we may think about the details of his narrative.[79] Herodotus, however, says that the total number was two hundred and it has been conjectured that to him the object or the result of the naval bill was to bring the size of the Athenian fleet, including existing ships, up to a total of two hundred; but this is not the most natural interpretation of his text.[80] It does, however, seem credible that he may be anticipating (albeit illogically) in his figure of two hundred the additional triremes which he explains were of necessity subsequently built and available for the battle of Salamis. Thus the initial proposal of Themistocles may have been for one hundred triremes with the provision for the building of others subsequently; or perhaps more than one naval bill had to be passed before Salamis for the construction of additional ships. As the Persian menace became more imminent, the Athenians may very well have seen fit to increase further the size of their navy; presumably the new vein of silver was not immediately depleted and extra money continued to be available. But a distinction between one bill to make the money from the extraordinary strike at Maroneia available to the hundred most wealthy Athenians and another to discontinue a customary dole out of the regular income from Laurium represents a needless hypothetical subtlety.[81]

Whatever stage or stages there may have been in the naval legislation, I conclude that at the time of Salamis the Athenians had available a fleet of about two hundred ships, whether or not this total represents only the new triremes built after 483 or includes as well previously constructed ships that were still sea-worthy and available.[82]

The evidence does not tell us whether or not Themistocles proposed any other naval reforms at this time.[83] We do not know if he held an official position when he made his naval proposal. He could have done so as a private citizen. But I wonder if he might have been general in 483/2 (if not before) and continued to be elected to this office until Salamis. There is no doubt, of course, that he was general in 480 at the time of the battle. After all there were ten generals elected every year. Re-election was in no way prohibited. Since Themistocles succeeded in his naval programme because of the war against Aegina, is it not probable that as general he was very much involved in the strategy of the campaign and as a result his arguments appeared even more convincing? At any rate I see no need to invent a special office for Themistocles in connection with his naval programme of 483/2.

We do not know the name of the archon for the year 482/1 and it has been argued that this, and not 493/2, is the correct year for Themistocles' archonship, even though the office was now filled by lot; and furthermore that his fortification of the Piraeus was begun in this period of his successful naval bill. My previous arguments have shown that his archonship should legitimately be placed in 493/2, and the initiation of his plans for the Piraeus probably belongs in this same year. Yet admittedly work on the Piraeus could have been begun or continued in the period 483–481; but for this and the archonship in 482/1 there is no indisputable direct evidence.

The difficulty arises from the fact that our ancient sources generally begin their focus upon the culmination of Themistocles' career: his bill of 483/2, his subsequent victory at Salamis and his fortification of both Athens and the Piraeus in the years following – and it is only natural that they should. No wonder, then, that his earlier activities often became either obscured or forgotten. In keeping with this emphasis upon the beginning of Themistocles' achievement in 483/2, Herodotus (quoted above) tells us that at the time of Salamis Themistocles recently had entered the ranks of those in first place and then he describes the naval bill of a few years earlier. But there nevertheless remains reliable evidence elsewhere for Themistocles' appearance in the 490s and the 480s, before 483, which cannot be dismissed lightly as hypothetical invention.

Finally, a word about Herodotus' curious introduction of Themistocles, 'his name was Themistocles but he was called the son [child? boy?] of Neocles' (τῷ οὔνομα μὲν ἦν Θεμιστοκλέης παῖς δὲ Νεοκλέος ἐκαλέετο). It has generally been assumed that Herodotus' intention is to be deliberately derogatory in keeping with his alleged bias against Themistocles elsewhere. I shall have more to say about this alleged bias later. But I am by no means certain what connotations Herodotus' introduction is meant to convey. Does it reflect the dubious ancestry of Themistocles on his mother's side which we have detected in Chapter II? Does it only mean that, although his name was Themistocles as a boy or in younger days, he was more often than not called the son of Neocles? Is it even too fanciful to imagine that the genitive Νεοκλέος is a correction or corruption of an original nominative, the meaning actually having once been: 'his name was Themistocles but as a boy he used to be called Neocles'?

THEMISTOCLES AND ARISTEIDES

Aristeides the Just was ostracized in the year 483/2 and there can be no doubt that the major reason for his removal from Athens was conflict with Themistocles over the naval programme.[84] Their hostility is reported as deep and long-standing and so it would be worth-while at this point to review part of what Plutarch in his *Life of Aristeides* has to say about their relationship. Plutarch stresses the moral antithesis between a just Aristeides and a corrupt Themistocles in his explanation of their rivalry; the following synopsis will suggest how anecdotal and dubious are many of the details of his narrative.[85] That the two were often politically opposed on certain issues is of course indisputable.

Aristeides favoured aristocracy and therefore had as his opponent Themistocles, the democrat. Their antagonism began when they were boys and fellow-students and from the outset their opposite natures were revealed: Themistocles being impetuous, versatile and unscrupulous; Aristeides stable, tried and true. According to Ariston of Ceos (Plutarch maintains) their rivalry originated in a love affair. Both became enamoured of the handsomest of youths, a lad from Ceos named Stesilaüs; and once the beauty of the boy had faded, they transferred their passionate hostility from love to politics.

So intense was their rivalry that Aristeides would often feel compelled to introduce measures expedient for the state through other men, so that Themistocles would refrain from opposing them. He was even driven to desperate lengths to curtail the aggressive power of his rival. On one occasion he opposed and caused to be defeated a proposal advocated by Themistocles, even though it was advantageous for the people. As Aristeides left the Assembly he is supposed to have remarked that, unless both Themistocles and he were hurled into the death-pit, there would be no security for the Athenian state.

When Aristeides had been elected curator of public revenues (ἐπιμελητὴς τῶν δημοσίων προσόδων),[86] he disclosed that large embezzlements of money had been made not only by his fellow officers but also by those of earlier years, especially Themistocles. Therefore, in retaliation, Themistocles won enough support to have Aristeides himself prosecuted on a charge of theft when his own accounts were audited; and (Plutarch reports on the authority of Idomeneus) a verdict against Aristeides was actually pronounced. But the foremost and best men in Athens rallied around him and Aristeides not only was exempted from a fine but by a clever ruse became reinstated in the eyes of the citizens and succeeded in exposing the thefts of the corrupt officials.

I should be hard pressed to defend the truth of much of this legendary information; but the essential depiction of bitter political rivalry obviously has a factual basis. Yet the two men could act in consort in more than one crisis. And when Aristeides was recalled from ostracism as a result of the threat of Xerxes' invasion, he joined Themistocles at Salamis in his greatest hour of triumph.

The Second Persian War[87]

In 486/5 Xerxes (Pl. 21) succeeded his father, Darius, to the
throne of Persia and before long his commitment to avenge the
Persian defeat at Marathon become only too apparent. The plan
that he put into effect was to attack both by land and sea with
an expedition under his personal command. By 480 he was
ready; his army proceeded across the Hellespont, over which
bridges had been constructed, and marched into Thrace for an
invasion of Hellas from the north; his fleet, after joining the
land forces at Doriscus in Thrace, sailed along the coast ready
for joint action. A canal was even dug through the Isthmus of
Mount Athos, where Mardonius' expedition in 492 had met
disaster.

Herodotus' account of the war dramatically highlights the
amazing victory of the Hellenes against overwhelming odds;
and his catalogue of the Persian forces is fantastically exaggerated
in its epic proportions: e.g. 1,700,000 foot-soldiers with 80,000
cavalry and more besides; 1207 triremes and 3000 penteconters
carrying 2,317,000 men; after their arrival in Hellas additional
recruits brought the total of fighting men to 2,641,610.[88] His
depiction of the Persians, in stark contrast with that of the
Hellenes, is also conceived on a grand and tragic scale. Xerxes
emerges as the brutal despot of enslaved minions who, through
his hubris and impiety, is finally brought low by the hand of
god and the righteous bravery, intelligence and cunning of
freedom-loving Greeks. The personalities of his *History* are
brought to life by the techniques of literary art; theatrical
scenes are cleverly constructed and speeches and dialogue freely
invented. In his interpretative manipulation of moral, religious
and political themes, Herodotus illuminates fundamental and
universal truths. Specific and generic historical facts, to be sure,
abound but they have been so splendidly embellished by anecdote, legend and mythology that his *History of the Persian Wars*
moves and inspires the reader very much in the legendary
manner of an epic. It is in this emotional and miraculous context
of saga, then, that the Herodotean portrait of Themistocles is

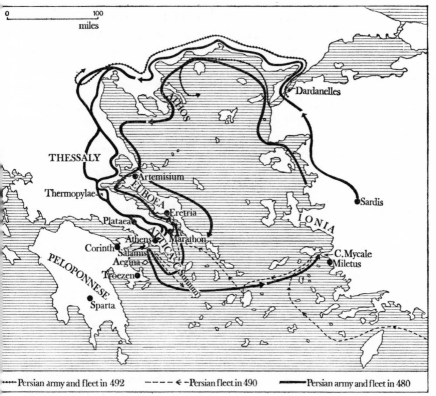

THESSALY

Thermopylae

Artemisium

Plataea

Corinth
Athens
Salamis
Aegina
Troezen

Sparta

PELOPONNESE

EUBOEA

ATTICA

Eretria

Marathon

Dardanelles

Sardis

IONIA

C. Mycale
Miletus

0   100
        miles

•••• Persian army and fleet in 492   – – – ◄ –Persian fleet in 490   ━━━ Persian army and fleet in 480

Map II   The Persian offensives against the Greeks

conceived and executed; and it is upon this portrait that I should like to concentrate.

Historians vary in their logical estimates of Xerxes' forces on the basis of Herodotus' information: perhaps his land army included at most 200,000 men plus a minimum of 800 triremes with their contingents. By 480 the Hellenes were well aware of their critical danger; to meet the emergency a Hellenic League was formed and a Congress of representatives of the member states convened at the Isthmus of Corinth to decide upon strategy. Since Sparta was the acknowledged military leader, the supreme command of both the army and the fleet was placed in her hands, and the Athenians bowed to the inevitable. King Leonidas was appointed as leader for the land forces and a

Spartan, Eurybiades, for the allied fleet. It was initially decided to defend the pass of Tempe, which led from lower Macedonia into Thessaly. Herodotus informs us that a Greek force of about 10,000 hoplites was dispatched under the Spartan Evaenetus and the Athenian Themistocles, son of Neocles.[89] But the area proved to be indefensible, since the Persians could have proceeded south by other routes, and so the Hellenes returned home. As a result most of northern Hellas submitted to the invaders, for the Hellenic Congress next resolved upon a double defensive farther south against the army and navy of Xerxes; they would guard the pass of Thermopylae, leading between mountains and sea from Trachis into Locris; their fleet would be stationed opposite, off the promontory of Artemisium at the northern tip of the island of Euboea.

Leonidas was dispatched to defend Thermopylae with a force of about 7000 men and so valiant was their defence that the repeated attacks of Xerxes' army proved of no avail. It was only through the betrayal of a Hellene named Ephialtes, who disclosed to the enemy that they could take the position by means of a mountain pass around to the rear, that the Persians finally achieved success. Despite the knowledge that all was now lost, Leonidas with a core of followers remained to face certain death. Their steadfast bravery, immortalized in the pages of Herodotus, did much to enhance the glory of the Spartans in particular as staunch defenders of Hellenic freedom. Xerxes and his army now poured down farther south, into Hellas, and news of the defeat at Thermopylae was conveyed to the Hellenic naval contingent at Artemisium, which at this same time had been in conflict with the Persian fleet.

ARTEMISIUM

In the naval defensive of the Hellenes at Artemisium the Athenians played a leading role. Herodotus tells us that of the 271 triremes in the fleet the Athenians contributed 147.[90] Although the Spartan Eurybiades was commander-in-chief of the entire naval forces, Themistocles as general of the Athenians was most influential in determining strategy both at Artemisium and in critical events during the course of the war.

Themistocles' election to the generalship in Athens for 480/79 apparently had not been easy, at least according to a story related only by Plutarch, which may be paraphrased as follows:[91]

> When the Persians were approaching Hellas, all the others [of the Leontid tribe] voluntarily withdrew from the election because of panic; but Epicydes, the son of Euphemides, a demagogue and clever speaker but a weak man subject to bribery, aimed at the office and seemed likely to win. Themistocles was afraid lest all would be ruined if such a man were elected and so he bribed him to withdraw his candidacy and thus won the generalship for himself.

The tale sounds like a later invention to reaffirm Themistocles' wily character. Whatever the case, it was indeed fortunate for Athens and for Hellas that Themistocles was elected to office at this critical time. As we have seen, he had been sent as one of the commanders to the pass of Tempe. He was very much present now with the naval forces at Artemisium.

Before the Persians took up their position at Aphetae at the tip of the peninsula of Magnesia, their fleet had suffered severe losses as a result of a storm; nevertheless the Hellenes at Artemisium were intimidated by the numbers of the enemy, which were still substantial. Herodotus' account continues as follows, with emphasis upon the clever manipulation of Eurybiades by a corrupt Themistocles:[92]

> When the Hellenes came to Artemisium they saw the many ships of the enemy anchored near Aphetae and the whole place full of soldiers. Since the fortunes of the Persians had gone completely contrary to their expectations, the Hellenes were frightened and deliberated about fleeing from Artemisium to the inner regions of Hellas. The Euboeans, upon hearing of these prospects, begged Eurybiades to remain for a short time until they could move their children and families to safety. When they did not persuade him, they next approached the Athenian general, Themistocles. They convinced Themistocles by the payment of thirty talents on condition that the Hellenes would stay and fight a sea battle in defence of Euboea.
>
> Themistocles got the Hellenes to remain in the following way: He passed on to Eurybiades five talents out of the money he had received,

pretending as he gave it that it was his own. Thus he won over Eurybiades; and since the Corinthian Adeimantus, the son of Ocytus, alone of the rest of the generals resisted and said that he would sail away from Artemisium and would not remain, Themistocles addressed him with an oath: 'You will not desert us, for I will give you a greater gift than the King of the Persians would send you if you abandoned the allies.' And as he said these words he sent three talents of silver to the ship of Adeimantus. These generals then were influenced and won over by the bribes and the wishes of the Euboeans were gratified. Themistocles himself also made a profit; no one knew that he had the rest of the money but the two who got a share of it thought that it came from Athens for this purpose. Thus the Hellenes remained in Euboea and faced the enemy with their ships.

But the engagements between the Persians and the Hellenes at Artemisium resulted in losses on both sides with no clear advantage for either; and so Abronichus (i.e. Habronichus), son of Lysicles, an Athenian, arrived in his thirty-oared ship (he had been stationed near Leonidas) with the news of the defeat at Thermopylae. Herodotus' narrative continues with another illustration of Themistocles' ingenuity:[93]

When they learned about Thermopylae the Hellenes no longer delayed their retreat and withdrew as they were stationed, the Corinthians first, the Athenians last.

Themistocles, having picked out the best sailing ships of the Athenians, proceeded to places where there was drinking water and cut into the rocks a message which the Ionians read the next day when they came to Artemisium.[94] The message read as follows: 'Men of Ionia, you do not do what is just in campaigning against your own fathers and enslaving Hellas. But come over to us. This would be best, but if it is not possible for you to do so, still at least do not now engage on either side yourselves and ask the Carians to act in the same way as you. If neither of these courses is possible but you are bound by a necessity too great to withstand, when we are engaged in actual conflict, fight badly remembering that you are of our blood and that our enmity against the Persians arose to begin with because of you.' Themistocles wrote this message, it seems to me, with two purposes in mind: either the King would not discover the message and he would make the Ionians change and come over to his side or, when it was reported to the King and the Ionians were incriminated, he would make them untrustworthy and remove them from subsequent sea battles. This is what Themistocles wrote.

The defences at Thermopylae and Artemisium had both been failures. What were the Hellenes now to do as the enemy was literally descending upon Hellas? Their course of action in the face of their immediate and dire crisis was largely determined by events that had transpired in Athens earlier.

THE WOODEN WALL

In Herodotus' account preliminary to the decisions of the Hellenic Congress to defend the pass of Tempe and then to take up positions at Thermopylae and Artemisium, the Athenians, as Xerxes was coming against Greece, anxiously sent messengers to consult the oracle at Delphi. Herodotus reports that the Pythian prophetess, whose name was Aristonice, urged them to flee, in verse as follows:[95]

> Poor wretches, why do you sit here?
> Flee to the ends of the earth.
> Leave your homes and the lofty citadel
> of your city with its circular wall.
> For neither the head remains firm
> nor the body nor the feet below
> nor, indeed, the hands,
> nor is any part in the middle left steadfast.
> But all is in a plight not to be envied.
> For fire and swift Ares, driving a Syrian chariot,
> lays her low.
> He will destroy many other citadels too,
> not yours alone.
> And he will give to raging fire
> many temples of the gods,
> which even now stand streaming with sweat
> and quaking with fear,
> and black blood pours down from the roof tops,
> portending the inevitable evil to come.
> But leave this sanctuary now
> and dwell upon your woes.

The Athenian ambassadors were terribly disturbed by this oracle when, in their despair, a distinguished man of Delphi named Timon, the son of Androboulus, advised them to enter the sanctuary and consult the oracle again, this time as suppliants with olive-branches in their hands. The Athenians followed his advice and spoke as follows: 'Lord Apollo, prophesy something better for our country, in respect of these suppliant olive branches that we bear or else we will not leave the sanctuary but remain in this place until we die.' The prophetess responded with this second oracle:

> Pallas Athena is not able to appease Olympian Zeus
> as she appeals to him
> with many arguments and sound wisdom.
> To you I speak again with these words,
> firm as adamant.
> When all else has been taken
> – as much as the boundary of Cecrops contains
> and the hollows of holy Cithaeron –
> far-seeing Zeus grants to the prayers
> of Athena Tritogeneia
> that the wooden wall alone remains unassailable,
> a protection for you and your children.
> Do not quietly await the hordes of cavalry and infantry
> of the invader from Asia.
> But turn your backs and retire.
> In time you will still meet him face to face.
> Divine Salamis, you will destroy the offspring of women
> when Demeter's grain is scattered at seed time
> or gathered in harvest.

At this point I shall continue with a direct translation of Herodotus, whose every word is vital for our understanding of Themistocles' career:[96]

This second reply seemed to be less severe than the first to the ambassadors (and indeed it was); and so they wrote it down and returned to Athens. When they arrived they presented it to the people. And there were many different opinions among those who sought the meaning of the oracle; the following two in particular were in direct opposition. Some of the elders said that they thought the god meant that the Acropolis would remain safe, for the Acropolis of Athens in those days was surrounded by a rampart and they concluded that this rampart was the wooden wall of the oracle.[97] Others, however, said that the god meant the ships and they urged that everything else be abandoned in favour of getting these ships ready. Nevertheless those who maintained that the wooden wall meant the ships were perplexed by the last two lines prophesied by the Priestess:

> Divine Salamis, you will destroy the offspring of women
> when Demeter's grain is scattered at seed time
> or gathered in harvest.

These were the words that created difficulties for the interpretation of those who maintained that the ships were the wooden wall. For the professional interpreters took them to mean that, if they prepared for a naval battle at Salamis, they would inevitably be defeated.

Now there was a certain man among the Athenians, who recently had entered the ranks of those in first place; his name was Themistocles but he was called the son of Neocles. This Themistocles said that the professional interpreters had not understood the whole oracle correctly. He argued as follows: If the disputed phrase really referred to the Athenians it would not appear to have been expressed so mildly but the words 'hateful Salamis' would have been used instead of 'divine Salamis' – if indeed those to whom the island belonged were going to die there. But instead the correct interpretation was that the god had uttered his oracle against the enemy, not against the Athenians. And so he advised that they prepare to fight on the sea with their ships, since that was what was meant by the wooden wall. Once Themistocles had explained the oracle in his way, the Athenians acknowledged that his interpretation was preferable to that of the professionals who forbade preparations for a naval battle and, in a word, were against lifting even a hand against the enemy; instead they insisted upon leaving Attica and settling in some other place.

Herodotus then goes on to comment how on a previous occasion another opinion of Themistocles proved to be best at a critical moment, providing an explanation of his naval bill that has already been translated early in this chapter. Then Herodotus continues:

In deliberation after the oracle, being convinced by the god, they resolved to receive the Persians who were coming against Hellas, with all the people in their ships along with those of the Hellenes who were willing [to join with them].

Among the many problems inherent in Herodotus, several emerge as especially significant at this point. Can we believe literally in his account of the role of the Delphic oracle in the determination of events? Was it a lucky coincidence or a deliberate manoeuvre that made the allusions to the wooden wall and

divine Salamis suit Themistocles' plans for the salvation of
Athens and Hellas? Were the oracles really either delivered or
confirmed by Delphi only after the fact of the Hellenic victory
against the Persians? If not, at what time in the period 481/0
were they pronounced? Were they in some way fabricated in
their entirety to fit the occasion or merely judiciously adjusted
through the machinations of Themistocles, with or without the
cooperation of the priests of Delphi? Such are the questions
debated by modern scholarship and I do not know of any
confident solutions. It seems to me preferable to believe that the
clever and political Delphic priesthood did make their ambiguous utterances as Herodotus has recorded; that the ingenious
and unscrupulous Themistocles, by whatever means, manipulated the whole proceedings for his own ends also appears not
unlikely. But we simply do not know.

Another major problem concerns the chronology of events
particularly in connection with the question of the formal
ratification by the Athenian Assembly of a decree by Themistocles that the Athenians should take to their ships. Herodotus'
narrative certainly cannot be pressed for chronological precision.
His method is generally to complete his discussion of one topic
before moving on to the next. Initial consultation of Delphi by
the Athenians could have begun before the Hellenic Congress
had decided to send a force to Tempe; and the final debate
(presumably one of many) in the Athenian Assembly about the
second utterance of the god could have occurred at any time
thereafter before the actual evacuation of the city. Herodotus'
statement that their naval resolution was made in deliberation
(after the oracle ἔδοξέ τέ σφι μετὰ τὸ χρηστήριον βουλευομένοισι)
seems to refer to an actual decree that was passed. If so, does the
decree of Themistocles that has been discovered authentically
reproduce either in whole or in part the decision reported by
Herodotus in this context? Was this decree passed before the
Hellenic Congress made their plans to defend Tempe, after
Thermopylae and Artemisium had been decided upon, or
perhaps later once both these defensive positions also proved to
be failures – more questions that must remain debatable. But

we need to postpone discussion until further literary evidence and the extant decree of Themistocles have been considered.

THE EVACUATION OF ATHENS

Herodotus[98] tells us that upon the departure of the Hellenic fleet from Artemisium it proceeded to Salamis and cast anchor there upon the insistent request of the Athenians. For the Athenians had expected that the Peloponnesian forces would be prepared to oppose the Persians, who by this time had made their way into Boeotia and threatened Attica and Athens itself. But instead they were busy constructing a wall across the Isthmus for their own protection, heedless of the perils of their fellow Hellenes. The rest of the Hellenic sea-force, upon learning that the fleet had arrived at Salamis, joined them there; the commander was still the Spartan Eurybiades, but the largest number of ships and the best sailors were Athenian. Herodotus provides a catalogue of the naval forces; the total number of triremes was 366 or 378. Herodotus' account of the Athenian measures upon the return of the fleet to Salamis runs as follows:[99]

While the rest of the fleet was anchored off Salamis, the Athenians returned to their own harbour. Upon their arrival a proclamation (κήρυγμα) was made that each and every Athenian should, in whatever way he was able, save his children and his household. Thereupon most of them were sent to Troezen, but some went to Aegina and others to Salamis. They made all haste for the removal of their families in their desire to fulfil the dictates of the oracle, but they were also, to be sure, motivated not least of all by the following circumstance. The Athenians say that a great snake guards the Acropolis and lives in the temple there; this is what they say and besides, in confirmation, each month they actually set out food for it, as though it really existed; and its monthly ration consists of a honey-cake. Previously the honey-cake had always been consumed but now it was untouched. When the priestess told the Athenians this, they were all the more eager to evacuate Athens since they believed that even the goddess had abandoned the Acropolis.

A natural reading of Herodotus suggests that a proposal made by Themistocles to take to their ships was agreed upon by the

Athenians at some time before going to Artemisium; now that they had returned, the proclamation to evacuate the city meant that decisions previously reached were now made final and put into effect. But the evidence of Plutarch must be also considered; for his text echoes, even more closely than Herodotus, language in the preliminary section of the extant Themistoclean decree. Plutarch in addition assures us that the omen of the serpent was used (if not actually contrived) by Themistocles for his own purpose and his account may also imply some devious manipulation of the Delphic oracle itself; at this point in Plutarch's narrative the Athenians have come back from Artemisium and the Peloponnesians have begun their construction of a wall across the Isthmus:[100]

Then indeed Themistocles, being at a loss to win over the multitude by human logic, set up stage machinery as in tragedy and brought before them divine omens and oracles. He took as a religious sign the business of the snake, which seemed to have disappeared from the sanctuary at this very time; and, when the priests discovered that the daily offerings made to it were untouched, they announced to the people what Themistocles told them to say – namely that the goddess had abandoned the city and was leading the way for them to the sea. He again used the oracle as an argument to persuade them, maintaining that the wooden wall meant nothing other than the ships; and therefore the god called Salamis divine and not dreadful or hateful because it would be a synonym of great good fortune for the Hellenes. He prevailed in his opinion and he introduced a decree (ψήφισμα γράφει) stipulating that the city be entrusted to Athena the guardian of Athens but that all men of military age board the triremes and provide safety for their children, wives and slaves, each as best he could. When the decree had been passed, most of the Athenians evacuated their children[101] to Troezen where the people welcomed them eagerly; for they even voted to give each (family) two obols and to allow the boys to pick the fruit everywhere and to pay teachers for them besides. The decree was introduced by Nicagoras.

Since the Athenians did not have any public money available, the Areopagus, according to Aristotle, by providing eight drachmas for each man who was to fight aboard his ship, became most responsible for the manning of the triremes.[102]

Plutarch, then, seems to place the decree of Themistocles after the return of the Athenians from Artemisium, although he alludes to Themistocles' earlier arguments concerning the oracle about the wooden wall. We can have no secure faith in Plutarch's ordering of events in any specific context. But perhaps he can be of some help, if used in connection with the testimony of Herodotus and the epigraphical evidence of the decree itself.

THE DECREE OF THEMISTOCLES FROM TROEZEN (Pls 15, 16)

The discovery in Troezen by Michael Jameson in 1959 of an inscription that purports to be the actual decree proposed by Themistocles has very quickly inspired a wealth of literature. I have no intention of reviewing the various facets of the controversy that have been covered so well and so often. Scholars are about equally divided in their acceptance or rejection of this inscription as authentic; and one more vote by anyone for one side or the other can hardly weigh very heavily, without the benefit of new solid evidence. Epigraphical experts assure us that the extant decree was inscribed in the third century BC; thus we apparently know for certain that we do not have the original inscription. The major issue is whether it is an outright forgery or actually represents (however faithfully) a decree or decrees actually passed. I am going to assume that it is in essence authentic and on this assumption (and not necessarily firm belief) I shall try in so far as possible to place it in its most probable historical context or contexts. But first here is a translation of the text of the stone; I make no attempt to reproduce the line divisions:[103]

Gods.
This decree was passed by the Council and the people; Themistocles, the son of Neocles, of Phrearrhioi, proposed it: The city is to be entrusted to Athena, the guardian of Athens, and to all the other gods for protection against the foreign enemy and to ward him off on behalf of the land; as for the Athenians themselves and the foreigners dwelling in Athens, children and women are to be taken to Troezen and the protection of Pittheus, founder of the place; old men and property (κτήματα, slaves) are to be taken to Salamis; treasurers and priestesses are to remain on the Acropolis watching over the things of the gods; all other Athenians and foreigners of military age are to

embark on the two hundred ships, which have been made ready, and ward off the foreign enemy for the sake of freedom, both their own and that of the other Hellenes, with the help of Lacedaemonians, Corinthians, Aeginetans and others who wish to share in the danger; the generals, beginning tomorrow, are to appoint two hundred ship-commanders (trierarchs), one for each ship, from among those who possess both land and a home at Athens and have legitimate children and who are not over fifty years of age, and to these men they are to assign the ships by lot; they are to enlist ten heavy-armed soldiers (ἐπιβάτας) for each ship from among those who are over twenty and under thirty years of age and four archers; and they are to choose by lot the crew (ὑπερεσίας)[104] for the ships at the time when they allot the ship-commanders; and the generals are to post on white notice-boards the names of the others, ship by ship, those of Athenians taken from the deme registers, those of foreigners from the records of the Polemarch; they are to post the lists of names, distributing them, by hundreds, into companies, no more than two hundred in number, and they are to write at the head of each company the name of the trireme, of the ship-commander and the crew (ὑπερεσίας) so that each company may know on which trireme it will embark. When all the companies have been made up and allotted to the triremes, the Council and the generals, after making a propitiatory sacrifice to Zeus the Almighty, Athena Nike and Poseidon the Preserver, are to man all the two hundred ships; when the ships have been manned, with a hundred of them they are to render service at Artemisium in Euboea and with the other hundred they are to lie in wait around Salamis and the rest of Attica and guard the land. In order that all the Athenians may be of one mind in warding off the foreign enemy, those who have [or had] been expelled for ten years are to go to Salamis and remain there until something has been decided about them by the people; and those (who have [or had] lost their rights?). . . .

If the decree is authentic, the measures it embodies will presumably have been determined early, i.e. perhaps even before the Hellenic Congress had agreed to send a force to Tempe or immediately after, once Tempe had been abandoned. For the decision of the Hellenic allies to make their defence at Thermopylae and Artemisium in all likelihood was decisively influenced by Athens herself, as a result of policies independently inaugurated by the assembly for the city's own protection, through the vehement advocacy of Themistocles. Thus preliminary plans to abandon the city and send ships to Artemisium

and Salamis were provisional. If evacuation did become necessary, children and women were to be taken to Troezen, old
men and slaves to Salamis; when deportation became a reality,
Aegina (as Herodotus relates) also became a place of refuge;
surely by this time her conflict with Athens must have been
resolved.

The assignment of ship-commanders, military contingents
and crews could have been initiated 'immediately' so that the
triremes would be ready to be dispatched both to Artemisium
and to Salamis. The total of two hundred may suggest that this
was, after all, the number of new ships built as a result of
Themistocles' naval bill. In any case, one hundred were designated for Artemisium; that this does not tally with Herodotus'
figure of 127[105] (assuming his text is correct) means again that
an adjustment became necessary when the actual conflict there
became a fact. Some ships assigned to Salamis, for example, may
have been transferred to Artemisium; or one hundred new
triremes, accounted for in the decree, may have been reinforced
by additional ships made available as a result of the indecisive
encounters with the Persians. The difficult last lines of the
decree as preserved, which seem to refer to the disposition of
those who had *already* been recalled from ostracism and exile
need not conflict with the testimony of Aristotle, who places
the formal resolution for their return in 481/0.[106] Upon the
Athenian withdrawal from Artemisium, the measures for the
final evacuation of the city were implemented. Arguments that
the haste and confusion inherent in Herodotus' depiction of the
abandonment of the city are in conflict with the belief that
specific stipulations for evacuation had been determined earlier
are exaggerated. Anguish and panic would naturally prevail
during the very hours of actual departure, whatever decisions
had been arrived at in less trying circumstances. Yet it may even
be possible that some evacuation of the city had already taken
place. It is nevertheless understandable that Plutarch places
Themistocles' decree in the final moments of the crisis, when
the Athenians departed from their city; for it was then that all
its stipulations were finally fulfilled. Perhaps the decree from

Troezen represents a subsequent commitment to stone of individual measures that had been taken at different times – an amalgamation, as it were, of various historical stages in the whole chain of events, most of which can be suspected and logically deduced from the literary testimony itself.

THE BATTLE OF SALAMIS

While the Hellenic navy was stationed at Salamis the Persian fleet had also proceeded south and taken its position in the bay of Phalerum. Xerxes' army by this time had descended from Boeotia into Attica for an attack on Athens itself. The Persians found the city abandoned except for a small group entrenched on the Acropolis behind the barricade that served as their 'wooden wall'. The Acropolis was taken, its defenders massacred and its temples looted and burned.

Herodotus narrates events at Salamis, after Xerxes had occupied Athens, as follows:[107]

When it was reported to the Hellenes at Salamis what had happened to the Acropolis of the Athenians, there was such an uproar that some of the generals did not even wait for the business on hand to be settled but rushed to their ships and raised their sails for flight; it was decided by those who remained to fight a sea-battle in defence of the Isthmus. Night fell, the meeting broke up, and they went to their ships.

Then, as Themistocles was approaching his ship, Mnesiphilus, an Athenian, asked what had been decided. When he learned from him that it was thought best to bring the ships to the Isthmus and defend the Peloponnesus by a sea battle, Mnesiphilus exclaimed: 'If they remove their ships from Salamis, you will be fighting for one country no longer. For each will return to his city and neither Eurybiades nor any other person will be able to hinder them and prevent the complete dissolution of the army, and Hellas will be destroyed by lack of good counsel. But if there is any way, go and try to upset these plans, if somehow you are able to persuade Eurybiades to change the decision and remain here.'

This suggestion appealed very much to Themistocles and without answering a word he went to the ship of Eurybiades. Once there he said that he had come to discuss some business for the common good. Eurybiades bade him board the ship and say whatever he wanted.

Thereupon Themistocles sat down beside Eurybiades and told him all
that he had heard from Mnesiphilus, pretending that it was his own
and adding many other arguments as well, until he convinced him by
his appeals to leave the ship and summon the generals to a meeting.

When they had been gathered together, before Eurybiades could
explain to the generals the reason why he had called them, Themistocles,
as one who is very insistent is wont to do, plunged into speech.
Adeimantus, the son of Ocytus, general of the Corinthians, interrupted
him by saying: 'Themistocles, in the games, those who start too soon
get whipped.' 'Yes,' Themistocles retorted in self-defence, 'but those
who start too late are not crowned as winners.' At this point his reply
to the Corinthian was mild and to Eurybiades he no longer used any
of those previous arguments to the effect that when they left Salamis
they would be dispersed, for it would have been unbecoming for him
to accuse the allies while they were present. But he resorted to another
argument and spoke as follows:

'It is in your power, Eurybiades, to save Hellas, if you listen to me
and remain here to fight a sea-battle and do not, through the persuasion
of others, leave with the ships for the Isthmus. Hear and weigh the
two courses. In a battle at the Isthmus you will fight on the open sea,
which is to our least advantage since we have ships that are heavier
and fewer in number. Besides you will lose Salamis, Megara and
Aegina, even if the rest goes well with us. Then too the land army will
follow their fleet and thus you will yourself lead them right down to
the Peloponnesus and endanger the whole of Hellas. But if you do what
I say, you will find all these advantages in my advice: First, by encountering many ships with few in narrow waters, we shall win a great
victory if the battle goes as one would expect; for a sea battle in a
confined space is to our advantage, but one in the open sea is to theirs.
Furthermore, Salamis where our women and children have been sent
for safety will be protected. And in addition the point to which you
cling most will be accomplished by this course of action: if you remain
here you will fight in defence of the Peloponnesians just as much as if
you went to the Isthmus and you will not lead the enemy, if you have
good sense, right down to the Peloponnesus. If what I expect turns
out and we win the victory with our ships, the Persians will not be a
threat to you at the Isthmus but will reach no further than Attica; they
will retreat in disorder and we shall gain by the safety of Megara,
Aegina and Salamis, where, according to an oracle, we are to triumph
over the enemy. Success is generally sure to follow those who make the
proper plans; but not even god is on the side of those who do not.'

As Themistocles spoke these words, once again the Corinthian
Adeimantus attacked him, commanding one who had no city to be

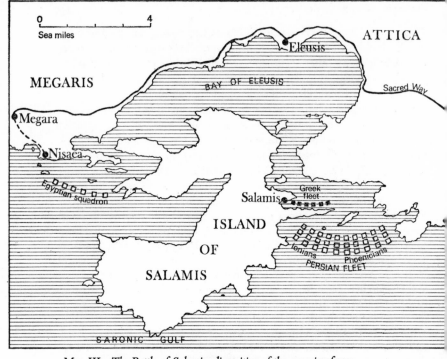

Map III   The Battle of Salamis: disposition of the opposing forces

silent and forbidding Eurybiades to put a question raised by a man without a country to the vote; for he ordered Themistocles to name the city that he represented before he offered any opinion. He made these jibes because the city of Athens had been captured and was being held by the enemy. Thereupon Themistocles did indeed pour many bitter abuses upon both Adeimantus and the Corinthians, and he made it quite clear that the Athenians, as long as they possessed two hundred ships fully manned, had a city and a country greater than theirs and none of the Hellenes could withstand their attack.

After this assertion he turned and addressed Eurybiades with even greater vehemence: 'If you remain here, you will be a good man by doing so; but if you do not, you will destroy Hellas. For the whole outcome of the war depends upon our ships. If you do not follow my advice, we will put our families on board our ships and sail to Siris in Italy, which is still ours from of old and which, an oracle says, we must colonize. When you are bereft of allies like us, you will remember my words.'

Eurybiades was induced to change his mind by Themistocles' speech, mainly because (as it seems to me) he was afraid that the

Athenians would desert them if he brought the ships to the Isthmus; for with the Athenians gone, the rest would no longer be worthy of battle. He chose the advice to remain at Salamis and offer battle.[108]

But when the Peloponnesians who were at Salamis learned that Hellenic troops had been assembled at the Isthmus, across which a wall was hastily being built, great consternation once again arose; for they were waiting, in their view, to fight on behalf of Athenian territory while their own was in jeopardy, with the risk of possible defeat. Thus open hostility against Eurybiades' decision to remain broke out and another meeting was held. Herodotus reports as follows:[109]

There was much talk about the same questions. Some argued that they must sail away to the Peloponnesus and risk all in its defence rather than remain at Salamis to fight on behalf of a land that had already fallen to the enemy's sword; but the Athenians, Aeginetans and Megarians were for staying and making their defence where they were.

Then Themistocles, as his proposal was being defeated by the Peloponnesians, slipped away from the meeting, unnoticed; after he had left he sent a man in a boat to the fleet of the Persians with instructions about what he had to say. The man's name was Sicinnus and he was one of Themistocles' domestics who attended to his children.[110] At a time after these events, Themistocles made him a citizen of Thespiae (as the Thespians used to welcome additional citizens) and financially prosperous. He then was the one who came to the generals of the Persians and spoke these words: 'The general of the Athenians has sent me without the knowledge of the other Hellenes (for he happens to be concerned about the prospects of the King and would prefer that you rather than the Hellenes be victorious) to disclose to you that the Hellenes in their terror are planning a retreat and now the opportunity presents itself for you to accomplish the finest of all your achievements, if you do not let them escape. For they do not agree with one another and they will no longer oppose you – you will see them fighting among themselves, one faction on your side, the other opposed to you.' After those disclosures, Sicinnus made a quick departure.

The Persians believed the message and began their preparation for the occupation of the islet of Psyttaleia and the blockading of the Hellenes at Salamis. Then Herodotus continues:[111]

A vehement and lengthy verbal dispute was taking place among the generals at Salamis. They did not as yet know that the enemy was encircling them with their ships but they thought that they were positioned in the same place, just as they had seen them during the day. The generals were at loggerheads when Aristeides, the son of Lysimachus, an Athenian who had been ostracized by the people, arrived from Aegina. From what I have learned about his character I have come to believe that he was the best and most just man in Athens. Aristeides held aloof from the meeting and called Themistocles outside, even though he was not friendly to him but in fact most hostile. Under the weight of the present misfortunes Aristeides made himself forget his enmity, and called Themistocles outside in his desire to confer with him. He had already heard that the Peloponnesians were anxious to bring the ships to the Isthmus and, when Themistocles came out, he spoke to him as follows:

'In any crisis and especially in this one we ought to be in conflict over which of us can do more good for our country. I tell you that it is all the same whether the Peloponnesians talk little or much about sailing away from here, for I tell you that I have seen with my own eyes that the Corinthians and Eurybiades himself will not be able to sail away, not even if they wish, since we are surrounded by the enemy. Go in to them and let them know this.'

Themistocles answered with these words: 'Splendid directions and excellent news. You yourself have come here as a witness who has seen happen what I have begged for. For I want you to know that the Persians have acted under my influence. For since the Hellenes did not want to engage in battle willingly, it was necessary to make them do so, like it or not. Since you have come here with these good tidings, tell them yourself. For, if I do so, they will think that I made it all up and I shall not convince them that the enemy has surrounded us. But you go before them and explain how matters stand. When you have done so, if they believe you that would be best of all, but if they do not, it is all the same to us. For they still will not run away, if indeed we are surrounded on all sides as you say.'

Aristeides made his appearance and told them these things. He had come from Aegina, his boat with difficulty escaping detection by those who were forming the blockade; for the army of the Hellenes was encircled by Xerxes' ships. He advised them to get ready for their self-defence. With these words, he left.

The generals for the most part did not believe him and the argument broke out once again until a Tenian trireme commanded by Panaetius, the son of Sosimenes, deserted from the Persian fleet and gave a full account confirming that of Aristeides. Herodotus continues:[112]

The Hellenes believed the report of the Tenians and prepared for battle. Dawn broke, the fighting men were assembled together, and Themistocles gave the best speech of all. The gist of his words contrasted the better with the worst in all that had to do with human nature and the human condition. He urged them to choose the better rather than the worse of these alternatives and at the conclusion of his speech he ordered them to board their ships.

Herodotus records nothing about Themistocles' role in the course of the battle itself except for an anecdote involving Themistocles and Polycritus, the son of Crius, a citizen of Aegina. At the very moment when Polycritus was about to ram a Sidonian trireme of the Persian fleet and accomplish a daring exploit, he noticed an Athenian ship which ran close by in pursuit of another enemy vessel. This ship was commanded by Themistocles, and, when Polycritus recognized the insignia of generalship, he shouted to Themistocles, reminding him in words of mocking reproach of the charges of Medism that had been made against the Aeginetans.[113]

Plutarch adds what appear to be fictitious details about Themistocles at Salamis.[114] He maintains that Themistocles not only knew the best place for the battle but also realized the best time. For he waited to direct the bows of the Hellenic triremes against the vessels of the enemy until the hour when there was always a fresh breeze and a swelling roll on the waters; this was disadvantageous for the towering Persian ships but did no harm to the smaller and lower Hellenic triremes. All the Hellenes kept their eyes on Themistocles because they realized that he knew the best course of action and because Ariamenes, the admiral of Xerxes, confronted him with a barrage of arrows and javelins. But Ariamenes' ship was rammed by another Hellenic vessel and he himself was killed.

On the authority of Phanias, Plutarch[115] also includes an even more incredible tale. As Themistocles was sacrificing before the battle, three handsome and richly dressed prisoners of war, sons of the King's sister, were brought to him. Because of certain omens the seer Euphrantides insisted that the youths be sacrificed to Dionysus Carnivorous (ὠμηστής) as assurance for victory.

Themistocles was appalled at the monstrous request but the multitude insisted that the sacrifice be carried out.

Such are the fantastic accretions that became part of the Themistoclean legend.[116]

There has been a great deal of discussion about the position and tactics of the opposing forces at Salamis. In conjunction with Herodotus, the divergent and poetic treatment of Aeschylus in *The Persians* provides the most crucial additional evidence, and I present a complete translation of his stirring account in the concluding section of Chapter VII. It is impossible, however, because of its length, to reproduce Herodotus' exciting account of Salamis, replete with epic invention and miraculous anecdote. Instead I shall attempt to provide only the briefest outline of the basic strategies, which amidst all the controversy seems to have attained a measure of general acceptance and which will provide some elucidation for Aeschylus' version to follow later.[117]

As a result of Themistocles' message, Xerxes marshalled his naval forces. His fleet blocked all the escape routes from Salamis: an Egyptian squadron was sent to the channel off the Megarian mainland and outside the main entrance between Salamis and Attica. Ionian and Phoenician squadrons were drawn up in preparation for the attack. A small force of soldiers was stationed on the small island of Psyttaleia (situated at this very entrance) to afford whatever help they could. At daybreak the Persians advanced into the straits, confident that they would find the Hellenes in confused dissension. Quite the contrary turned out to be the case, for they faced instead a disciplined array of ships, ready and waiting for action. As they advanced the Greeks at first back-watered in order to draw them further into the narrows and then rowed forward to the attack. In the narrows the superior numbers of the Persian fleet turned out to be a great liability. A heroic battle was waged by both sides but the Persians were decisively overcome. Not only were the Hellenes victorious on the sea but a force directed against the island of Psyttaleia destroyed the Persians there. Xerxes, who had seated himself on a high throne constructed on the mainland of Attica opposite to witness the spectacle of victory, was instead utterly dismayed at his terrifying defeat. After the battle his only recourse was to return home with the remnants of his fleet, leaving his best troops behind in Greece. In the next year (479) his land army faced the Hellenic military forces at Plataea in Boeotia; again the Hellenes were victorious, with the Peloponnesians and the Spartan commander Pausanias achieving particular glory. At Mycale on the coast of Asia Minor the allied fleet of the Hellenes also won a spectacular victory against the enemy; tradition has it that this battle was fought on the very same day as that at Plataea. We have, however, ignored some important events immediately following upon Salamis; and so we should return now to Herodotus' narrative.

THE AFTERMATH OF SALAMIS

Herodotus explains how, after Salamis, Xerxes ordered his captains with his fleet to leave Phalerum and speed to the Hellespont so that they might protect the bridges there and safeguard Xerxes' return; for Xerxes was to retire with Mardonius and his army by land, north to Boeotia and Thessaly and from there proceed home, leaving, for the time being, Mardonius and the rest of the army behind. When the Hellenes were assured that the enemy ships had all left, they immediately resolved to sail after them. Herodotus' account at this point focuses once again upon Themistocles.[118]

The Hellenes pursued the fleet of Xerxes as far as Andros without sighting them; they stopped at Andros and held a conference. At this point Themistocles voiced the opinion that they should continue their pursuit in their ships, proceeding from island to island straight for the Hellespont to destroy the bridges there. But Eurybiades opposed him, saying that if they were to destroy these bridges they would inflict upon Hellas the worst of all possible harm. For if the Persians were cut off from retreat and compelled to remain in Europe, they would not attempt to stay quiet, since by doing nothing they would not be able to achieve any success nor would any way back be open for them and their army would be destroyed by starvation; but if they were aggressive and tenacious it would be possible that all of Europe fall before them, city by city and people by people either through conquest or diplomacy.

And they would have for their continual sustenance the annual crops of the Hellenes. But since Xerxes intended not to remain in Europe after his defeat in the sea-battle of Salamis, he ought to be allowed to make his escape until he reached his own country. In this way, Eurybiades urged, the struggle would then be over Persian territory, not Greek.

The other Peloponnesian generals concurred with Eurybiades' opinion. When Themistocles realized that he would not persuade the majority to sail to the Hellespont, he shifted ground and spoke to the Athenians as follows (for the Athenians most of all were disturbed by the escape of the enemy and were eager to sail to the Hellespont and do the job themselves, if the others were unwilling):

'I myself have already been involved in many instances and I have heard about many more which have turned out in such a way that men who were reduced to desperation and conquered have renewed the battle and repaired their former misfortune. Both we ourselves and all Hellas have had the startling good fortune to repel a vast cloud of men and so let us not persist in pursuing them as they flee. For it is not we who have accomplished such achievements but gods and heroes who were envious that one man who is unholy and presumptious should be King of both Asia and Europe – a man who holds both the sacred and profane in like esteem, having burned and destroyed the statues of the gods, and who has violently scourged the sea and bound it in fetters. But for the present all is well for us if we remain in Hellas now and look out for ourselves and our families. In the assurance that the enemy have been completely driven out, let each rebuild his own house and plant his own crops diligently. With the coming of spring let us sail to the Hellespont and Ionia.'

Themistocles said these things with the intention of establishing a claim upon Persian gratitude, so that if he should ever suffer anything at the hands of the Athenians, he would have a refuge; and indeed this is what actually did happen. By these words then Themistocles was deceptive and the Athenians were convinced. For since he had previously been considered to be a wise man and now he actually appeared to be truly wise and of prudent counsel, they were completely disposed to be persuaded by whatever he said; and so they were won over.

Immediately afterwards Themistocles sent off in a boat men who he trusted would not reveal under any kind of torture the message that he instructed them to deliver to the King. Once again his domestic Sicinnus was one of the group. When they came to Attica, the others remained on the boat but Sicinnus disembarked and said the following to Xerxes:

'Themistocles, the son of Neocles, general of the Athenians, the best and the wisest of all the allies, has sent me to inform you that he, Themistocles, wishing to be of service to you, has kept the Hellenes from pursuing your ships and destroying the bridges on the Hellespont, although this was their desire. And now proceed on your way with great tranquillity.' When they had delivered their message they sailed back.

After the Hellenes had decided not to pursue the ships of the enemy any farther and not to sail to the Hellespont to destroy the way across, they laid siege to Andros wishing to capture it. For the people of Andros were the first of the islanders from whom Themistocles demanded money but they refused, and when Themistocles presented the argument that the Athenians had come having with them two great gods, Persuasion and Compulsion [or Necessity], and thus the money certainly had to be paid, the Andrians replied that it was evident from his argument that Athens was great and blessed and well off in terms of profitable deities, but since they were extremely poor in land and frequented by two unprofitable gods, Poverty and Helplessness, who always loved to frequent their island and would not leave, they could not pay the money. For the power of the Athenians could never be greater than the powerlessness of the Andrians [and thus force them to do the impossible]. This is what they answered, and since they did not pay up, they were subjected to a siege.

Themistocles (since he was ceaseless in his quest for gain) sent out to the other islands similar threatening messages in his demand for money, making use of the same messengers as he had used for Xerxes. He told them that, if they would not give what he demanded, he would lead the army of the Hellenes to subject them to siege and capitulation. By these threats he succeeded in gathering a great sum of money from the Carystians and Parians, who, when they learned that the Andrians were being besieged because they Medized and that Themistocles of all the generals was held in the greatest esteem, were afraid and sent money. But whether any other of the islanders gave anything I am not able to say; I think some others did and not only these mentioned. Although they paid, the Carystians were not spared from harm. But the Parians succeeded in conciliating Themistocles by the money that they gave and so escaped from the fleet's aggression. In this way Themistocles beginning with Andros as his base exacted money from the islanders without the knowledge of the other generals.

THEMISTOCLES' HONOURS AFTER SALAMIS

After the siege of Andros and their failure to capture the island, the Hellenes devastated the land of the Carystians and then

returned to Salamis, where they turned their attention to the
booty that was to be dedicated to the gods and distributed
among themselves.[119] Herodotus then relates the following
episodes concerning Themistocles:[120]

After the division of the booty, the Hellenes sailed to the Isthmus to
present a prize for valour to the Hellenes who had been most worthy
throughout this war. The generals met at the altar of Poseidon where
they cast their votes to determine who of all was to be ranked first and
second. Each of the voters thought that he was best but many agreed
in their judgment of Themistocles as second best. Indeed they all
claimed first place but Themistocles won by a large majority as their
second choice. Since they did not want to resolve the matter because
of envy, each sailed to his own home without a final decision. Nevertheless, Themistocles was acclaimed throughout the whole of Hellas
and deemed to be the wisest man by far of the Hellenes.

Since those who had fought at Salamis had not given him the honour
that he had won, Themistocles immediately afterwards went to
Sparta in his desire to receive his due. The Spartans received him
magnificently and honoured him greatly. To be sure as a prize for
valour they gave Eurybiades a crown of olive but they also gave one
to Themistocles, in his case for clever dexterity and wisdom. They also
gave him the gift of a chariot, the most beautiful in Sparta. After being
showered with praises, he was escorted as far as the borders of Tegea
by three hundred picked Spartans who are called the knights. He is the
only person we have ever known to have been escorted in this way.

Herodotus goes on to tell of the abuse that Themistocles
received when he returned to Athens from Timodemus, an
envious countryman from Aphidnae; this incident I have
recounted in Chapter XIV.[121]

Herodotus' Depiction of Themistocles

There are many disputed problems inherent in Herodotus'
account of Themistocles' actions during the second Persian
invasion. The message of Sicinnus, for example, has been
seriously questioned by modern scholars and some go so far as
to reject it completely as fictitious. How could Xerxes possibly
be so gullible? Was not the whole story a later invention inspired by charges of Medism subsequently brought against

Themistocles and seemingly confirmed by his flight to Persia and successful reception there? But a message to Xerxes is an integral part of the tradition and this cannot be dismissed lightly, however embellished it may have become after the event. Besides Xerxes, at least as characterized by Herodotus, was above all hubristically overconfident in his supreme power and the might of his forces. What had he to lose? And had not a Hellene, Ephialtes, betrayed his fellow Greeks at Thermopylae? That Themistocles used the argument of his encouragement of the Persians to join battle at Salamis when he actually did seek refuge in Persia presents a different problem. Thucydides is ambiguous on this point but Plutarch omits any reference to this first message in Themistocles' later appeal to the King for help; yet Epistle 20 clearly presents it as one of Themistocles' appeals, perhaps on the basis of an interpretation or misinterpretation of Thucydides' text.[122] The first message then could be a fact; I can imagine how it might have been later used (but not invented outright) against Themistocles by his political opponents through devious misrepresentation. But it is more difficult to see how Themistocles later could pretend that he had Xerxes' interests at heart in delivering the message, and our early sources are by no means clear that he did so; maybe he pretended that his communication was sincere and accurate and he did not anticipate that the Hellenes would present a united front or under any circumstances would be able to defeat the Persian armada.

The second message delivered to Xerxes, in which Themistocles claimed responsibility for deterring the Hellenes from destroying the bridges across the Hellespont and thereby insuring the safe return of his forces, is even more problematical. How could Xerxes conceivably trust Themistocles a second time? Plutarch's account of the same events is strikingly different from that of Herodotus.[123] After the battle of Salamis, Themistocles, in order to sound out Aristeides, pretended that he wanted to sail with the fleet to the Hellespont to destroy the bridges; Aristeides argued against this proposal and suggested that instead another bridge should be constructed to hasten Xerxes' exodus. Themistocles then agreed that they should contrive some means to get Xerxes out of Hellas by the quickest route. Thereupon Themistocles sent a royal eunuch and prisoner of war named Arnaces to tell the King that the Hellenes had decided to sail to the Hellespont to destroy the bridges but that Themistocles in his concern for Xerxes urged him to return as quickly as possible, while he would do his best to delay the allies in their pursuit.

Herodotus maintains that Themistocles sent this second message to establish Persian gratitude in case he might need refuge at some future time and thus the episode sounds very much like an invention inspired by Themistocles' subsequent career. But Thucydides (in the same passage referred to above) clearly states that Themistocles in his letter to Artaxerxes falsely claimed that he was responsible for the preservation of the bridges and the meaning seems to be that he had told him so after Salamis by means of a message; and our other sources are all agreed on both the message and its use as an argument to win the King's favour. The charges of Medism brought against Themistocles by both Athenians and Spartans could possibly have led to the invention of this second message as well as the first. I can well believe that Themistocles lied to the King about his role in assuring the safe return of Persian forces. But could he do so successfully, even to Artaxerxes, if no message had even been sent at all? The ancient tradition compels us to believe in the second message even more strongly than in the first; but we have every right to have sceptical reservations about both.

Most significant of all is the portrait of Themistocles that emerges from the pages of Herodotus. The standard opinion is that the historian is maliciously biased, probably as a result of his prejudiced Alcmaeonid sources. Bias there may be, whatever its origins, but in my view his hostility has been grossly exaggerated.[124]

The most damning criticism has been directed against Herodotus' contention that Mnesiphilus, the fellow demesman and (as we have seen in Chapter II) mentor of Themistocles, made the suggestion to him that he must at all costs devise some means to persuade Eurybiades to stay and fight at Salamis. Themistocles was pleased with this advice but without a word he proceeded to Eurybiades' ship and using Mnesiphilus' idea without acknowledgement convinced Eurybiades himself and later the assembled leaders by adding many arguments of his own. This all may very well be true, although it is hard to believe that Themistocles would not himself have wanted to insist on a naval engagement where the Greek fleet was already located rather than at the Isthmus. But if the story is true, would it have been in any way politically expedient to give Mnesiphilus credit? For all we know, to do so might have even been detrimental to his case. Furthermore, why did Mnesiphilus himself not approach Eurybiades? Was it because he knew that a sympathetic and forceful Themistocles was the one who could find ways to win by persuasion? How many great men have employed the ideas of others and through the amplifications wrought by their own genius brought them to successful and brilliant fruition? The essential point, however, remains: Herodotus does not really obscure the fact that Themistocles was ultimately responsible for the crucial decisions at Salamis.

Other judgments against Themistocles, either direct or by innuendo, abound. He bribed Eurybiades and Adeimantus to stay at Artemisium with money from the Euboeans and kept what was left for himself; after Salamis he acted brutally and venally against the islanders, and so forth. Yet none of our sources deny these charges, which bear all the earmarks of truth. In fact later writers (even Plutarch!) add to the list of his unscrupulous activities – many but not all of which are necessarily invention. Herodotus approves of Aristeides but does not seem to like the corrupt Themistocles. Historians have a right to make judgments, moral or otherwise, on the basis of their evidence; and I believe that in general Herodotus had fairly accurate and substantial proof for many of his allegations.

Two dominant aspects of Themistocles' ingenuity and character are vividly portrayed by Herodotus. He was responsible for the momentous decision of the Athenians to create a significant naval force; he played a major role in the determination of crucial strategies in the second Persian War; and it was through his devious and brilliant genius that the amazing and critical battle of Salamis was won. In addition to this appreciative assessment of Themistocles' worth, Herodotus also presents a shockingly candid portrait of an ambitious man, aggressive general and unscrupulous politician – a terrifyingly real depiction, certainly more credible than a generic idealization of a heroic paragon. It is upon both of these two essential aspects of Themistocles' character, crystallized by Herodotus, that the subsequent tradition plays.

Finally, a few words about Herodotus' inspired perception concerning Themistocles' unprincipled aggression against the Andrians will not be out of place. In his demands for money and his threats of violence, Themistocles' arguments from Persuasion and Compulsion sound frighteningly sophistic. The poor and weak Andrians nevertheless hopefully defend themselves against superior odds – surely an ominous foreshadowing of things to come. The year is only 479; yet the Andrians find themselves very much in the same position as the Melians in 416, when, according to the common view, Athenian imperialistic aggression finally reveals itself in its most blatant form. This undertaking against the Andrians explains most clearly why Themistocles found no place in the Delian Confederacy with its pan-Hellenic and idealistic goals. Cimon and Aristeides, at least in the beginning, were more diplomatic, honest and tactful. The brutality and greed of a Themistocles would eventually and inevitably come into their own soon enough.

CHAPTER V

THE FORTIFICATION OF ATHENS
AND THE PIRAEUS:
A HERO'S WILES

Immediately after the battle of Plataea Athens rebuilt the walls of her city and fortified the Piraeus as her major harbour. Our sources hold Themistocles responsible for these actions, which were so significant in the future development of Athenian power.

THUCYDIDES, OUR EARLIEST SOURCE

Thucydides gives us the details,[125] focusing upon the characteristic feature of Themistocles' cleverness, his ability to size up a situation and do something about it in terms of the best interest of his city:

After the Persian invaders had departed from their territory, the Athenian people immediately brought back their children, their wives and their surviving goods from where they had sent them for safety[126] and prepared to rebuild the city and the walls. For only small sections of the encircling wall were standing and many of their homes lay fallen in ruins, with only those few remaining that had been occupied by the leaders of the Persians.

When the Spartans found out what was intended, they sent an embassy because they themselves would not have liked to see either the Athenians or anyone else have a wall and especially because they were being prodded by their allies, who were frightened at the size of the Athenian navy (which had been inconsequential before) and Athenian daring in the war against the Persians. They asked them not to rebuild their walls but rather to join them in demolishing any fortifications still standing around cities outside the Peloponnesus; they did not reveal to the Athenians their real purpose or intent or their suspicions but maintained that, if the Persians were to attack again, they would not have any stronghold from which to operate, as they had found in Thebes, and claimed the Peloponnesus to be a sufficient

place of refuge or base of attack for everyone. The Athenians, at the
suggestion of Themistocles, answered the Spartans' proposals by
saying that they would send them ambassadors to discuss their suggestions and thus got rid of them at once. Themistocles also urged them
to send him to Sparta as quickly as possible and to choose other
ambassadors in addition to him but not to send them out immediately
but to wait until they had built up the wall sufficiently to the maximum
height necessary for defensive battle; he also urged all the people in
the city together, men, women and children, to take part in the erection
of the wall, without sparing any building, private or public, that would
be helpful to the project but destroying them all. After giving these
instructions and implying that he would take care of everything else
in Sparta, he departed.

Once he arrived in Sparta, he did not approach the government but
he made excuses and delayed. Whenever anyone of those in power
asked why he did not come forward, he said that he was waiting for
his fellow ambassadors who had been detained by some business, but
they would come soon and he was surprised that they were not already
there.

The Spartans listened to and believed Themistocles because of their
friendship towards him;[127] but when others came from Athens,
charging that the wall was being built and was already high, they did
not know how they could remain incredulous. Themistocles, being
aware of the situation, urged them not to be led astray by reports but
instead to send men of their own number who were reliable and who
would bring back a trustworthy report. And so they sent the men but
Themistocles secretly warned the Athenians about them, bidding them
to detain the Spartan envoys as inconspicuously as possible and not to
let them go until he and his colleagues returned to Athens; for his
fellow ambassadors had now joined him (namely Habronichus, the
son of Lysicles, and Aristeides, the son of Lysimachus) and he feared
that the Spartans would not let them go when they heard the truth.
Therefore the Athenians detained the envoys, just as they had been
told, and Themistocles now came before the Spartans and openly
revealed that his city was already sufficiently walled to protect the
inhabitants and, if the Spartans or their allies wished to negotiate, they
should realize from now on that they would be dealing with Athenians
who knew how to determine what was to their own advantage and
the common good. For when it seemed better to abandon their city
and to take to their ships, they knew what to do and dared to do it,
without the Spartans; on the other hand, concerning whatever matters
they deliberated along with the Spartans, they showed themselves
inferior to no one in good judgment. Therefore now too it seemed to

them that it was better for their city to have a wall and that it would be advantageous both for their own citizens and for all their allies. Indeed it was not possible to take council for the common good on any kind of similar or equal footing except on the basis of matching military preparation. Themistocles therefore concluded that either all those in the alliance should be without walls or what the Athenians had done should be considered as right.

When the Spartans heard this they did not openly display their resentment against the Athenians (to be sure they had not sent their ambassadors to Athens to stop the work but to offer advice and besides they happened at this time to be particularly friendly with the Athenians because of their vigour against the Persians); nevertheless they had failed in their purpose and were secretly upset. The envoys from both sides went home without voicing complaint.

In this way the Athenians built walls around their city in a short time and even now it is evident that the construction was done in haste. For the foundation consists of stones of every sort, in some places not even worked to fit but left just as each worker had originally brought them; and many tombstones and pieces already worked on were incorporated. Indeed the circuit of the city-wall was extended on all sides and for this reason they moved everything alike as they pressed on.

Themistocles also persuaded them to build what remained to be completed in the Piraeus; he had begun the project during the magistracy that he held for an annual term at Athens,[128] since he believed that the site was a splendid one with its three natural harbours and that the Athenians having become seamen was a great advantage towards acquisition of power. For he was the first to say that they must turn to the sea and straightway helped prepare the foundation of their empire. On his advice they built the wall around the Piraeus of a breadth which is now still evident; indeed two wagons, moving in opposite directions, brought up the stones on to the wall.[129] On the inside there was neither rubble nor clay but huge stones were cut into blocks and fitted together, while on the outside they were bound to one another by iron and lead. The wall was completed only to about half of the height that he intended; for he wished to repel the attacks of an enemy by its height and thickness and he considered that a garrison of a few least able-bodied men would be sufficient, while the rest could take to the ships. For he was an advocate of the navy because he observed, as it seems to me, that the invasion of the Persian King's army was easier by sea than by land. He thought the Piraeus was of greater use than the upper city of Athens and he often advised the Athenians to go down to the Piraeus and defy any opponents with their ships, if they were ever hard pressed on land. In this way the Athenians built their walls and made their other preparations right after the departure of the Persians.

DIODORUS, A FABRICATED TRADITION?

After Thucydides, it is fascinating to read the variations in Diodorus' account. He very carefully separates the building of the walls of Athens, narrated under the archonship of Timosthenes (478/7), from the work at the Piraeus (dated by the archonship of Adeimantus, 477/6). Other details and contradictions are causes for wonder and so let us read what Diodorus[130] has to say, presumably following Ephorus:

In Greece, after the victory at Plataea, the Athenians brought back their women and children to Athens from Troezen and Salamis, and thereupon undertook to put a wall around their city and turned their attention to other similar matters pertaining to their safety. But the Spartans, seeing that the Athenians had acquired great renown because of their sea power, were suspicious of their growing might and resolved to prevent the Athenians from building up their walls. Therefore they immediately sent out envoys who were to say to the Athenians that their advice was not to fortify Athens at present because it was not to the common advantage of the Hellenes in general; for, if Xerxes were to return with greater forces, he would have at his disposal outside the Peloponnesus walled cities from which as bases he would easily make war against the Hellenes. Since their words had no effect, the ambassadors went to those who were doing the building and directed them to desist from their work at once.

When the Athenians did not know what they ought to do, Themistocles, who at that time happened to be held in their highest esteem, advised them to hold their peace. For if they used force, he argued, the Spartans with the Peloponnesians would easily lead forces against them and put a stop to the fortification of their city. But he told the Council (*Boule*) in private that he would himself go with certain others as an ambassador to Sparta to offer an explanation of the wall to the Spartans and he gave directions to the magistrates; whenever ambassadors came from Sparta to Athens, they were to detain them until he himself returned from Sparta and in the meantime the whole population was to engage in fortifying the city. He made clear that in this way they would accomplish what they intended.

The Athenians listened to his words, Themistocles and his ambassadors set out for Sparta and the Athenians in great haste built their walls, without sparing house or tomb for material. Children and women, and every alien and slave, generally speaking, joined in the work, with no one lacking in zeal. When the task was being completed at an astonishing speed because of the number of workers and the enthusiasm of them all, Themistocles was summoned by the Spartan magistrates and reprimanded for the construction of the walls; he denied any building and urged the magistrates not to trust empty rumours but to send trustworthy ambassadors to Athens through whom, he argued, they would know the truth. As security for them he surrendered himself and his fellow ambassadors. The Spartans being convinced put Themistocles under guard and sent to Athens men of the highest repute to look closely at whatever needed investigation. Since time had elapsed the Athenians had already constructed the wall to a sufficient height; and when the Spartan ambassadors came to Athens and denounced them with violent threats, they put them under guard, saying that they would let them go at the time when the Spartans also released Themistocles and his fellow ambassadors. In this way the Spartans were outmanoeuvred and compelled to release the Athenian ambassadors to get back their own. Themistocles by such a strategem fortified his country quickly and safely and won great esteem among the citizens.

At this time [477/6] Themistocles because of his generalship and shrewdness won esteem not only among his fellow citizens but also among all the Hellenes. Therefore, because of his elation at his fame, he undertook other, much greater, enterprises relating to the growth of the hegemony of his native land. The Piraeus, as it is named, was not their harbour at that time but the Athenians used as their sea port the harbour called Phalerum, which was very small, and indeed it was Themistocles' idea to fit out the Piraeus as a harbour since it needed little reconstruction and could be converted into the finest and largest harbour in Hellas. Thus he hoped that once the Athenians possessed this additional advantage their city would be able to vie for hegemony of the sea. For at that time the Athenians had acquired the most ships and because of the succession of sea battles they had obtained experience and great renown in naval engagements. Besides, he reasoned that the Ionians would be on their side because of kinship and with Ionian help they would free the other Hellenes in Asia, who on account of gratitude for this good service would then align themselves with the Athenians, and that all the islanders, struck by the size of their naval power, would readily be numbered among those most capable of inflicting the worst harm or affording the greatest assistance. For he saw that the Spartans, although well equipped in terms of their land forces, were not naturally talented with respect to naval engagements.

Thus, as Themistocles thought these things over, he decided not to mention his plan openly, since he knew that the Spartans would oppose it, and he told the citizens in the Assembly (*Ecclesia*) that he wished to advise upon and propose significant matters of benefit to the city but to reveal them clearly was not to their advantage and it was appropriate to achieve their ends through a few men. Therefore he asked the people to select two men, whom they particularly trusted and to hand over the business to them. The majority were convinced, and the people selected two men, Aristeides and Xanthippus, choosing them not only for their good qualities (*arete*) but also because they saw that the two were competing with Themistocles for the glory of first place and on this account were not favourably disposed towards him. After these men heard Themistocles' plan in private, they divulged to the people that what Themistocles had told them was definitely significant, advantageous to the city and feasible.

The people marvelled at the man and at the same time were suspicious lest he one day attempt some kind of tyranny for himself, once he had contrived important plans of such sort, and they demanded that he reveal to them clearly what he intended. But he again replied that it was not to the advantage of the people to disclose his intentions openly.

The people were now much more amazed at the man's cleverness and greatness of mind and they directed him to tell the Council (*Boule*) in private what he intended; if the Council judged his words to be feasible and advantageous, then they too would recommend that his plan be carried out to completion. Therefore, when the Council learned the details and judged that his words were advantageous to the city and feasible, there remained only for the people to acknowledge their agreement with the Council; and Themistocles received the power to do whatever he wished and each member of the Assembly (*Ecclesia*) departed, awed by the excellence (*arete*) of the man and elated by the prospect of the completion of his plan.

When Themistocles had accepted the power to act and had every means ready at hand for the undertaking, he again devised a plan to outmanoeuvre the Spartans. For he was keenly aware that, just as the Spartans had tried to prevent the building of the wall of the city, in the same way they would attempt to obstruct the plans of the Athenians for the building of their harbour. And so he decided to send ambassadors to the Spartans to explain that it was advantageous for the general affairs of the Greeks to have an excellent harbour in the face of the campaign of the Persians to come. In this way, having made the Spartans less keen in their opposition, he himself turned to the task and, when everyone joined in enthusiastically, the harbour was quickly fitted out and completed contrary to expectation. And he persuaded the people each year to build twenty triremes to add to the existing fleet and to remit taxes for metics and artisans so that a great crowd might come from everywhere to the city and a greater number of skills might be made available. For he considered both these policies to be most useful for the building of naval power. Thus the Athenians were occupied with these concerns.

THUCYDIDES, DIODORUS (AND EPHORUS?)

It is impossible to know whether the variations in Diodorus' account merely represent an imaginative interpretation of Thucydides or rest upon independent reliable authorities, perhaps even an original common source. Most scholars accept Thucydides, although not uncritically, and treat anything that is unique in our later sources as of little value. But we need not assume that Thucydides alone represents an authentic original version. Indeed it is difficult to believe that Diodorus (or Ephorus) merely provided elaborated inventions upon Thucydides' account alone. Their modifications may reflect not only judgment (as sane as that of any historian) but also the narrative of someone like Hellanicus. We must recognize, therefore, that details in these subsequent accounts may well come from early sources and may even have been known to and suppressed by Thucydides for reasons of economy and emphasis, and not only because of their historical falsehood.

A comparative example from Thucydides and Diodorus will illustrate the problem. After explaining how Themistocles instructed the Athenians to send him to Sparta and later to dispatch other chosen ambassadors, and then to build up the wall around their city, Thucydides remarks: 'After giving these instructions and implying that he would take care of everything else in Sparta, he [Themistocles] departed.' The Greek verb ὑπειπών translated as 'implying' could also mean 'adding the suggestion' or 'saying in secret'. The latter interpretation would transform the whole clause into: 'and secretly disclosing the other things that he would do, he departed'.

With this possibility in mind, compare Diodorus' version

according to which Themistocles tells 'the Council (*Boule*) in private that he would go with certain others as an ambassador to Sparta'. Does Diodorus merely represent an interpretation of Thucydides' text, or independent and reliable authority? Diodorus does *not* (like Thucydides) make the distinction between Themistocles' departure for Sparta and the later arrival of the other Athenian ambassadors. Why? There are no easy and final answers to these and many other such questions.[131]

Although Diodorus' account is generally dismissed as merely inventive embellishment upon Thucydides, historians on occasion are not averse to accepting a unique detail as a historical fact rather than a hypothetical invention. For example, some believe that Diodorus or Ephorus had good authority for the statement that Themistocles persuaded the people to build twenty triremes each year and remit taxes for metics and artisans with the purpose of increasing Athenian naval power. If this is true, and therefore reflects a source not completely unreliable, perhaps other information, not found in Thucydides, may be of independent value, but we cannot be sure.

PLUTARCH, THE ECLECTIC, AND OTHERS

In addition to Thucydides and Diodorus, Plutarch[132] also tells us that immediately after Salamis Themistocles rebuilt the walls. Since his brief account offers further interesting variations and details (including Themistocles' supposed bribery of the Spartan ephors)[133] it too is worth quoting:

Themistocles undertook to rebuild and wall the city, by persuading the ephors with money not to oppose him, as Theopompus records, but, according to the majority of writers, by deceiving them. For on the pretext of an embassy he came to Sparta; and when the Spartans charged that the Athenians were building a wall around their city and Polyarchus, who had been expressly sent from Aegina, made the same accusation, Themistocles denied the charge and urged that they send men to Athens to investigate; his intention was to obtain more time for the wall by the delay and to put those who had been sent into the hands of the Athenians as hostages in his place. This is what in fact happened; for when the Spartans realized the truth they did not harm him but hiding their displeasure sent him away.

After this he fortified the Piraeus, because he realized the potential of its natural harbours for his policy of attaching the whole city to the sea, a policy that in some ways ran counter to that of the ancient kings of the Athenians. For they, as it is said, strove to draw the citizens away from the sea and to make them accustomed to live not by sailing but by cultivating the land; thus they spread the story about how Athena contended with Poseidon for control of the land and by producing the sacred olive tree was given the victory by the judges. And Themistocles did not attach the Piraeus to the city as the comic poet Aristophanes[134] says but joined the city to the Piraeus and the land to the sea; as a result he increased the power of the people as opposed to the aristocrats and filled them full of boldness now that power came into the hands of sailors, boatswains, and helmsmen. For this reason too the speaker's platform ($\beta\hat{\eta}\mu\alpha$) on the Pnyx hill [where the democratic assembly met], which had been made to look towards the sea, was later turned around towards the land by the Thirty Tyrants [in 404/3] in their belief that the sea empire had brought democracy into being, whereas farmers were less displeased by democracy.

We may be surprised that Plutarch can specifically name Polyarchus, the Aeginetan, as one who came to Sparta to denounce the Athenians, although Aegina's hostility to Athens in general was notorious.[135] Plutarch certainly appreciates the ramifications of Themistocles' programme for the subsequent destiny of Athens. And who is to say that his interpretation, commonplace to be sure, is not ultimately just and correct?

Two of the Epistles of Themistocles (nos 4 and 10) are to Habronichus, his fellow ambassador to Sparta. Several letters too (nos 3, 4, 18 and 19) reflect the fluctuating relationship between Themistocles and Aristeides, another of his colleagues in the ruse concerning the walls.[136] These two rivals could in a crisis once again unite in their efforts for the common good of Athens just as they had done against the Persians at Salamis. An anecdote succinctly illustrates this aspect of their relationship: When they were going out on an embassy or on a military campaign Aristeides was wont to remark to Themistocles: 'Let us agree to leave our hostility at the boundary and work together for the city; we can pick it up again, if we feel it is right, when we return.'[137]

The Walls and their Remains[138] (Pls 22–24)

No remains of the ancient (pre-Themistoclean) circuit wall of Athens have as yet been discovered. But the outline of the Themistoclean wall and later construction, such as that of Conon in 395, can be traced with confidence from the archaeological evidence. The sections that are to be identified as Themistoclean fit well with the description, given by our ancient sources, of co-operative haste. Column drums from temples and statue bases with sculpture in relief (belonging to buildings and monuments erected before the Persian sack of the city) have been found incorporated into the construction. The portions of the existing wall that is Themistoclean exist only in their lower courses (upper sections remaining belong to later rebuilding) and consist of a foundation of squared blocks of poros (ashlar type), upon which are placed rows of limestone blocks. It is conjectured that, in Themistocles' time, a superstructure of mud-brick was built above the lower course to reach quickly a height sufficient for defence.

Our knowledge of the Themistoclean wall in the Piraeus on the basis of the archaeological remains is much more tenuous. What does exist today seems to belong to the construction undertaken by Conon in 395 and it is a question whether or not his and the earlier wall of Themistocles follow the same line, i.e. around the outer circuit of the Acte peninsula; for there are some indications that another wall (originally Themistocles'?) may have cut across rather than have completely surrounded the peninsula. Since the ancient testimony allows for more than one stage to Themistocles' own programme in the harbour both lines of fortification (indicated on map I) could have originated with him. On the basis of existing archaeological reports nothing conclusive can be established and a new and complete examination of the ruins needs to be made.

Some General Conclusions

Diodorus and Plutarch place the entire fortification of the Piraeus at one time (c. 477) with no implication that Themis-

tocles had begun work earlier. But their testimony is contra-
dicted as we have seen by other weighty evidence (including
Thucydides), which puts the beginning of the construction as
early as 493/2 or at some time in the 480s.[139]

Further amplifications of the fortification of Athens and the
Piraeus were made later in the fifth century. Cimon was
responsible for the building of two long walls (the Phaleric and
North) joining the city and the harbour; then in 445 Pericles
advised the erection of a middle (or south wall) between these
two walls – telling proofs of Themistocles' brilliant political
and military foresight.

I have presented the reader with all the major sources for
Themistocles' fortification of Athens and the Piraeus in direct
translation rather than paraphrase (even though the narratives
of both Thucydides and Diodorus are lengthy) because they
afford a particularly striking illustration of basic and persistent
problems. The subtle and multifaceted variations in these
diverse accounts raise serious questions, many of which unfortunately as yet cannot be confidently answered. Should we
accept Thucydides' version alone because he is our earliest and
most authoritative evidence? Do later versions represent any
independent reliable sources, or are their deviations and additions merely the result of interpretative hypotheses, not unlike
those of modern scholarship? To be sure, we know essential
facts about Themistocles' role in the fortification of his city and
its harbour. But perhaps a recurring motif of secretive diplomacy
has determined details in Diodorus' account; and Plutarch may
accuse Themistocles of bribing the ephorate because this would
only be appropriate for the traditional conception of him as a
devious and corrupt politician. It is in such ways that the
historical legend was created and factual detail within it
obscured.

CHAPTER VI

THE DOWNFALL OF A HERO

Themistocles was to pay dearly for the enmity that he incurred
with the Spartans as a result of his deception concerning the
walls of Athens. For it was the Spartans who played a most
prominent and vigorous role in his subsequent eclipse and ruin.
They found willing allies in Athens – especially Cimon (son of
Miltiades the great hero of Marathon), who shot into promin-
ence shortly after Salamis, and Aristeides the Just, who had once
again resumed his career at the expense of Themistocles. One of
the most significant achievements in these years was the formation of the confederacy of allied Greek states, with its head-
quarters on the island of Delos, to wage vigorous warfare to
free Greeks from Persian domination. This naval confederacy
under the aegis of Athens was formally ratified in the spring of
477 with Cimon an aggressive general and Aristeides a shrewd
and honest financial administrator. Curiously enough, our
sources are completely silent about Themistocles' relationship
to this new confederacy, which surely represented the logical
outcome of *his* political and military philosophy.

While Themistocles was busy fortifying his city and its
port at home, Cimon was active against the Persians in the
establishment of the Delian league. The walls of the Piraeus
were finished to only one half their intended height – is this
fact any indication of the weakening of Themistocles' position
in the face of Cimon's success?[140]

We have many indications of Themistocles' fall from favour,
which is said to have been initiated in the very year of Salamis.
But our sources, which are conflicting, oblique and confused,
pose many difficulties, not the least of which are chronological.[141]

GROWING HOSTILITY TOWARDS THEMISTOCLES

As we have seen, Herodotus[142] tells how Themistocles extorted

money from the islanders and Plutarch[143] presents essentially
the same story, explaining that this was why Themistocles
became hateful to the allies. No wonder, then, that he could
find no place in the new confederacy. Herodotus also states
that at the Isthmus Themistocles was ranked second for the
prize for valour by the majority of the voters, since each put
himself in first place. Still, Themistocles was held in the highest
esteem throughout Hellas and at Sparta he was granted magnificent honours; to be sure, upon his return home he was roundly
abused by the envious Timodemus, but the hostility here seems
to be more personal than general.[144]

Diodorus,[145] however, has this to say concerning the award
for valour. The Spartans wanted to humble Athens' pride after
Salamis because they feared her rival naval power. So through
their prestige they influenced the decision concerning the prizes
for valour – the island of Aegina won and also an individual,
Ameinias of Athens (the brother of Aeschylus, the dramatist).
The Athenians became angry at this and the Spartans were
concerned lest Themistocles retaliate in some way. Therefore
they bestowed upon him double the number of gifts they had
given those who had won the prizes for valour. Themistocles
accepted and the Athenians in assembly removed him from the
generalship and gave the office to Xanthippus. Epistle 11, translated below,[146] further maintains that Themistocles supported
Ameinias for the award and thus created ill-will for himself.

These events belong presumably to 480 or at latest 479. We
have no concrete evidence that Themistocles was re-elected to
the generalship after the year of Salamis, although one might
assume automatically that he was. Yet it need not have been as
general that he negotiated the rebuilding of the walls.

Plutarch[147] tells us that, at a meeting of the Amphictyonic
league, the Spartans attempted to exclude all those who had not
taken part in fighting against the Persians. Through the efforts
of Themistocles the Spartan proposal was defeated and they in
revenge furthered the political ambitions of Cimon. This would
be the year 479 or 478.

Plutarch also relates[148] Themistocles' plan for assuring the

naval supremacy of Athens. When the fleet had stopped at
Pagasae, after Xerxes' departure, it was Themistocles' intention
that the Athenians should burn the other Hellenic ships but
Aristeides with the people's support was successful in opposing
the scheme. If the incident is true it should belong in the period
479–477; again we have the picture of a high-handed Themistocles unwilling to co-operate with his fellow Hellenes in any
kind of naval union. Cimon and Aristeides were presumably
more realistic and diplomatic.

The rivalry for power between Themistocles on the one hand
and Cimon and Aristeides on the other must have been bitter;
yet our sources are hopelessly inadequate in their details.
Scholars, nevertheless, unintimidated by the lack of evidence,
reconstruct what they imagine to be various facets of the
struggle. It has been suggested, for example, that Cimon and
Themistocles vied one with the other in their championship of
the great Athenian hero Theseus and his cult; for we are told
that Cimon, at the behest of an oracle from Delphi (476/5),
brought the bones of Theseus from Scyrus (where, according
to legend, he had been treacherously killed) back to Athens.[149]

Themistocles' Personal Building Programme

As we have seen, Plutarch[150] tells us, on the authority of
Stesimbrotus, that Themistocles had the chapel shrine at Phlya,
which belonged to the family of the Lycomidae and had been
destroyed by the Persians, restored at his own expense and
decorated with frescoes. It could be that Themistocles deliberately associates himself with the family of the Lycomidae at this
time to rival the noble Philaid connections of his opponent
Cimon. Gestures such as this therefore probably represent a bid
for power that may not have sat well with the majority of the
Athenians. For Plutarch recounts the following concerning
another project of Themistocles, the construction of a temple
to Artemis Aristoboule (Pls 25, 26):

Themistocles distressed many by building a temple of Artemis to whom he gave the name Aristoboule ('Best Counsellor'), implying that he was the one who had provided for the city and the Hellenes the best counsel. He erected the temple near his home in Melite, where the public officials now cast out the bodies of those who have been executed and deposit the clothes and the nooses of those who have hanged themselves. A portrait-statue of Themistocles has still stood in the temple of Aristoboule down to my own day, from which he appears to have been heroic, not only in spirit but also in appearance.[151]

A small temple discovered in 1948 just west of Theseion Square in Athens has been identified (probably correctly) as Themistocles' temple of Aristoboule on the basis of an inscription referring to Artemis. Miniature kraters or votive jugs of the early fifth century characteristically associated with Artemis were found near the foundations for the altar in the court in front of the temple. Only the foundations of the pronaos and a large anta block remain from the fifth-century structure. It is conjectured that the temple was abandoned and destroyed after Themistocles' exile and rebuilt c. 330.[152]

Other buildings have been linked to Themistocles in one way or another but the associations are much more tenuous – namely an odeion or recital hall for musical performance in Athens and a temple of Artemis Proseoia ('Dawnward-facing') near Artemisium; thus one must be careful lest the argument that Themistocles and Cimon were engaged in a battle of propaganda on all fronts, including architectural and artistic compositions, be overstated.[153]

THEMISTOCLES AND THE POETS[154]

There is some evidence, for the most part indirect, to suggest that Themistocles and the poet Simonides of Ceos were friends. At least that is the standard interpretation of the anecdotes recording Themistocles' purported jibes against the poet's physical ugliness and lack of integrity, among other things.[155] Perhaps such remarks (made solely in jest?) do reflect an easy and real familiarity between the two men; if so, we must also assume that Simonides possessed, at least on some occasions, a

lively and charitable sense of humour. Then too tradition had
it that Simonides offered to teach Themistocles his system for
strengthening the memory. That Themistocles may have used
the poet for his own political purposes is not, in itself, unlikely
or impossible. After all Simonides was a free-lance writer,
available to any and everyone – at a price.

Simonides had originally come to Athens upon the invitation
of the Peisistratid tyrant, Hipparchus, for high pay. With the
fall of the tyranny, he went to Thessaly but later returned to
Athens, c. 490. He can be linked to no single political sect or
family for any length of time. Fragments of his poetry, for
example, reflect an association with the Philaid Miltiades and
his circle; but he wrote as well an elegiac couplet bewailing the
death of the Alcmaeonid Megacles, who was ostracized in 487/6.

Certain it is that Simonides became at various times the poet
laureate, as it were, of the Greeks in their victories over the
Persians, but at whose instigation and expense we cannot always
be sure. He defeated Aeschylus in writing an epitaph for those
who died at Marathon; and the second Persian invasion provided
him with the inspiration for at least two poems, 'The Sea-fight
at Artemisium' and 'The Sea-fight at Salamis', and possibly a
third piece (if indeed it is distinct from the other two), 'The
Sea-fight with Xerxes'. Themistocles' role in the poems both as
hero and sponsor rests in large part upon conjecture – and conjecture has run rampant. But it seems to be true at least that
Simonides did single out Themistocles for commendation at
Salamis; for Plutarch, offering a brief paraphrase, writes as
follows:[156]

[In the battle of Salamis, the Hellenes], as Simonides has said, won that
beautiful and famous victory, no more glorious achievement than
which has ever been accomplished on the sea, because of the bravery
and ardour shared by those who fought in their ships and because of the
judgment (γνώμῃ) and cleverness (δεινότητι) of Themistocles.

Simonides also wrote for the Spartans in tribute to the dead
at Thermopylae; and curiously enough he became associated
with the Spartan Pausanias, the notorious friend of Themistocles. Indeed Simonides is credited with composing the dedica-

tion gracing the Persian spoils at Delphi, which became one of the issues in the prosecution of Pausanias.[157]

In 476, Simonides went to Sicily; is it mere coincidence that about this very time we can detect Themistocles' imminent fall from favour? When Themistocles himself saw fit to flee, did he originally plan in his voyage westward to follow in Simonides' wake?

However ambiguous the links between Themistocles and Simonides, when we turn to another contemporary poet, Timocreon of Rhodes, we can speak with much greater confidence. In fact Timocreon's fame today rests almost solely upon the lines etched in hatred, that Plutarch has preserved. The verses themselves are extremely difficult to interpret precisely, yet the general purport of vehement invective against Themistocles emerges with passionate clarity:[158]

> But if you praise Pausanias,
> and you, Xanthippus,
> or you, Leotychidas,
> then I praise Aristeides,
> the one best man
> to come from holy Athens;
> since Leto hated Themistocles,
> who was bribed by dirty silver
> not to bring back Timocreon,
> even though he was his host,
> to his city Ialysus [in his native Rhodes].
> But he took three talents of silver
> and went sailing off for ruin,
> bringing back some unjustly,
> pursuing some and killing others,
> glutted with silver coins.
> And at the Isthmus, he acted as host
> ridiculously offering cold meats;
> but they ate and prayed
> that the hour of Themistocles
> would never be.

Scholars can by no means agree about the date of composition for these verses by Timocreon; they must belong in the decade 480–470 but it is impossible to date them precisely with any

real confidence. Plutarch perhaps implies that they refer to
events in 480/79 since he quotes them after explaining how
Themistocles made himself hateful to islanders (e.g. the Andrians)
by trying to exact money from them.[159] The last lines with
their obscure reference to events at the Isthmus may allude to the
awarding of the prizes for valour there. The ecstatic praise of
Aristeides in contrast to the scathing denunciation of Themistocles and the puzzling allusion that Leto hated (or came to
hate) Themistocles may suggest the years 478/7, when Aristeides
and the Delian Confederacy emerged triumphant – Leto had
given birth to Apollo on the island of Delos, which was sacred
to the god. At any rate the poem alludes to some incident
(otherwise unknown) when Themistocles, who had been entertained by Timocreon, refused, because of a bribe, to bring him
back home to Rhodes. Arguments that the poem belongs as
late as the period of Themistocles' ostracism or exile (e.g. after
471) are not compelling. Plutarch at least makes a clear distinction between the verses quoted above and lines later written by
Timocreon, charging Themistocles with Medism, collusion
with the Persians:[160]

Timocreon used much more licentious and explicit invective against
Themistocles after Themistocles' flight and condemnation in a song
beginning:

> Muse make the fame
> of my song
> resound throughout Hellas,
> as is fitting and just.

It is said that Timocreon was exiled for Medism and Themistocles
joined in the vote of condemnation. Therefore when Themistocles
was charged with Medism, he wrote these lines against him:

> And so Timocreon is not the only one
> who swears compacts with the Persians;
> but there are other villains too.
> I am not the only 'stump-tailed';[161]
> there are other foxes too.

Some are dubious about Plutarch's statement concerning
Timocreon's condemnation, but other evidence does attest the
poet's presence at the Persian court.[162]

Themistocles in these years of personal and political crisis was also associated with the dramatist Phrynichus. We know from Plutarch that in the spring of 476, when Adeimantus was archon, Themistocles as *choregos* (i.e. he was financially responsible for the production) won a victory with tragedies. Even in this early period the dramatic contest entailed eager and ambitious rivalry, and Themistocles set up an inscription as follows:[163] 'Themistocles of the Phrearrhian deme was *choregos*, Phrynichus the poet, and Adeimantus the archon.'

It is generally assumed that the play was *The Phoenician Women*, whose subject, the Persian Wars, influenced Aeschylus in his composition of *The Persians*. *The Phoenician Women* may have been Phrynichus' presentation in 476 but I cannot help but wonder if he might also have produced his *Sack of Miletus* at this same festival. As we have seen, the standard view, on the basis of Herodotus,[164] has been that *The Sack of Miletus* belongs in the 490s, perhaps in the very year of Themistocles' archonship; and Phrynichus was fined for upsetting the Athenians by his stirring presentation of such a heart-breaking subject. But there are problems. It seems curious that Phrynichus, if he had suffered earlier because of his treatment of a contemporary theme (at Themistocles' instigation?), would run the same risks again in 476. It is true that Herodotus tells us that the Athenians burst into tears upon witnessing Phrynichus' tragedy and he narrates the incident in the context of his account of the fall of Miletus; but his sequence need not be immediately chronological. The Athenians might well be extremely sensitive in 476 after their decisive victories against the Persians, upon being reminded of what the Milesians had suffered under such dubious circumstances in the years when their troubles all began.

There is a possibility that *The Sack of Miletus* is not a separate play at all but merely a designation for *The Phoenician Women* either under a different title or with particular reference to the thematic material or specific scene (perhaps a messenger's speech), which the Athenians found particularly offensive. Suidas lists as one of Phrynichus' plays *The Persians* with two alternative titles (i.e. Δίκαιοι ἢ Πέρσαι ἢ Σύνθωκοι) which may be very well another name for either *The Phoenician Women* (Φοίνισσαι) or *The Sack of Miletus* (Μιλήτου *Ἅλωσις*). With so many available titles for at least one play about the Persian Wars, one begins to wonder if Phrynichus may not have written a trilogy (or tetralogy) on the subject.[165]

A play or trilogy about the Persian Wars by Phrynichus on only one occasion, not in 493 or 492, but in 476 is perfectly credible; for it was in this period that Themistocles appears to have used every means in his desperate attempts to maintain power. Phrynichus was victorious, presumably on artistic grounds. But the political and emotional backlash represented by the subsequent fining of the playwright would then appropriately represent another facet of the attack against Themistocles himself (the *choregos*) in the 470s, which reached its triumphant culmination in his ostracism and exile.

In this view Aeschylus' presentation of *The Persians* in the Spring of 472 becomes even more timely, controversial and daring; and perhaps we can better appreciate the guarded nature of his treatment particularly with reference to Themistocles. Aeschylus then is still another poet to be linked to Themistocles' career but we shall examine their association subsequently in a more meaningful context.

The Fall of Themistocles

Our sources indicate that the archon year of Praxiergus, 471/0, is to be associated in some way with Themistocles' downfall; but they are unclear whether the ostracism or the exile (or both) should be dated in that year. I have argued at length in support of 471/0 for the flight with the ostracism belonging somewhere in the period 476–471 and this chronology still has much to recommend it.[166] Yet I have come to realize that dogmatism is unwarranted because of the inadequacy of our evidence. It is virtually impossible, however, to date the ostracism after 471/0 (but it may have been earlier); the flight may have occurred in this same year, but it could have followed later.

We must realize that the last specific chronological information for Themistocles in Athens before 471 belongs to 476. In addition to acting as *choregos* for Phrynichus, he appeared at the Olympic festival (almost certainly in this same year); when Themistocles entered the stadium all the Hellenes rose and applauded and he received more admiration and attention than the contestants themselves.[167] It appears that Themistocles is still a figure to reckon with, at least outside Athens.

But his eclipse was soon to follow. Plutarch observes that the Athenians because of jealousy were ready to accept any slander against Themistocles; thus he was compelled to remind them over and over again of his own achievements and as a result he became obnoxious to them.[168]

CHAPTER VII

OSTRACISM AND EXILE:
A HERO DISOWNED

Our sources are in general agreement that Themistocles was incriminated because of his association with the Spartan hero of Plataea, Pausanias, son of Cleombrotus, of the royal family of the Agiadae and regent for his young cousin Pleistarchus. The investigation and death of Pausanias culminated in charges against Themistocles himself, while he was residing at Argos in ostracism. Before we can proceed then with a closer analysis of the case against Themistocles (in conjunction with both his ostracism and his exile), it is imperative to review the career of Pausanias subsequent to his victory over the Persians at Plataea in 479.

PAUSANIAS, THE RENEGADE SPARTAN

Thucydides is our most significant source for Pausanias; the following account represents a close paraphrase of his text, with a direct translation of the purported correspondence between Pausanias and the King that it contains – amazing, if not incredible, historical documentation![169] The ephors referred to were powerful Spartan magistrates, who supervised the authority of the two Kings and other officials of the state; the Helots were the large discontented slave population of Sparta.

Pausanias was sent by the Spartans to lead the Hellenic allies in their pursuit of the Persians and their efforts to free fellow Hellenes. Their combined forces won over most of the island of Cyprus and besieged and captured Byzantium from the Persians. In the capture of Byzantium certain friends and relatives of the King were taken prisoner. Pausanias sent these prisoners back to the King and thus incurred his gratitude; he did not, however, let the allies know what he had done but pretended that the prisoners had escaped. In all of this Pausanias acted in concert with an Eretrian named Gongylus, the man whom he had placed in charge of Byzantium and the prisoners; and he also sent Gongylus to the King with a letter, in which, as was later revealed, he wrote as follows:

Pausanias, the commander of Sparta, in his desire to do you a favour, sends back these men captured by the spear; and I make the proposal, if it is your pleasure, of marrying your daughter and bringing both Sparta and the rest of Hellas under your control. I think that I can accomplish this in collaboration with you. If, then, you find any of these proposals to your liking, send to the sea-coast a trusty man through whom we may communicate in future.

Xerxes was pleased and he sent Artabazus, the son of Pharnaces, to the sea-coast to replace Megabates as governor of the satrapy of Dascylium; and he dispatched Megabates to Pausanias, and ordered him to pledge the King's support and deliver a written reply which went as follows:

So King Xerxes speaks to Pausanias. For the men whom you saved from Byzantium beyond the sea for me, a record of gratitude will be stored up for you in our house forever; and I am pleased with your words. Let neither night nor day keep you from accomplishing any of your promises to me and do not be hindered by any lack of gold or silver to spend or number of troops, if they be required anywhere. But with Artabazus, a good man whom I have sent to you, confidently fulfil my interests and yours in whatever way will be finest and best for us both.[170]

Pausanias already was highly esteemed by the Hellenes because of his leadership at Plataea; now, after receiving this letter from the King, he became inordinate in his elation and his behaviour. He would leave Byzantium dressed in Persian garb, and whenever he travelled through Thrace he was attended by a body-guard of Persians and Egyptians; he even dined in Persian style. By his aloofness and violent temper he made clear to all his grandiose ambitions and alienated his fellow Hellenes. Thus, when Pausanias became unpopular in his command, the Hellenes, especially the Ionians, appealed to the Athenians to assume leadership and help them get rid of

Pausanias. Athens agreed and, at this very juncture, the Spartans recalled Pausanias for questioning about the reports of his great wrongdoings and his tyrannical behaviour. In Sparta Pausanias was called to account for his personal injustices against individuals but he was acquitted of the most serious charges; for he was accused of Medism (i.e. collaboration with the Persians) and, Thucydides pointedly observes, it seemed to be the clearest case against him. The Spartans then sent out instead of Pausanias Dorcis with a small force as commander of the allies, but they would no longer accept him and so he returned home. Thereafter the Spartans sent out no other commanders, fearing that they might be corrupted like Pausanias; they also wanted to be free of the war against Persia and considered the Athenians at that time friends and competent for leadership.[171]

After his recall, trial and acquittal, Pausanias was not sent out again in a public, official capacity. But privately of his own accord he took a trireme from the town of Hermione without Spartan authority and sailed once again to the Hellespont. He said that his purpose was to engage in the war against Persia; in actual fact he intended to pursue his intrigue with the King and become master of all Hellas.

It was readily apparent that Pausanias was acting in the very same manner as he had before; and, when the Athenians laid siege to Byzantium and evicted him by force, Pausanias did not return to Sparta but instead settled at Colonae in the Troad. The report came back to Sparta that he was intriguing with the Persians and lingering there for no good purpose, and so the ephors could restrain themselves no longer; they sent a herald with a formal dispatch (σκυταλή) commanding him either to return at once with the herald or else face a Spartan declaration of war. Since Pausanias wanted to avoid suspicion as much as possible and fully expected that he could by the use of money dispose of the accusation, he returned to Sparta for the second time. At first he was thrown into prison by the ephors but later managed to obtain release and offered to submit himself to a trial by those who wished to subject him to scrutiny.

The Spartans – either his personal enemies or the state as a whole – possessed no clear evidence trustworthy enough to be relied upon for the condemnation of a man of royal blood such as he who was at that time acting as regent for the young King Pleistarchus, son of Leonidas. But his former behaviour provided ample ground for suspicion that he was not content to abide by the normal order of things. As they scrutinized his past for confirmation of his ambition they recalled in particular that he had previously on his own authority seen fit to have inscribed on the tripod in Delphi, which the Hellenes dedicated as the first fruits of their Persian spoils, this elegiac couplet:

When as leader of the Hellenes he destroyed the army of the Persians Pausanias dedicated this memorial to Phoebus Apollo.

The Spartans had immediately removed these verses from the tripod and inscribed by name all the cities which had joined in the defeat of the Persians and set up the monument.[172] At the time this act of Pausanias was thought to have been wrong; in the present circumstances it appeared as an indication of his prevailing disposition. It was also found out that he was conspiring with the Helots – and so he was; for he promised them freedom and citizenship if they would join him in a revolt to accomplish his designs. But even when some Helots turned informers no action was taken against Pausanias, in keeping with typical Spartan caution and the desire for irrefutable evidence.

Finally (as it is said), a man from Argilus, who as a boy had been a friend of Pausanias and had remained most loyal, turned informer; for, as he was about to deliver to Artabazus Pausanias' last letter to the King, he became frightened when he realized that no previous messenger had ever returned. So he opened the letter (having made a counterfeit seal to avoid discovery) and found, as he had suspected, written directions for his own death.

The ephors still demanded further evidence: actually to hear Pausanias incriminate himself by his own words. They concocted a plan whereby the man of Argilus went as a suppliant to the temple at Taenarus; there he took quarters in a hut, divided by a partition, on the other side of which some of the ephors were hidden.

When Pausanias came to him and asked what he was doing there as a suppliant, the man reminded Pausanias of his devotion in all his negotiations with the King and complained bitterly that his reward was to be that of the most ordinary servant – death. Pausanias admitted everything but asked the man not to be angry; he gave him assurances of safety and urged him to proceed with his mission as quickly as possible.

Now that the ephors heard with their own ears Pausanias' admission of guilt they left with the avowed intention of arresting him in the city. It is said that as he was about to be arrested in the street he realized from the face of one of the approaching ephors the reason why he was coming and that another ephor out of friendship gave him a secret sign of warning. Thereupon he ran to the temple of Athena Goddess of the Brazen House, and hid in a small room within. The ephors discovered where he had taken refuge; they removed the roof of the room, walled up the doors, stationed sentries as guards and proceeded to starve him to death. But just as he was about to expire they brought him, still breathing, out of the temple; whereupon he died immediately.[173] Their first intention was to cast his body into the Caeadas – a cavern in the mountains where criminals were thrown – but later they decided to bury him somewhere near by. Afterwards Apollo in Delphi ordered the Spartans to move his tomb to the place where he died – an inscription makes clear that he now lies in the entrance to the sacred precinct. Apollo also directed that they should repay two bodies instead of one to the Goddess of the Brazen House, since their treatment of Pausanias had brought down a curse upon them. Therefore the Spartans had two bronze statues made to dedicate to Athena.

As Thucydides continues he briefly comments on the link between Pausanias' downfall and Themistocles. These important lines had better be translated directly; notice that, after Pausanius' death, Themistocles is in ostracism at Argos.

The Spartans sent ambassadors to the Athenians and accused Themistocles, along with Pausanias, of collaboration with the Persians (Medism) on the grounds of what they had found in their investigation of Pausanias; they thought it right that Themistocles be punished in the same way and they convinced the Athenians. Now, Themistocles had already been ostracized and, while he was living in Argos, he used to visit the rest of the Peloponnesus; and so the Athenians sent men with the Spartans who were ready to join in the pursuit, ordering them to arrest him wherever they found him.

There is hardly anything in this account of Pausanias' career that has not been challenged by one scholar or another.[174] The narrative in some respects appears for some uncharacteristic of Thucydides' stark analytical style elsewhere; as we shall see in the next chapter his treatment of Themistocles is in similar fashion replete with a Herodotean penchant for the details of a dramatic story.[175] What was Thucydides' source for such intimate information? Has he succumbed to some 'official' Spartan version promulgated for the outside world as a façade for the realities of the situation? Could the correspondence between Pausanias and Xerxes possibly be authentic? And so forth. But after reviewing (at times with amazement!) the plethora of fanciful modern theories, one returns to Thucydides' account with renewed confidence. At any rate we cannot get behind, as it were, this evidence – we cannot guess what transpired and pretend in the process to have established any kind of historical fact. The essentials of the story seem feasible – that Pausanias negotiated with Xerxes, i.e. Medized; that upon being evicted from Byzantium a second time he attempted once again to further his ambition for power, this time by fostering a revolt in Sparta and threatening the powerful office of the ephorate. That Themistocles Medized as well, in league with Pausanias, is another question which demands that we examine further, crucial testimony, in striking contrast to the terse remarks of Thucydides.

THE EVIDENCE OF DIODORUS AND PLUTARCH

Under the archon year 471/0 Diodorus provided the following account of Themistocles' ostracism and exile. It is important, if only because our other sources are so meagre and ambiguous

about this crucial turning-point in Themistocles' career. Epistles
8 and 11, translated below (pp. 167, 174), should be consulted
in this context; Epistle 8 in particular offers striking similarities
to Diodorus, with the addition of fascinating details; perhaps
they have Ephorus as a common source:[176]

When the Spartans saw that Sparta had been humiliated by the
treason of Pausanias, their general, whereas the Athenians were in
good repute because no citizen of theirs had been found guilty of
treason, they were anxious to incriminate Athens on similar charges.
Therefore, since Themistocles was held in the highest repute and
greatest esteem among the Athenians for his excellence (*arete*), they
charged him with treason (προδοσίαν), claiming that he was a very good
friend of Pausanias and had contrived with him that they would together betray Hellas to Xerxes. They also talked with Themistocles'
enemies, urging them to bring a charge against Themistocles and
Pausanias, and they gave them money; they informed them that, when
Pausanias had decided to betray the Hellenes, he revealed his own plan
to Themistocles and urged him to join in the scheme, but Themistocles
did not accept the offer and did not think that he should accuse a man
who was his friend. At any rate, Themistocles was charged but at that
time he was found not guilty of treason. And so at first, after his
acquittal, he was still great among the Athenians, for his fellow citizens
were extremely devoted to him because of his achievements; but
afterwards some who feared his pre-eminence and others who envied
his renown forgot his good services and strove to bring his power low
and humble his pride.

First, therefore, they removed him from the city through ostracism
. . . and Themistocles having been ostracized fled from his native city
to Argos; but when the Spartans learned of this they considered that
chance (τύχη) had offered them an opportune moment to attack Themistocles. They sent ambassadors to Athens once again to accuse him of
complicity in treason with Pausanias and demanded that, since their
crimes affected all Hellas, the trial must not be held privately among the
Athenians but before the general congress (κοινοῦ συνεδρίου) of the
Hellenes, which customarily met at that time.

When Themistocles saw that the Spartans were pressing to defame
and humble Athens and that the Athenians wished to acquit themselves
of the charge which was being made, he assumed that he would be
handed over to the General Congress. On the basis of previous
decisions, including the awards for valour that had been assigned, he
knew that this body made judgments which were not just but favourable to the Spartans. For in the case of the awards for valour those

controlling the vote were so jealously disposed towards the Athenians that they made them out to be in no way better than the rest of the Hellenes, even though they provided more triremes than all the others who engaged in the war. It was for these reasons, then, that Themistocles was not disposed to trust the members of the congress. Indeed the Spartans had derived the basis of this later charge against him out of the previous defence that he had made in Athens. For in that instance Themistocles confessed that Pausanias had sent letters to him urging that he be party to treason and he used this as his strongest evidence for the argument of his case, i.e. Pausanias would not have continued to urge him, if he had not continued to reject his offer.

For these reasons Themistocles fled from Argos to Admetus. . . .

And finally this is how Plutarch relates these crucial events; as we have seen in the previous chapter, he claims that it was jealousy against a pre-eminent Themistocles that brought about his ostracism and exile:[177]

The Athenians ostracized Themistocles and eclipsed his excessive reputation and esteem, just as they were accustomed to do against all whom they believed to be oppressive in power and beyond the limits of democratic equality. . . .

When he had been banished from Athens and was living in Argos, circumstances in connection with Pausanias provided his enemies with an opportunity to attack him. The man who actually indicted (γραψάμενος) Themistocles for treason (προδοσίας) was Leobotes[178] the son of Alcmeon of the deme Agraule, and the Spartans joined in support of the charge. Pausanias at first kept his treasonous schemes hidden from Themistocles, although he was his friend; but when he saw that Themistocles was banished from his homeland and taking such treatment badly, he became bold enough to invite him to share in his undertaking. He showed Themistocles a letter from the Persian King and attempted to incite him against the base and ungrateful Hellenes. But Themistocles rejected Pausanias' appeal and utterly refused to become his partner in crime. Yet he told no one about their communications and did not denounce the project of Pausanias because he expected either Pausanias would abandon it of his own accord or otherwise would be caught striving so irrationally for such extraordinary and hazardous goals.

Thus after Pausanias had been put to death some letters and documents pertaining to these matters were found which threw suspicion upon Themistocles. The Spartans persisted in their outcries against him and so did his jealous fellow citizens; because he could not defend himself in person, he did so in writing, with particular reference to

previous charges that had been brought against him. For he wrote to
the Athenians that, since he was slanderously accused by his enemies of
being a man who always sought to rule but was neither by nature nor
desire one to be ruled, he would never have sold himself, along with
Hellas, to barbarians, much less to an enemy of his country. Nevertheless the people were persuaded by his accusers and they sent men who
were ordered to arrest him and to bring him to be tried before the
Hellenes.

But he was forewarned and crossed over to Corcyra. . . .

What in the world are we to deduce from all this? Our sources
distinguish a first trial and acquittal, ostracism in Argos, and
a second formal accusation from which Themistocles fled. But
the issues and the charges are so blurred and confused that it is
extremely difficult to reconstruct with any satisfactory precision
the course of the whole proceedings.[179]

THE FIRST TRIAL

The first trial described by Diodorus and probably alluded to
indirectly by Plutarch has been deemed an invention for one
reason or another. Certainly among the doublets in the parallel
careers of Pausanias and Themistocles a first trial and acquittal
for both could in itself appear dubious. This first accusation
against Themistocles, which according to Diodorus charged
collusion in the Medism of Pausanias, seems too early, if Themistocles' involvement could be alleged by the Spartans only as a
result of discoveries after Pausanias' death. In fact both Plutarch
and the Epistles have it that Pausanias approached Themistocles
while he was residing in Argos and not before. Some such charge
as Medism at Salamis and during its aftermath is more credible
than collaboration with Pausanias for an early trial; in fact
betrayal of his generalship is one of the charges named in Epistle
11. Perhaps his actions against the Andrians and other islanders
were also included in the incriminations? When Plutarch mentions letters which Themistocles wrote from Argos, referring to
earlier charges, one wonders if he knew some collection of
Epistles, such as the one that we possess.

Yet the fiction of Themistocles' collusion with Xerxes at

Salamis and possibly in connection with the Persian retreat was very likely fostered by the Spartan allegations linking Themistocles with Pausanias. If so, the first trial itself (whatever the charges) also might be invention, further inspired by the actual fact of Themistocles' eventual flight to Persia; the legend then was even more elaborately embellished by having Themistocles turn to Xerxes himself, whereas, in reality, he was received and accepted by Xerxes' son and successor, Artaxerxes.

Assuming, however, that this first trial with acquittal was a reality, one is hard pressed to conjecture a date. It can hardly have occurred before 477 or later than 471. Perhaps c. 476 is a reasonable assumption, after, rather than before, the production of Phrynichus' *The Phoenician Women*.

In the later tradition, at any rate, among the rhetorical inventions inspired by Themistocles' career we find a stirring appeal intended to echo his defence, presumably at this first trial:[180]

If you condemn me to death, let the inscription on my grave clearly enumerate each of my achievements, on account of which I now face envy and judgment. Let Artemisium and Salamis be inscribed and the Athenian fleet and every other worthy addition.

The late epigrams composed for Themistocles' sepulchre (translated in a subsequent chapter)[181] echo this same theme in their listing of his achievements.

THE OSTRACISM, CONDEMNATION AND EXILE

The circumstances surrounding Themictocles' ostracism are equally troublesome. But that he was ostracized we can have no doubt. Overweening ambition and tyrannical behaviour are the reasons cited, coupled with the envy of his fellow Athenians for his glorious victory at Salamis. Hostility and fear on the part of political rivals and the anger of Sparta also hastened his downfall; and it is not too difficult to imagine that issues revolving about the formation of the Delian Confederacy were very much at stake. Cimon, backed by Spartan hatred, would be delighted to see the last of Themistocles. But ostracism apparently was not enough.

Epistles 1 and 2 (below, pp. 156ff.) claim that Themistocles, after being ostracized from Athens, was on his way to live in Delphi, when he was prevailed upon by Argive friends to sojourn in Argos, where his father had once lived. Upon his arrival there he refused to accept the offer of power extended to him. While in Argos, Themistocles was faced with a formal charge of treason – specifically collaboration with Pausanias in his intrigues with the Great King of Persia. It is disconcerting to realize how vehemently the Spartans acted as prime movers in the prosecution. The ancient testimony forces us to believe that the accusations that were overtly disclosed must have been false – although Thucydides does not say so directly. It would be an impossible task to attempt a reconstruction of the alleged correspondence, papers or whatever, that the Spartans produced, if indeed they produced anything concrete or 'factual' at all. In order to save face for their treatment of Pausanias, they demanded from the Athenians the blood of Themistocles.

Thucydides does tell us that while at Argos Themistocles used to visit the rest of the Peloponnesus; and one cannot help but wonder what he was up to. Argos was forever at odds with Sparta; and if, by some chance, Themistocles was in touch with Pausanias' intrigues upon his final return to Sparta, the Spartans might have every reason to be angry and afraid. But perhaps I too need to curb my historical imagination; for real evidence is in the last analysis sadly lacking.[182]

Themistocles in his absence from Athens was formally indicted by the Athenians; Plutarch names Leobotes, the son of Alcmeon, of the powerful Alcmaeonid family, as the accuser in language that suggests an authentic source.[183] In another context Plutarch lists Alcmeon (not necessarily a slip for Leobotes), Cimon and many other enemies, but we cannot be sure that the specific occasion of this indictment is referred to; in the same passage Aristeides is said to have remained aloof, even though Themistocles had been responsible for his ostracism. But Aristeides' participation in Themistocles' downfall is variously reported in our sources; he either befriends or opposes Themistocles.[184] Perhaps he actually played different roles in the various stages of the attack.

In Epistle 8 several others are named as Themistocles' enemies, some of whom may be historically real – Alcmeonides (son of Alcmeon) appears on *ostraka* and both Leager (son of Glaucon) and Pronapes can be identified in other sources; and Epistle 11 lists other opponents of Themistocles who may not be mere inventions.[185] The indictment against Themistocles, then, is by no means merely an Alcmaeonid vendetta. For what it is worth a reference in Theodorus Metochites (late thirteenth or early fourteenth century AD) states that a Lycomedes (of the same Lycomid family as Themistocles) was one of Themistocles' attackers.[186]

Scholars have identified the charge as the legal procedure in Athens known as an εἰσαγγελία, initiated by Solon to be used in indictment for major cases to be tried by the Areopagus.[187] But our sources raise the question whether in the case of Themistocles some other Athenian jury or the *Ecclesia* itself was involved, or even if he was to be tried by an Athenian court at all. Diodorus and the Epistle 11 (below, p. 174) explicitly maintain that the Spartans and the Athenians came after Themistocles in Argos to bring him before the General Congress of the Hellenes and that it was particularly because of the summons to this prejudiced court that he feared to face judgment. It is not inappropriate that the Hellenes in concert would act upon this accusation of Medism, particularly since both Sparta and Athens and not Athens alone were the initiators of the prosecution. How then does a specific Athenian indictment (εἰσαγγελία) apply? It looks as though Leobotes' charge belongs to the first trial of Themistocles in Athens – thereby lending it much greater credibility. The second charge – Medism in conjunction with Pausanias – would then logically be tried by the General Congress of the Hellenes. But the untidy evidence does not seem to allow us to have it so; and such an hypothesis must rest in large part on the insecure assumption that Plutarch has hopelessly garbled the tradition. One thing, however, is certain. We are unable, as yet, to provide final, satisfactory answers.

FURTHER PROBLEMS, MAINLY CHRONOLOGICAL

The chronology for Pausanias' career after Plataea is as problematical as that for Themistocles; and the preceding discussion
has revealed that questions concerning both hang closely one
upon the other. In the last chapter I concluded that Themistocles,
in all probability, was in ostracism by 471/0. The complex and
evasive evidence for Pausanias could allow for his death at about
this very time; thus Themistocles' flight may belong in this
same archon year. I have supported such a chronology elsewhere, and I still find it attractive. But many scholars have felt
that the ancient testimony more easily implies a later date for
Pausanias' death within the period after 471 – perhaps even as
late as 466.[188] I am more than willing to concede that the
present state of our knowledge militates against any kind of
absolute certainty. Thus Themistocles' summons and flight may
have occurred at any time within the period 471/0–465/4.
Evidence to be introduced in the next chapter will provide still
further complications which need to be considered in connection
with the chronology of his journey from Argos to Persia.

Yet at this point it is pertinent to mention a curious story
reported in the *Constitution of Athens*.[189] In 462, when Ephialtes
attacked the Areopagus and stripped it of its political powers,
Themistocles was one of his allies. For Themistocles, an Areo-
pagite himself, was about to be tried by his fellow members for
Medism and thus he wanted the Council to be destroyed.

All our other evidence makes it difficult, if not impossible, to
believe that Themistocles was in Athens as late as 462; and
nowhere else do we find Themistocles associated with Ephialtes
even in earlier years. Since the story, then, in so far as it involves
Themistocles, must be false, it provides weak evidence indeed
for assuming that the trial of Themistocles was actually intended
for the Areopagus. It is true, however, that, if Themistocles had
in fact previously held the archonship, he would as a matter of
course have become a member of the Areopagus.

Perhaps Themistocles, the democrat, particularly in the later tradition, had to be associated, however incorrectly, with this most democratic of reforms – the stripping of the august Areopagus of its traditional political prestige; or perhaps Themistocles' name appears here in association with the notorious Ephialtes merely through inadvertent error. Aristotle in the *Politics* joins Pericles, not Themistocles, with Ephialtes in the attack and this inevitably makes much better sense.[190]

AESCHYLUS' *The Persians*

Aeschylus' *The Persians* was produced in the spring of 472, a critical year in the life of Themistocles. Since the subject concentrates on the glorious victory at Salamis with oblique references to Themistocles himself, the play has been interpreted in terms of Themistocles' career. There follows, therefore, a translation of the messenger's speech, which is particularly crucial to the argument. In it we have presented an account of Salamis to complement that of Herodotus, which for all its poetic cast is historically important, since Aeschylus himself fought in the battle.[191] But the tenor of his tragedy (not unlike that of Herodotus' *History*!) is poetic, religious and dramatic, qualities which even my prose translation cannot obliterate completely. The depiction is of a despotic and hubristic Xerxes lured to his doom by a jealous god and a man of guile, in the context of Hellenic freedom, confidence, joy and patriotic valour. Thus only some eight years after the event the heroic aura of saga was irreparably cast over Themistocles' most glorious achievement. The Messenger presents his account to Queen Atossa, widow of Darius and mother of Xerxes:[192]

O lady, an avenging or evil deity ($\delta\alpha\acute{\iota}\mu\omega\nu$) appeared from somewhere and began the entire disaster. For a Hellenic man came from the camp of the Athenians and spoke as follows to your son Xerxes: once the darkness of black night were to come, the Hellenes would not remain but each would leap in disorder upon the benches of the ships to save his life in secret flight. As soon as Xerxes heard this, not understanding either the treachery ($\delta\acute{o}\lambda o\nu$) of a Hellenic man or the envy of the

gods, he proclaimed to all his captains this command: when the sun
would cease to heat the earth with its rays and darkness take over the
realm of the sky, they were to draw up a dense array of ships in three
divisions to guard the exits of the sea-resounding straights and position
others in a circle about the island of Ajax [Salamis]. It was decreed by
Xerxes for all, 'Off with their heads,' if the Hellenes should find a
secret escape with their ships and avoid an evil fate. Thus he spoke
with very cheerful heart, for he did not know what was about to
come from the gods. His men, not in unruly spirit but with obedient
hearts, prepared their meal and each sailor fastened his oar by its thong
to its nicely fitting peg. When the light of the sun had set and night
came on, every man, the master of the oar and the one in charge of
arms, boarded his ship. And one called out to the other in their lines
of ships, sailing in order as each had been assigned. All night long the
captains of the ships supervised the patrolling of the naval host; night
departed and the army of the Hellenes had made no attempt to sail
away secretly. But when the white steeds of dawning day, bright to
behold, illuminated the whole earth, first a joyful sound rang out
triumphantly from the Hellenes, like a song, and at the same time the
echo answered clearly among the island's rocks. Fear seized all the
Persians as they realized their error in judgment, for the Hellenes then
were singing out a holy paean not as if in flight but rushing into battle
with confident courage; and over all a trumpet blazened forth its
blare. Immediately at the command they struck the depths of sea with
resounding oars in unison, and swiftly all were clearly to be seen. The
right wing first in order led the disciplined attack and then the whole
array came on and at the same time a great shout could be heard: 'O
sons of Hellenes come, make free your fatherland, make free your
children, wives, the seats of your ancestral gods and graves of your
forefathers. Now the contest is for all.' Indeed from us a clamour of
Persian tongues made answer, and there was no longer any time for
delay. Straightway ship struck ship with brazen-plated beaks. A Hellenic
ship began the ramming and broke off the whole stern of a Phoenician
ship; and spears were shot by men on either side. Now at first the
stream of the Persian force endured but when the numbers of their
ships were crowded in the narrows, and no assistance at all could be
given to one another but they struck each other with the blows from
their ships' brazen beaks, they kept smashing all their equipage of
oars; the Hellenic ships in orderly fashion struck them in a circle
round about and the hulls of their ships were overturned and the sea
no longer could be seen, full as it was with shipwrecks and the slaughter
of mortals. The beaches and the reefs were filled with corpses. Every
ship of the Persian armament was being rowed away in disorderly

flight; and they kept striking us with broken oars and pieces of
wreckage and hewing us down like mackerel or a catch of fish.
Moaning mingled with shrieks filled the stretches of sea until the eye of
black night brought oblivion. Not even if I were to go on for ten
days, should I be able to recount the full measure of misfortune. For
you may be sure of this – never in one day did so great a number of
men lose their lives.

After a short exchange with Atossa, the Messenger continues
with a description of the slaughter on the island of Psyttaleia
and so, for the record, let us complete his stirring account of the
events:[193]

There is an island in front of Salamis, a small one with bad anchorage
for ships on its shore, which is the haunt of Pan who loves the dance.
There Xerxes had sent some men so that, when the enemy had been
shipwrecked and were struggling to reach the island from their ships,
they might easily finish the slaughter of the surviving Hellenes; but
they were to rescue their friends from the stream of the sea – so badly
did he know what was to be. For when god gave the glory of victory
in the naval battle to the Hellenes, before the day was out they fitted
their bodies with armour of fine bronze and thus girt, leapt from their
ships. They encircled the whole island so that the Persians were at a
loss where to turn. For the Hellenes hurled many stones at them and
shot arrows from their bow strings that destroyed them. Finally the
Hellenes attacked in a single rush, struck and butchered the limbs of
their wretched enemy, until they had taken the lives of all. Xerxes
groaned aloud on seeing the depth of the disaster, for he had a seat in
clear view of the whole army, on a lofty hill near the sea-shore. He
rent his garments and gave a shrill cry; thereupon he passed on his
orders to his land army and left in disorderly flight. You may lament
over this misfortune along with the one before.

There can be no doubt that, in the year 472 when *The Persians*
was performed, Themistocles was in trouble, for his ostracism
can hardly be dated after 471/0. But if we ask what specific
relationship the production of Aeschylus' play bears to Themistocles' career, a precise answer is impossible. Was it performed
before, after, or in the very year of his ostracism? Unfortunately
there is nothing in the text itself to provide us with secure
historical evidence one way or the other. Any interpretation of
Aeschylus' personal or political relationship with Themistocles

or analysis of his motives for the composition of *The Persians*
must be based on very subjective grounds.[194]

It is quite possible that Aeschylus and Themistocles were
friends. They both fought at Salamis and Epistle 1, written to
the playwright, assumes some intimacy between the two men.
Yet the allusions to Themistocles in the play itself are curious;
for example, it is 'the treachery' of this 'Hellenic man' that is
emphasized. Is this a compliment, suggesting a typically Hellenic
admiration for clever duplicity?[195] Are the lines about Themistocles and his message deliberately oblique because of dramatic
conventions that might not allow too direct a reference in a
historical play to contemporaries and their achievements? Or
are they slyly evasive and even perhaps suggestively derogatory?

We do know from an inscription that Pericles of the deme
Cholargus was *choregos* for the production of *The Persians*.[196]
This is a startling piece of information, for I assume that the
reference is to the great Pericles, who in 472 would have been a
young man. How is it that he, an Alcmaeonid, would act as
financial backer for a play in support of Themistocles? Perhaps
Alcmaeonid hatred was not as all-pervasive as many historians
have thought and an individual like Pericles could appreciate
the accomplishments of a Themistocles. Yet, on the other hand,
The Persians may not be intended to be a tribute to Themistocles
at all. Rather, Aeschylus and Pericles might have been primarily
concerned about arousing anti-Persian sentiment and support
for the activities of the Delian Confederacy. It is even possible
that they were deliberately responding, not necessarily favourably, to the dramatic production by Phrynichus in 476, for which
Themistocles was *choregos*. If Phrynichus also dealt with the
subject of the Persian Wars in that year and consequently was
fined, as I have conjectured in the previous chapter, Aeschylus
might very well be wary of any supportive allusions to Themistocles. Since *The Persians* was supposed to have been directly
influenced by *The Phoenician Women* by Phrynichus,[197] it may
also be possible that Aeschylus (along with Pericles) was actually
expressing his disapproval of Themistocles' hubristic attempts
to glorify his own role against the Persians through the medium

of tragedy. Hypotheses to be sure! But they are prompted by
the nagging suspicion that Aeschylus in a play about the
Persian Wars, supported by Pericles, need not inevitably be
primarily motivated by the desire to rescue Themistocles from
political or personal disaster.

CHAPTER VIII

THEMISTOCLES' ODYSSEY: A HERO'S FLIGHT

As we have seen in the last chapter, after reviewing the career of the Spartan Pausanias and recounting his ignominious death, Thucydides tells how Themistocles was incriminated by the Athenians and Spartans who sent men to Argos to summon him while in ostracism to face charges. This is the way Thucydides, our earliest extant source, continues with his account of Themistocles' flight:

> But Themistocles was forewarned [about his pursuers] and fled from the Peloponnesus to Corcyra, where he was their benefactor. The Corcyraeans alleged that they were afraid to keep him at the risk of incurring the enmity of the Spartans and the Athenians, and they conveyed him to the mainland opposite.[198]

IN CORCYRA

Themistocles' first stop, then, according to Thucydides, is Corcyra; but it should be noted that, in the letters (3, 17 and 20, below, pp. 158f., 184 and 186ff.), he is delayed by a storm at Cyllene, on the northwest coast of the Peloponnesus, while en route from Argos to Corcyra. How can we know for sure whether this is a factual, but minor detail, omitted by our other sources, or an epistolary invention?

Although Thucydides tells us that Themistocles was a benefactor of the Corcyraeans and thus sought refuge with them, he does not provide any further elucidation. A scholiast on this passage offers a unique explanation of Themistocles' service:

> Since the Corcyraeans had not fought with Hellas against the Persians, the Hellenes, who had participated in the war, wished to take action against them; Themistocles opposed, saying that such a policy would be a worse experience for Hellas than if the Persians themselves had

become masters of the Hellenes and gone to the attack. For this reason, Themistocles was a benefactor.

The veracity of this explanation is suspect, since it seems only to be an inference, reminiscent of an episode, recorded by Plutarch alone, according to which Themistocles opposed the Spartans at the Amphictyonic meetings (of the Delphic League) when they proposed that all cities that had not joined in the war against the Persians be excluded from the Amphictyonic alliance; if there is any truth at all in this episode, we have at least confirmation of the Corcyraeans' friendliness towards Themistocles.[199]

But a more credible specific reason (if only one is to be isolated) for the designation of Themistocles as a benefactor (εὐεργέτης), which we know from inscriptions was an official title of honour, is given by Plutarch when he recounts Themistocles' flight to Corcyra, and the same explanation is recorded in a papyrus fragment. In a quarrel between the Corcyraeans and the Corinthians, he acted as arbitrator and settled their dispute by deciding that the Corinthians should pay twenty talents to the Corcyraeans and that the two parties together should administer Leucas (an island in the Adriatic, off the northwest coast of Hellas) as a common colony. Leucas had been colonized in the seventh century (c. 635); and the conflict of interests between Corinth and Corcyra in that area was always a source of contention. Yet this explanation too has been dismissed by the sceptical because parallels may be detected with events later in the fifth century.[200]

With Admetus

But, as Thucydides says, the Corcyraeans were afraid to harbour Themistocles; and so he sought refuge with Admetus, in Epirus in northwestern Greece. Let us continue with Thucydides' account.

Followed by his assigned pursuers as they learned of his movements, he was compelled by some desperate strait to take refuge with Admetus, King of the Molossians, who was not friendly towards him. Admetus happened not to be at home and Themistocles became a suppliant of the King's wife, who instructed him to take their child and sit at the hearth. Not much later, Admetus returned and Themistocles revealed who he was and claimed that, even if he had in any way opposed any request that the King had made of the Athenians, it was not right that he take vengeance on a fugitive. Indeed in this present circumstance he was at anyone's mercy and might be the victim of someone much weaker than Admetus and the noble thing to do was to take vengeance on equals on the basis of equality.[201] Besides he had opposed Admetus on the matter of a request, not on the matter of saving his life; but Admetus, if he gave him up, would put his life in jeopardy (he told him by whom and for what he was being pursued). When Admetus had heard his plea, he lifted him up along with his son; Themistocles was holding him as he sat, and this indeed was the most potent element in his supplication. When the Spartans and the Athenians came and made their many appeals, Admetus did not give Themistocles up; but since he wished to go to the King he sent him off by land to Pydna on the Thermaic Gulf in the Aegean, in the territory of Alexander [I of Macedon].[202]

The historicity of details in various stages of Themistocles' flight has inevitably been challenged and the story about the nature of his suppliancy at the hearth of Admetus is no exception. Even the account of Thucydides, here and elsewhere, includes elements that to some appear uncharacteristically romantic for so sober a historian. Suspicion grows when it is recognized that the episode bears certain similarities to an incident in Athenian drama, apparently well known by the ancients.

The legend of Telephus, a hero in the Trojan War, tells how he came, at Apollo's direction, as a suppliant of Agamemnon to find the cure for a festering wound that had been inflicted by Achilles. In order to achieve his ends, Telephus seized Agamemnon's infant son Orestes, at the instigation of the child's mother Clytemnestra, rushed to the altar and threatened to kill him; and so Agamemnon agreed to help Telephus. The tragedy of Telephus was treated by all three dramatists, Aeschylus, Sophocles and Euripides, in plays that survive for us only in fragments; but the scene of the seizure of Orestes as depicted by Euripides in his *Telephus* (produced in 438), in particular, is parodied more than once in the extant comedies of Aristophanes.[203]

1–5 *Ostraka* for five of Themistocles' contemporaries: 1 Aristeides Lysima-
chou. Fragment of the rim of a mortar. P20044. 2 Hippokrates Alkmeonidou.
Fragment of the rim of a semi-glazed krater. P17648. 3 Kallixenos Aristonymou,
the Alcmaeonid. Fragment of a semi-glazed krater. P17769. 4 Kimon Miltiadou,
Fragment of a glazed roof tile. P18339. 5 Megakles ho Hippokratous. Fragment
of a heavy krater. P2651

6–10 *Ostraka* for Themistocles: 6 Themistokles Neokleous. Fragment of black glazed foot of a large pot. P17138. 7 Themistokles Neokleous Phrearrhios. From the Agora excavations, Athens. P9950. 8 Themistokles Neokleous. Fragment of a closed pot. P5963. 9 Themistokles Neokleous, inscribed boustrophedon. P19836. 10 Themistokles Neokleous. Fragment of a black glazed krater. P17629

11 Largest of the *ostraka*, inscribed with the name of Themistokles Neokleous Phrearrhios. P15727

12 Nine *ostraka* of Themistokles Neokleous from the large find on the north slope of the Acropolis, Athens. Fragments of kylix bases. The top row are all by one hand, the second row by another, the last row by a third

13 *Ostrakon* for Themistokles Neokleous, with ITO added. AO49

14 Large group of *ostraka* for Themistocles from the north slope of the Acropolis, exhibited in the Stoa of the Attalos Museum, Athens

15 Stone bearing Themistocles' Troezen decree, in the National (Epigraphical) Museum, Athens

16 The Greek text of the Troezen decree

[θεοί]

ἔδοξ[εν] τῆι βουλῆι καὶ τῶι δήμωι

Θεμισ[τοκλ]ῆς Νεοκλέους Φρεάρριος εἶπεν

τὴ[μ] μὲν πό[λιν παρ]ακατ[αθέ]σθαι τῆι ᾿Αθηνᾶι τῆι ᾿Αθηνῶ

5 μ [μεδεο]ύ[σηι] κ[αὶ τοῖς ἄλλ]οις θεοῖς ἅπασιν φυλάττει

ν κα[ὶ] ἀμ[ύνειν τὸμ βά]ρβαρ[ο]ν ὑπὲρ τῆς χώρας· ᾿Αθηναίου

[ς δὲ α]ὐτ[οὺς καὶ τοὺς ξένο]υς τοὺς οἰκοῦντας ᾿Αθήνησι

[τὰ τέκ]ν[α καὶ τὰς γυναῖκ]ας ε[ἰς] Τροιζῆνα καταθέσθαι

[προστάτου ὄντος Πιτθέως] τοῦ ἀρχηγέτου τῆς χώρας· τ

10 [οὺς δὲ πρεσβύτας καὶ τὰ] κτήματα εἰς Σαλαμῖνα καταθ

ἐ[σ]θ[αι· τοὺς δὲ ταμίας καὶ τ]ὰς ἱερέας ἐν τῆι ἀκροπόλε

[ι μένειν φυλάττοντας τὰ τῶ]ν θεῶν· τοὺς δὲ ἄλλους ᾿Αθη

[ναίους ἅπαντας καὶ τοὺς ξέ]νους τοὺς ἡβῶντας εἰσβαί

νειν ε[ἰς τὰς ἑτοιμασθ]ε[ί]σ[α]ς διακοσίας ναῦς καὶ ἀμύ

15 νεσ[θαι] τ[ὸμ βάρβαρον ὑπὲρ τῆ]ς ἐλευθερίας τῆς τε ἑαυ

τῶν [καὶ τῶν ἄλλων ῾Ελλήνων] μετὰ Λακεδαιμονίων καὶ Κο

ριν[θίων καὶ Αἰγινητῶν] καὶ τῶν ἄλλων τῶμ βουλομένω

[ν] κοινω[νήσειν τοῦ κινδύνο]υ· καταστῆσαι δὲ καὶ τριη

[ρ]ά[ρχους διακοσίους, ἕνα ἐπὶ] τὴν ναῦν ἑκάστην τοὺς [σ]

20 τρατη[γ]οὺ[ς ἀρχομένους τ]ῆι αὔριον ἡμέραι ἐκ τῶν κ[εκ]

τημέν[ω]ν γ[ῆν] τ[ε κ]αὶ [οἰκί]αν ᾿Αθ[ή]νησι καὶ οἷς ἀμ παῖδ[ες]

ὦσι γνή[σιοι μὴ πρεσβυτέρο]υς πεντήκοντα ἐτῶν κα[ὶ ἐ]

πικλ[ηρῶσαι αὐτ]οῖς [τ]ὰς ναῦς· ʹʹ καταλέξαι δὲ καὶ ἐπ[ι]

βάτας [δ]έκα [ἐφ᾿ ἑκάστη]ν ναῦν ἐκ τῶν ὑπὲρ εἴκοσιν ἔτη [γ]

25 εγονότω[ν μέχρι τριά]κοντα ἐτῶν καὶ τοξότας τέτταρ

ας· δια[κληρῶσαι δὲ κ]αὶ [τ]ὰς ὑπηρεσίας ἐπὶ τὰς ναῦς ὅτ

αμπερ κ[αὶ τοὺς τριηράρ]χους ἐπικληρῶσιν· ἀναγράψα

ι δὲ κα[ὶ τοὺς ἄλλους κατὰ] ναῦν τοὺς στρατηγοὺς εἰς λ

ευκώ[ματα τοὺς μὲν ᾿Α]θηναίους ἐκ τῶν ληξιαρχικῶν γρ

30 αμματεί[ων τοὺς] δὲ ξ[έν]ους ἐκ τῶν ἀπογεγραμμένων πα

[ρ]ὰ τῶι [πολε]μ[άρχ]ω[ι·] ἀναγράφειν δὲ νέμοντας κατὰ τάξ

εις [εἰς διακοσί]α[ς] ἀ[ν]ὰ ἑκατὸν ἀριθμὸν καὶ ἐπιγράψα

ι τῆι [τάξ]ει ἑκάστηι τῆς τριήρους τοὔνομα καὶ τοῦ τρι

ηράρχου καὶ τ[ὰ]ς ὑπηρε[σί]ας ὅπως ἂν εἰδῶσιν εἰς ὁποί

35 αν τριήρη ἐ[μ]βήσεται ἡ [τ]άξις ἑ[κ]άστη· ἐπειδὰν δὲ νεμη

θῶσιν ἅπα[σ]αι αἱ τάξεις καὶ ἐπικληρωθῶσι ταῖς τριή

ρεσι πληροῦν ἁ[π]άσας τὰς διακοσίας ναῦς τὴμ βουλὴν

καὶ τ[ο]ὺς τρατηγοὺ[ς θύ]σαντας ἀρεστήριον τῶι Διὶ τῶι

Παγκρατεῖ καὶ τῆι ᾿Αθηνᾶι καὶ τῆι Νίκηι καὶ τῶι Ποσει

40 δῶνι τῶι ᾿Ασφα[λ]είωι· ʹʹ ἐπειδὰν δὲ πεπληρωμέναι ὦσιν

αἱ νῆες τα[ῖ]ς μὲν ἑκατὸν αὐτῶν βοηθεῖν ἐπὶ τὸ ᾿Αρτεμίσ

[ι]ον τὸ Εὐβοϊκὸν ταῖς δὲ ἑκατὸν αὐτῶν περὶ τὴν Σαλαμ

ῖνα καὶ τὴν ἄλλην ᾿Αττικὴν ναυλοχεῖν καὶ φυλάττειν

τὴν χώραν· ὅπως δ᾿ ἂν καὶ ὁμονοοῦντες ἅπαντες ᾿Αθηναῖοι

45 ἀμύνωνται τὸμ βάρβαρον τοὺς μὲν μεθεστηκότας τὰ [δ]

[έκα] ἔτη ἀπιέναι εἰς Σαλαμῖνα καὶ μένειν αὐτοὺς ἐ[κε]

[ῖ ἕως ἄν τι τῶι δήμ]ωι δόξηι περὶ αὐτῶν· τοὺς δὲ [ἀτίμου]

[ς – – – – – – – – – –] traces [– – – – – – – – –]

17 Model of a trireme made by Sinclair Morrison in 1939, in the Nautical Museum, Greenwich

18 Drawing of a trireme

19 Forward section of the hull of a trireme. The so-called Lenormant relief from the Erechtheum on the Acropolis, Athens. Cast in the British Museum

Scale 1:180
Height of deck above waterline: 8 ft
Draught: 3 ft 9 ins
Length: 115 ft
(Breadth of Hull amidships: 12 ft
(Overall breadth including
 outriggers: 16 ft)

Waterline

20 Marble grave-stele from Salamis, with names of Chaeredemus and Lynceus

21   Xerxes as Crown Prince. Detail from the Treasury Frieze at Persepolis

22   Section of the Themistoclean wall west of the Sacred Gate, with repairs made in the fourth century BC by Conon and Demosthenes

23   Section of the Themistoclean wall near the Sacred Gate. The lower part of the wall, 0·75 m. high, is of Acropolis limestone, the upper part of poros

24   Section of the Themistoclean wall showing the fourth-century BC repair at Gate XIII

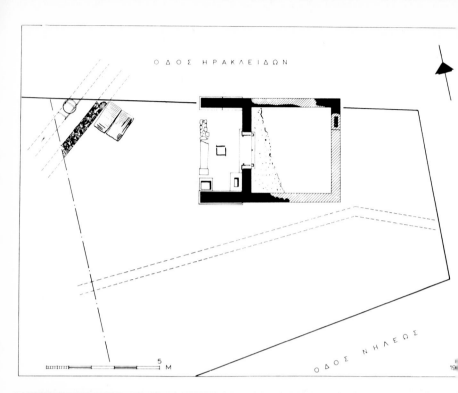

Ο Δ Ο Σ   Η Ρ Α Κ Λ Ε Ι Δ Ω Ν

Ο Δ Ο Σ   Ν Η Λ Ε Ω Σ

5 M

25 Temple and altar of the shrine of Artemis Aristoboule at Athens

26 Remains of the temple of Artemis Aristoboule. General view from the southwest

27   Solid silver didrachm. Obv. Apollo with his right hand extended to dispatch a bird. Rev. A bird (raven, hawk or eagle?) with spread wings

28   Silver-plated didrachm. Obv. As for Plate 29. Rev. As for Plate 27

29   Solid silver didrachm. Obv. Apollo holding a long staff (of, or entwined with, olive or laurel?). Rev. As for Plate 27

30 Bronze coin of Magnesia issued by Antoninus Pius. Rev. Male figure grasping a sheathed sword with his left hand and pouring a libation over a lighted altar from a phiale held in his right. The name Themistocles is inscribed with the year designated as that of the Secretary (to the Council), Dioscourides Gratus, of the metropolis of the Magnesians

31 Persepolis. Artaxerxes giving audience

32 Persepolis. Persian dignitaries, sixth–fifth centuries BC

33 Codex Palatinus Graecus 398. Title-page of the Epistles of Themistocles

34 The tomb of Themistocles. Photograph of the column and tomb on the Acte peninsula, Piraeus

35 Portrait-herm from Ostia, with the name of Themistocles inscribed, in the
Ostia Museum. Total height 20·47 in. (57 cm.), max. width 11·81 in. (30 cm.);
head only: height 10·63 in. (27 cm.), width 7·87 in. (20 cm.)

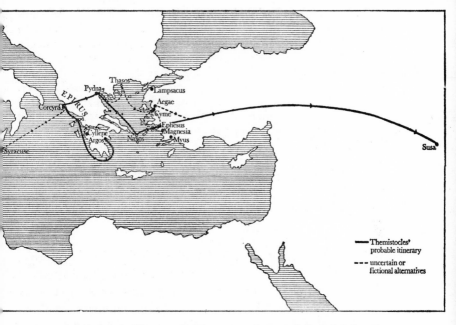

Map IV   Themistocles' Odyssey. The place-names shown include the King's gifts, Magnesia, Lampsacus and Myus.

A heroic parallel for Themistocles may also be found in the *Odyssey* where Odysseus becomes the suppliant of King Alcinous through the instructions of Queen Arete.[204]

Plutarch points to the dramatic character of Themistocles' encounter with Admetus and for this reason alone his version is worth quoting in full; notice especially the verbs 'contrived' and 'acted out the tragic scene' in the last sentence. Although there are similarities to Thucydides' account, Plutarch does provide variations and additions.

Themistocles fled from Corcyra to Epirus and, since he was pursued by the Athenians and the Spartans, he abandoned himself to desperate and difficult hopes and sought refuge with Admetus, who was King of the Molossians; for Admetus had made some request of the Athenians, which was scornfully rejected by Themistocles when he

was at the height of political power. The King continued to be angry
with Themistocles and made it clear that, if he got hold of him, he
would exact vengeance. But in his present misfortune Themistocles
feared the recent enmity of his countrymen more than the older
hostility of the King. He placed himself at the mercy of Admetus,
making himself his suppliant in a most startling and peculiar way.
For he took the young son of the King and fell down at his hearth –
this form of supplication is considered by the Molossians the most
potent and the only one that is virtually irrefutable. Some say that
Phthia, the wife of the King, suggested this manner of entreaty to
Themistocles and that she sat her son down with him. Others maintain that Admetus contrived (διαθεῖναι) and acted out the tragic scene
of supplication (συντραγῳδῆσαι) in order that he might allege as an
excuse to the pursuers a religious necessity for not surrendering
Themistocles.[205]

   This last interpretation, which Plutarch found in his sources,
perhaps represents an inventive rationalization of the apparent
theatrical elements in the scene. Thus ancient writers may very
well have been as dubious as their modern counterparts about
the drama of Themistocles' encounter with Admetus. Is this
why Diodorus (or his source Ephorus?) omits entirely any
details about the nature of the episode and does not even mention
the original hostility of Admetus? A paraphrase of Diodorus'
account will reveal the differences in point of view of his
narrative.
   According to Diodorus Themistocles took refuge at the
hearth to become the suppliant of Admetus, who at first received
him in a friendly way, until the arrival of the most distinguished
ambassadors of the Spartans who had been sent in pursuit.[206]
For the Spartans denounced Themistocles as the betrayer and
destroyer of the whole of Hellas and maintained that they, along
with all the Hellenes, would make war against him, if he refused.
In fear of this threat, out of pity for his suppliant, and to avoid
the shame of surrendering him, he persuaded Themistocles to
depart as quickly as possible, without the Spartans' knowledge;
and he gave him a large amount of gold for the expenses of his
flight.[207]
   In the multiple versions of this episode, with their variations

in details and of emphasis, we can detect two major traditions which in the last analysis are not inevitably contradictory: the Thucydidean (the earliest for us) that stresses Themistocles' desperation in turning to his enemy Admetus and describes the unusual nature of his suppliancy; and another (as far as we can tell, later) version that, for some reason, omits the original hostility of Admetus and neglects to describe the character of Themistocles' suppliancy.[208] Both versions appear to be reflected by the letters (5 and 20) translated below, and perhaps by Nepos.[209]

The best that we can do is accept Thucydides' testimony, whether or not it has been influenced by dramatic considerations or coloured by the desire to characterize most forcefully Themistocles' desperate ingenuity. We cannot know for sure that later writers had any good evidence for the suppression of dubious details.[210]

We learn from later ancient commentators that the request made by Admetus to the Athenians which was rejected upon the advice of Themistocles was for an alliance ($\sigma\upsilon\mu\mu\alpha\chi\acute{\iota}\alpha$). Whether this explanation for Admetus' hostility is based upon factual knowledge or merely represents a logical inference, it is impossible to say.[211]

Thus Themistocles fled to Admetus. But at this point we must consider conflicting testimony concerning Themistocles and Sicily.

To Sicily?

Plutarch tells us that, according to Stesimbrotus, a man named Epicrates of the deme Acharnae stole the wife and children of Themistocles out of Athens and sent them to him at the court of Admetus. For this, Cimon later convicted Epicrates and put him to death. Then Plutarch observes:

I do not know how Stesimbrotus forgets this, or makes Themistocles forget this, when he says that Themistocles sailed to Hieron in Sicily and asked for the daughter of the tyrant in marriage, promising he

would make the Hellenes subject to him; but that Hieron sent him
away and thus he set sail for Asia.

Thus Plutarch not only doubts the voyage to Sicily because
Themistocles supposedly already had a wife and family with
him in Epirus, and the proposal of marriage was absurd, but he
goes on to add, giving Theophrastus *On Monarchy* as his source,
that the journey to Hieron is also unlikely because of Themistocles' speech urging the Hellenes to prevent Hieron from competing at Olympia.[212]

We cannot believe that Themistocles actually went to Sicily,
whether or not his family came to him in Epirus. But that he
contemplated the journey is not entirely impossible. In Epistle
20 we find that, when the Corcyraeans refused to harbour him,
he intended to sail to Gelon (not Hieron) in Sicily, since he was
friendly to him. But he was deterred from the voyage after
learning that Hieron, who had recently become King, was
embroiled in difficulties. Friendship with Gelon is reinforced by
Epistle 7, which establishes a tie between Themistocles and
Menyllus, the helmsman who once brought a grain ship of
Gelon's to the Piraeus.

The Letters are at least more credible than Plutarch, who for
all we know may have garbled Stesimbrotus' testimony. If
Themistocles contemplated going to Sicily, he might have done
so upon leaving Corcyra, rather than Epirus. The chronology
is difficult but not impossible: Gelon died *c.* 477; Themistocles
cannot be in Corcyra before 471.[213] If the story is not to be
dismissed completely, we have further confirmation of Themistocles' view towards the west; or was this view merely a later
inference? For whatever reasons, Diodorus omits any mention
of both Corcyra and Sicily in his account of the flight.

To Pydna and Asia Minor

Apparently Themistocles left Admetus and set out by land,
eventually arriving in Asia Minor. According to Thucydides,
Admetus directed Themistocles to Pydna, in the kingdom of

Alexander, since he wished to go to the King [of Persia]. But Diodorus' account is rather different: in his view, as we have already seen, Themistocles fled from Argos to Admetus and became a suppliant at the hearth. Not only is there no mention of Corcyra but the original hostility of Admetus upon Themistocles' arrival is also omitted completely. Thus, in terms of this itinerary, Themistocles' flight from Argos to Admetus is perhaps made more credible. Diodorus differs in other respects from Thucydides: no reference is made to Themistocles' intention of going to the King of Persia and his departure from Pydna is ignored; yet other specific details about his journey are included.

Themistocles, pressed as he was on all sides, accepted the gold (that Admetus offered) and fled during the night from the country of the Molossians, King Admetus making every effort to help him in his flight. And Themistocles found two young men, who were Lyncestians by birth; by travelling during the night he eluded the Spartans, and because of the good will and the perseverance of the young men he arrived in Asia.[214]

In Nepos it is Admetus' idea that Themistocles should flee far from his enemies:

Admetus did not hand over his suppliant but warned him to plan for his protection, since it was difficult for him to remain safe in a place so close to his enemies, and gave him what assistance would be sufficient.[215]

To be sure these variants are not completely irreconcilable with Thucydides and they need not represent a more reliable tradition. But one cannot help but wonder what Thucydides intends precisely when he says that since Themistocles, upon leaving Epirus, wished to go to the King, Admetus sent him to Pydna, in the territory of Alexander. Are we to think that Themistocles has already formulated the plan of actually approaching the King himself? Is this King supposed to be Xerxes or Artaxerxes? In fact, Thucydides seems to be using the common expression 'to the King' imprecisely and after the fact, with no specific King (Xerxes or Artaxerxes) in mind; and his evidence need imply little more than the fact that Themistocles, when he left Admetus, was on his way to Persia. Even if Themistocles' intention was already ultimately to approach the Persian King, circumstances have yet to determine the time and the manner for the fulfilment of his ambitions.

But let us continue with Thucydides' account; it is he and not Diodorus who relates the dramatic details concerning his journey from mainland Greece to Asia Minor.

At Pydna he found a merchant ship sailing for Ionia; he got on and was carried by a storm to the Athenian squadron that was besieging the island of Naxos. Since those on the ship did not know him and he was afraid, Themistocles told the captain who he was and why he was in flight; he said that if he would not save him he would claim that the captain had been won over by money to give him passage. Safety depended on no one leaving the ship until the voyage was resumed; if he agreed to this, he would repay the favour with a worthy recompense. The captain did as he was told and after waiting out the storm for a day and a night at a distance from the Athenian squadron, later arrived at Ephesus. And Themistocles took care of him with a gift of money (for later there came to him out of Athens from friends and out of Argos what had been stowed away).[216]

Plutarch[217] amplifies this last information given by Thucydides as follows:

Much of his money was stolen away for him by friends and sent across the sea to Asia; the total amount that was discovered and confiscated by the state amounted to 100 talents, according to Theopompus, but Theophrastus says 80. Yet Themistocles did not have the worth of as much as three talents before he entered politics.

Thus Themistocles arrived in Asia Minor. Nepos[218] and Epistle 20 follow Thucydides' narrative with no significant variations. But Plutarch, who acknowledges Thucydides as one of his sources, presents us with further complications. According to Plutarch, Themistocles landed at Cyme (at least that is the first stop mentioned), not Ephesus, and it is possible that he wrote that Themistocles encountered the Athenian fleet off the island of Thasos rather than Naxos.[219] Both readings are found in the manuscripts at this point and there are strong arguments to suggest that Thasos is to be preferred. If so, have we reflected here rival traditions for Themistocles' itinerary – Thasos to Cyme or Naxos to Ephesus – following a geographical logic that is confirmed by a glance at the map? The question of Thasos or Naxos has even more serious implications, especially chronological, which, as we shall see, are closely related to the subsequent problem of whether Themistocles eventually encountered Xerxes or Artaxerxes. The emendation of Naxos to Thasos in Thucydides' text is difficult and does not resolve all the difficulties; and so the best that we can do is to keep faith with Thucydides' version of Themistocles' journey from Pydna to Naxos to Ephesus.[220] It is not entirely impossible that Themistocles stopped at both Cyme and Ephesus in his travels, wherever he landed first.

Conclusions

An overall view of the nature and geography of Themistocles' flight, in terms of the unanimity of our sources, makes certain general conclusions inevitable, quite apart from the disturbing conflicts and problems. Themistocles was pursued by the Spartans and Athenians as he fled in haste from Argos westward. Very probably he first turned to the Corcyraeans, who were his friends. They were afraid to harbour him. He most certainly sought refuge with Admetus, King of the Molossians in Epirus. Possibly Admetus was an enemy of Themistocles but became his friend. At any rate Themistocles was the King's suppliant and the nature of his suppliancy may have been most startling and dramatic. We do not know how long Themistocles intended to remain with Admetus, and it is curious that his family was sent to him in Epirus, if only because of his precarious position. Indeed his sojourn there was cut short by the arrival of his pursuers and Admetus was most helpful to Themistocles in his escape. At some point, perhaps after leaving Corcyra (or Epirus), Themistocles may have toyed with the idea of fleeing farther west to Sicily. Could escape to Sicily have been his original intention? We cannot be sure how clearly Themistocles had formulated his plans for approaching the King of Persia as

he left Admetus. His immediate goal was Asia Minor. He set
sail (probably from Pydna) and because of a storm encountered
the Athenian fleet off Naxos (or Thasos) and arrived at Ephesus
(or Cyme).

These are not the actions of a man who, because of collusion
with Xerxes, is confident of a welcome reception in Persia.
Themistocles' first impulse was to run to the West, not to the
East. Chance and circumstance, turned at times ingeniously to
his own advantage, dictated in large measure the character of
his movements and the itinerary of his flight. After the rewards
of his suppliancy at the court of Admetus, he might very well
try his success with the King of Persia.

Various attempts have been made to distinguish which wife
and children of Themistocles were assisted in their escape by
Epicrates (whether to Epirus as Plutarch maintains, or perhaps
to Asia Minor). But since we have no assurance about either the
dates of Themistocles' marriages or the births of his children,
conjecture seems futile. We do not know that his family was
ever formally exiled by the Athenian state. Epistle 4 (below,
pp. 159ff.) expresses Themistocles' disbelief (but also his concern) that the Athenians might maltreat his wife and children
in his absence; in this same letter one of his daughters in Athens
is supposedly betrothed or married to Lysicles, son of Habronichus. Plutarch does, however, tell us about the official con-
fiscation of Themistocles' wealth and that money was secretly
dispatched to him in Asia. We know for a fact that Themistocles'
children resided in Athens later,[221] but we are under no compulsion to believe that a special decree had to be passed for a
return of his family. It has been conjectured that a reinstatement
of his children occurred at some time after 459, once the new
spirit initiated by the democratic reforms of Ephialtes had taken
effect and Themistocles' bitter enemy, Cimon, had died.[222]

NAXOS OR THASOS? ARTAXERXES OR XERXES?
CHRONOLOGICAL PROBLEMS AGAIN

In the last chapter I concluded that Themistocles was probably in ostracism by 471/0 and that his flight belongs in the period 471/0–465/4. Our sources above have indicated that in his journey to Asia Minor he encountered the Athenian fleet, which was besieging the island of Naxos or Thasos. The siege of Naxos cannot be dated with certainty – it has been placed as early as 470 or as late as 465.[223] The siege of Thasos can be more securely fixed as beginning in 465 or 464.

The authority of Thucydides for Naxos is on the face of it to be preferred,[224] but without a certain date for the siege we cannot confidently pinpoint the flight within the period 471/0– 465/4. If Themistocles did encounter the fleet off Thasos his journey from Pydna will probably have occurred in the year 465 or 464; but Thasos did not capitulate until 463/2 or at latest 461.

The problem is further complicated by the question whether Themistocles encountered Artaxerxes or Xerxes upon his arrival in Persia, and thus it is necessary at this point to anticipate further evidence, which will be more fully disclosed in the next chapter. Thucydides and Charon of Lampsacus, as we shall soon see, maintained that Themistocles approached Artaxerxes; Thucydides in fact says that, upon proceeding inland from the coast, Themistocles sent a letter to Artaxerxes who recently had become King. It seems to be securely established that Xerxes died in 465 to be succeeded by his son, Artaxerxes.

If Themistocles met Xerxes, as historians other than Thucydides and Charon reported, he will then have had to arrive in Persia at latest in 465 and probably earlier. It is extremely unlikely, however, that Themistocles did in actual fact approach Xerxes at all. Not only does the authority of Thucydides and Charon speak against it, but also such an encounter by its very nature smacks of dramatic invention. Themistocles, the hero of Salamis, was brought face to face with his former enemy (and friend!) Xerxes, in a theatrical scene which builds upon allegations that Themistocles had been in collusion with Xerxes all along – from the very time of the battle or at least its aftermath. The fiction of a meeting with Xerxes seeks to shed the final aura of truth upon the accusation that Themistocles actually betrayed his generalship and his fellow Hellenes in their struggle against the Persians.

If, then, a first encounter with Artaxerxes must be historical, Themistocles will have written his letter to the King no earlier than 465 and will not have been received by him before 464 or 463. With Themistocles' flight in the year 471/0, he *could* have encountered Xerxes at any time before 465; but if we are right in having him negotiate with Artaxerxes, there is no compulsion to make him reach Asia before 465. At any rate, there will have been about five years (471/0–465/4) for his journey to Asia (with its various stops) and perhaps a sojourn there before writing to Artaxerxes.

If, on the other hand, we place his departure from Argos at some time after 471/0, even as late as 465/4, we then curtail both the length of time for his journey before encountering Artaxerxes, and the period of his power under the aegis of the Persian King. Fundamental to the problem is the fact that we cannot, unfortunately, ascertain how long it took Themistocles to travel from Argos to Asia Minor and then to the King himself. We have already described how he was perhaps delayed at Cyllene, and actually spent some time in Corcyra and with Admetus in Epirus; and in the next chapter we shall see that he also may have stopped with friends on the coast of Asia Minor.

Our answers, therefore, to many of these questions must be tentative and flexible, until, perchance, some new evidence appears. Despite the risk of repetition, let me sum up as follows: Themistocles was ostracized in 471/0 or earlier; his flight belongs in the period 471–464 and probably no later; he very likely encountered the fleet off Naxos (rather than Thasos) and he almost certainly met first with Artaxerxes (not Xerxes) in 464 or not too long thereafter.[225]

CHAPTER IX

THEMISTOCLES JOINS THE PERSIAN KING: A HERO'S REFUGE

It is noteworthy that Thucydides does not mention details about Themistocles' adventures in Asia Minor, but concentrates instead upon his correspondence with the King and his preparations for joining him to 'become great by his side.' This is how Thucydides continues his account of Themistocles' flight:[226]

And proceeding inland (to Susa?) with one of the Persians from the coast,[227] he sent a letter to King Artaxerxes the son of Xerxes, who had recently (νεωστί) become king. The letter clearly stated the following: 'I have come to you, I Themistocles, who of all Hellenes wrought the most evil upon your house in all the time that I, by necessity, defended myself against your father as he attacked; but still I wrought much more good on the occasion of his retreat, when I was in safety and he in danger. A good turn is owed me (he wrote of the forewarning from Salamis about departure and the preservation of the bridges for which he falsely claimed he then was responsible),[228] and now, pursued by the Hellenes because of my friendship for you, I am here having it in my power to do you great good. I wish, after waiting a year, to make clear to you myself for what I have come.' The king, as it is said, was amazed at his perception[229] and bade him do as he wished. And Themistocles in the time that he waited learned as much as he could of the Persian language and the customs of the country. After a year he approached the King and became great by his side, as no one of the Hellenes ever had, because of his proven worth and the hope that he suggested of enslaving the Hellenic world and especially because of his keen intelligence of which he repeatedly gave clear and ample proof.

ON THE WAY TO THE KING

When we turn to the later versions of these same events by Diodorus and Plutarch we find significant amplifications and variations. Plutarch makes a point of noting that Thucydides and Charon of Lampsacus (is Thucydides dependent upon Charon?) relate that Xerxes was dead and that Themistocles had his interview with Artaxerxes, the son of Xerxes (Pl. 31). On the other hand, according to Ephorus, Dinon, Clitarchus, Heracleides and still other writers, Themistocles came to King Xerxes himself. Plutarch goes on to express his preference for the version of Thucydides (and Charon), i.e. the meeting with Artaxerxes, for chronological reasons, although he admits that the chronology is by no means established securely.[230] We know that Artaxerxes did not come to the throne until 465 and so according to Thucydides it was not until 464 at the earliest that Themistocles would have approached him personally.

In the later elaborative details there is much that one could automatically dismiss as romantic fiction, particularly in view of Thucydides' silence. But we do not know if Thucydides too was aware of any or all of these stories found in later authors and wilfully suppressed them. If he did wilfully suppress them was it because he thought *all* of them false or merely inappropriate to his narrative? It strikes me as extremely curious that Thucydides' account is full of romantic details (as we have seen) up until the time of Themistocles' arrival in Asia Minor in contrast to Diodorus' more sober version, whereas, after Themistocles reaches Asia, quite the reverse is true: Diodorus becomes the romantic historian (although perhaps not quite to the extent that Plutarch does) and Thucydides appears more sober because of his silence.

It is enough then at this point to combine the narratives of Diodorus and Plutarch in an attempt to trace Themistocles' movements. These historical legends that became part of the exciting saga of the heroic Themistocles cannot be ignored; and amidst all that is patently fanciful one should not be blind to truths that may be embedded in them. Certainly historians are not averse to accepting the itinerary of the later tradition and do not find it incredible that Themistocles turned to a friend or friends in Asia Minor for help.[231] Such facts could have been kept alive in the oral tradition and recorded by someone like

Charon. How in the world did Thucydides find credible evidence for his composition of Themistocles' letter to Artaxerxes? As we proceed it must be remembered, that Diodorus (like Ephorus) believed Themistocles approached Xerxes; we have seen that Plutarch prefers Thucydides' (and Charon's) version of a meeting with Artaxerxes, although his narrative seems to combine elements that belonged to the tradition uniting Themistocles and Xerxes.

Diodorus[232] reports that in Asia Themistocles had a personal friend named Lysitheides, who was esteemed for his reputation and wealth; this Lysitheides was also a friend of Xerxes and he had entertained his entire Persian force during their passage through Asia.[233] In Plutarch, when Themistocles came to Cyme he learned that there were many people (and two men in particular, Ergoteles and Pythodorus) who were watching and waiting to seize him; for his capture would be profitable to the unscrupulous, since the King had set a price of 200 talents on his head. Thus he fled to Aegae, a small Aeolic town; no one there knew him except his host, Nicogenes, who was the richest man in Aeolia and well known by the powerful and wealthy of the interior. Themistocles remained in hiding with Nicogenes for a few days. One night after a sacrifice and dinner, the pedagogue of Nicogenes' children, a man named Olbius, fell into an inspired trance and uttered the following verse: 'Night will speak to you, night will advise you, night will grant you victory.' Afterwards when Themistocles went to bed he had a dream in which he saw a serpent wind itself along his stomach all the way up to his neck. As it touched his face it turned into an eagle, which enfolded him with its wings, and lifting him aloft carried him a great distance. Then the golden staff of a herald appeared and as the eagle placed him upon it he was freed from his helpless anxiety and fear. It is not too difficult to interpret the eagle and the staff as symbols of the safety and peace that Themistocles is to find at last in the person of the King of Persia.

It was Nicogenes then (or according to Diodorus, Lysitheides) [234] who devised a scheme whereby Themistocles was

to be safely escorted to the Persian King. A Persian custom
was to conduct a concubine to the King's court in a closed
wagon; in fact Persians were particularly jealous of their
women – wives, slaves and concubines were guarded so as
never to be seen by strangers, not only at home but also when
they travelled, for they were carried in a covered four-wheeled
wagon, surrounded with curtains. Such a wagon was prepared
for Themistocles, who was safely hidden behind costly hangings;
his attendants explained to any enquirers that they were leading
a delicate girl from Ionia to one of the King's courtiers (or to
the King himself). According to Diodorus, Lysitheides, who
accompanied Themistocles on the journey, first approached the
King cautiously and on his own to obtain assurances for Themistocles' safety. Then he led in Themistocles himself, who upon
explaining that he had done no wrong was absolved from
punishment.

Plutarch, however, on the authority of Phanias and Eratosthenes in his book *On Wealth*, tells of how Themistocles first
had an audience with Artabanus, the Chiliarch or Grand Vizier,
noting that Eratosthenes added that it was through Artabanus'
wife, a woman of Eretria, that Themistocles had obtained his
interview with Artabanus.[235] Shades of the story concerning
Admetus? That interview, we are supposed to believe, went
something like this:

Themistocles: I am a Hellene and I wish to have an audience with the
   King about matters of the greatest importance and concern to him.
Artabanus: Stranger, customs differ among men; what is right for
   one is not right for another. But all agree that it is right to honour
   and preserve their own particular ways. And so it is said that you
   Hellenes admire liberty and equality most of all. But for a Persian
   the most beautiful of our customs is to honour our King and
   prostrate ourselves before him as the image of a god who preserves
   everything. If then you approve of our customs and will make
   obeisance to him, you may behold the King and speak to him; but
   if you think otherwise, you will have to use messengers as your
   intermediaries, since it is not Persian custom for the King to give
   audience to a man who has not prostrated himself before him.
Themistocles: But I have come, Artabanus, to increase the fame and

the power of the King. I shall myself abide by your ways, since this is the will of the god who exalts the Persians, and through me the number of men who now pay obeisance to the King will be increased. Therefore do not let Persian custom stand in the way of the words that I wish to speak to him.

Artabanus: Who of the Hellenes am I to say you are? You, who have come here, are certainly unlike any ordinary fellow in intelligence.

Themistocles: No one, Artabanus, before the King himself, is to learn my name.

THEMISTOCLES FACES THE KING

Plutarch goes on to relate that after Themistocles was led into the King's presence he prostrated himself, then stood up and remained silent; whereupon the King ordered an interpreter to ask the stranger who he was. And this was Themistocles' response:

O King, I, Themistocles the Athenian, have come to you, an exile pursued by the Hellenes; I am responsible for bringing many evils upon the Persians, but also many blessings greater in number than the evils, for I prevented the Hellenes from following in pursuit once Hellas itself was secure and the salvation of my own home and country gave me the opportunity of doing you a favour as well. Now then in my present circumstances I am resigned to anything; and I have come here to you either to receive the favour of your kind reconciliation or, if you still harbour the memory of past wrongs, to plead that you forget your anger. Make my enemies your witnesses, I beg you, of the good that I have done for the Persians, and use my present fortunes to display your virtue rather than satisfy your revenge. It is one who is your suppliant whom you will save; it is one who has become an enemy of the Hellenes whom you will destroy.

Plutarch[236] says that Themistocles went on to invoke the supernatural in support of his appeal. He told of his dream at the house of Nicogenes and of an oracle that he had received from Zeus at Dodona which had ordered him to go to the namesake of the god; he concluded that Zeus' meaning was to send him to the King of Persia since both were great and called King.

Upon hearing Themistocles' speech the Persian King made no reply, although he was struck with admiration for his intelligent and bold spirit. But it is said that in conversation with his friends he congratulated himself for this greatest good fortune and he prayed that the god Arimanius would always make his enemies of a mind to drive out their best men; and he sacrificed to the gods and directly gave himself up to drinking and during the night in the midst of his sleep he cried out three times in his joy: 'I have the Athenian Themistocles.'

Themistocles' letter to Artaxerxes has become a speech to the King (unnamed) in Plutarch. Thus Plutarch who had stated his preference for Thucydides' account of the meeting with Artaxerxes abandons it for the more dramatic details that probably embellished the encounter with Xerxes recounted by later writers.

THEMISTOCLES ESTABLISHES HIS POWER

Thus Themistocles was received by the King of Persia. But his reception by no means went unchallenged. Amidst the stories about his career in Persia under the aegis of the King, fundamental truths perhaps can once again be detected. Themistocles was clever and able and was well rewarded by the King for his loyalty and his intelligence. But the acceptance of the Greek Themistocles, the victorious general at Salamis, was met by jealous hostility among the Persians.

After recounting the King's jubilant cries in the night, 'I have Themistocles the Athenian', Plutarch[237] goes on to record that at daybreak he called together his friends and summoned Themistocles. As Themistocles made his way to the King he was anything but optimistic for the guards at the gates made their hostility apparent and spoke insultingly to him once they learned his identity. When he entered the King was seated and the court waited in hushed silence but, as he passed, the Chiliarch Roxanes groaned softly and whispered: 'You subtle serpent of Hellas, the guardian deity of the King has brought you here.' After Themistocles had again prostrated himself, the King welcomed him kindly and said that he already owed him the 200 talents offered for his capture, since he had delivered himself up of his own accord. He promised him much more than this, gave him encouragement and granted permission to speak as freely as he wished about Hellenic affairs. Thereupon Themistocles asked for a year in which to learn the Persian language and the King granted his request.[238] In that time Themistocles learned Persian well enough to converse with the King by himself without the help of interpreters. These conversations were not solely concerned with foreign Hellenic matters as outsiders thought. At this time the King introduced many innovations at court that affected his favourites and as a result the powerful became jealous and hostile towards Themistocles for presuming to use his freedom of speech with the King to their detriment. Indeed the honours enjoyed by Themistocles were far greater than those paid to other foreigners. He took part in the King's hunts and in his indoor diversions and had the honour of seeing the queen-mother and became her intimate associate and at the King's command he was instructed in the religion of the Magi. It is even said that, whenever later Persian Kings (in whose reigns closer relations were established between Persia and Hellas) needed a Hellene as an adviser, they promised in writing that each would be more influential in court than a Themistocles.[239]

To illustrate Themistocles' influence Plutarch tells the following story of his intercession on behalf of Demaratus the Spartan King who had been deposed and in earlier times had fled to Persia (like Themistocles) and become the King's confidant. When Demaratus was commanded to choose a gift for himself,[240] he asked to be permitted to ride in state through Sardis, wearing his tiara upright just like the Persian Kings. At this the King's cousin, Mithropaustes, touched Demaratus' tiara and remarked: 'This tiara of yours doesn't have any brains to cover; you will not become Zeus merely by grasping his thunderbolt.' The King himself was furious with Demaratus and seemed determined never to forgive him. But Themistocles pleaded on behalf of Demaratus and brought about a reconciliation.

Athenaeus mentions that the King of Persia gave Themistocles presents similar to those he had formerly given to Demaratus, among them Persian attire, and the stipulation was made that he abandon Greek dress completely (Cf. Pl. 32).[241]

Plutarch has told us of the hostility towards Themistocles in the Persian court. Diodorus[242] describes even more fanciful and specific dangers that Themistocles had to face because of the resentment of Mandane, the highly esteemed daughter of Darius the Great, sister of Xerxes. The people pitied her in her grief over the death of her children. She had lost her sons in the Persian defeat at Salamis and, when she learned that Themistocles was in the palace, she appeared there dressed in mourning and in tears begged her brother for vengeance upon Themistocles. When Xerxes refused, she went about to the Persian aristocrats and by her appeals aroused the people who rushed in a mob to the palace and demanded Themistocles for punishment. But the King answered that he would set up a jury of the noblest persons and their verdict would be final. Everyone agreed and, since sufficient time was given for the preparation of the trial, Themistocles was able to learn the Persian language, present his own defence and win acquittal. The King was delighted and honoured him with great gifts. He gave to Themistocles in marriage a Persian woman of exceptional birth and beauty and praiseworthy virtue and she brought with her as a dowry (or the King gave in addition) many household servants, drinking cups of all sorts and other expensive furnishings that contribute to a life of luxurious pleasure. This marriage of Themistocles, attested only by Diodorus, is questionable indeed. But we do not know when Themistocles' (first or second?) wife died. And it is just possible that he not only assumed Persian garb but also took a Persian wife or at least a concubine!

We have now been faced with three versions of when and why Themistocles learned Persian: (1) he wrote to Artaxerxes requesting leave of a year to learn the language before he approached the King personally; (2) he asked Artaxerxes or Xerxes personally for a year in which to study Persian; (3) he mastered the language to defend himself in a trial. The first (Thucydidean) version is probably correct.

SUBSEQUENT ADVENTURES

In this context two unique stories related by Plutarch[243] remain to be paraphrased. The first explains why Themistocles built a temple to the Great Mother goddess in Magnesia.

A Persian named Epixyes, satrap of Upper Phrygia, plotted to kill Themistocles as he was going down to the sea coast to deal with Hellenic affairs. This Epixyes had some Pisidians (mountain dwellers in the area) ready and waiting to accomplish the murder whenever Themistocles stopped for the night at a village called Lion's Head. But before Themistocles arrived there, the Great Mother of the Gods (called among many names Rhea, Cybele, and Dindymene after Mount Dindymon in Phrygia) appeared to him at midday while he was sleeping and said: 'Themistocles, avoid the head of lions so as not to encounter a lion. In recompense for this warning I demand your daughter Mnesiptolema as my priestess.' Themistocles, much disturbed, offered a prayer to the goddess and only after he had carefully bypassed the village of Lion's Head did he make his camp at nightfall. Now it happened that one of the draught animals carrying the equipment for his tent fell into a river and as a result his servants had to set it up to dry out. Whereupon the Pisidians, swords drawn, descended upon the tent, being unable to perceive in the moonlight that it was wet and empty and thus expecting to butcher the sleeping Themistocles inside.[244] But they were instead seized by guards and Themistocles was saved. In his wonder and appreciation, he built a temple to the Great Mother Goddess Dindymene and appointed his daughter as her priestess.[245]

The elements of truth in the next story (again found only in Plutarch) are difficult to assess. Certainly it illustrates once again the wily and dubious side of Themistocles' character.[246] When Themistocles came to Sardis he made a leisurely tour of the sanctuaries with their many dedicatory offerings. In the temple of the Great Mother goddess he saw the bronze statue of a maiden, about three feet in height (called the Water-Carrier), which he himself, when he was water commissioner at Athens,

had had made and dedicated there from the fines imposed upon
those convicted of tapping and stealing the water supply.[247]
Whether because of his feelings upon realizing that his dedicatory offering had been carried off or because he wanted to
demonstrate to the Athenians how great his honour and power
were with the King, Themistocles tried to get the satrap of
Lydia to send the maiden back to Athens. But the satrap was
angry at the proposition and threatened to write to the King.
At this Themistocles became frightened and sought safety in the
women's quarters where, through money, he won over the
concubines of the satrap and thus pacified the satrap himself.
After this, Themistocles behaved more cautiously as he realized
that he still had to fear the enmity of the Persians. And so he did
not travel all over Asia, as Theopompus says, but he had a house
in Magnesia where he reaped the benefits of great gifts and
received honours equal to those of the best of the Persians.
Thus he lived a great while without trouble, as long as the King
paid no attention to the affairs of the Hellenes and was occupied
instead with matters in the interior.

The Gifts of the King

Our sources (including Thucydides) generally agree in listing as
significant among the King's gifts three cities for Themistocles'
enjoyment and support: Magnesia on the Meander River for
bread (if had abundant grain fields and brought in fifty talents
a year); Lampsacus on the Hellespont for wine (it was considered
one of the best wine districts at that time); and Myus (in Ionia
near Miletus) for other provisions (i.e. especially fish in which
the sea there abounded).[248] Plutarch observes that Neanthes of
Cyzicus and Phanias added two others: Percote (in the Troad)
and Palaescepsis (in Phrygia near the Troad) for his bedding and
his clothes; and Athenaeus lists (if the text is correct) – for good
measure, as it were, – still another city, Gambreium (in southwest Mysia) for his raiment.[249]

LAMPSACUS AND MYUS

It is easy to discredit these last, Percote, Palaescepsis and Gambreium, as dubious because of the nature of the sources. For this
same reason, however, the presentation of Lampsacus and Myus
must be taken more seriously and ought not to be dismissed
lightly as mere show on the part of the King or the fabrication
of an anecdote.[250] It has been argued that Lampsacus and Myus
were early or even original members of the Athenian Confederacy of Delos and thus the King's gesture, if made at all,
must have been a hollow one. These gifts cannot have been
offered before 469 (at the very earliest) but it is much more
likely that they belong to the period after 464. What then could
have been the association of the exiled Themistocles (even under
the aegis of the powerful Persian King) with two cities that
were members of the Athenian Confederacy? Our lack of
knowledge makes a precise answer to this question impossible.
Besides we cannot be certain when Lampsacus and Myus
actually did join the Greek alliance.

As for Lampsacus we do indeed possess further evidence that
seems to confirm Themistocles' ties with the city as more real
than imaginary. An inscription from Lampsacus of the late
third century B C refers to an annual festival of Themistocles
and privileges granted to Cleophantus (Themistocles' son) and
his descendants.[251] This inscription poses many unanswerable
questions. But it seems to me that the festival could go back
to the time of Themistocles himself, although it may very well
have been inaugurated as a tribute after his death. At any rate
it must at least belong to the lifetime of Cleophantus.[252] But
why this special festival in honour of Themistocles and why
these privileges for his descendants, if the King's gift was merely
nominal or fiction? Further evidence is provided by Epistle 20
where Themistocles is made to write: 'He (The King) has taken
Myus, Lampsacus and Magnesia on the Meander from his own
kingdom and given them to me. I freed Lampsacus and remitted
all its great burden of tax (φόρος) and I reap the fruits of Myus

in Magnesia and Magnesia itself.' Since this evidence may come
from the historian Charon, who was himself from Lampsacus,
it is perhaps worthy of serious attention. If so, did Themistocles
remit Lampsacus' tribute to himself (and the King?) and was
this the reason for the festival in his honour and the fact that he
and his family were treated like benefactors? Or is it even too
absurd to imagine that somehow he kept Lampsacus safe (for a
while) from paying tribute to Athens?

Magnesia

But there can be no question about Themistocles' association
with Magnesia, which never belonged to the Delian Confederacy. Themistocles was 'governor' of Magnesia and its rich
district, he had a residence there and issued coinage in his own
name, and it was said that there he died and was buried. That
Magnesia was the most important of Themistocles' cities seems
to be confirmed by Athenaeus, who writes:

Possis in Book 3 of his *History of Magnesia* says that, after Themistocles
assumed the crowned magistracy (i.e. the office with the right to wear
a crown, ἡ στεφανηφόρος ἀρχή) in Magnesia, he sacrificed to Athena
and called the festival Panathenaea; and having sacrificed to Dionysus
Choopotes (Pitcher-drinker), he instituted the festival of the Choes
(Pitchers) there.[253]

The Panathenaic festival was one of the most significant of
Athenian celebrations; important too in Athens was the festival
of the Anthesteria in honour of Dionysus, the second day of
which, the Choes-day, provided the inspiration for Themistocles in Magnesia. Pausanias offers further support for the
strength of Themistocles' ties with the Magnesians. The sons of
Themistocles dedicated a bronze statue of the goddess Artemis,
surnamed Leucophryenian, on the Acropolis of Athens near
the statue of Olympiodorus, because the Magnesians, whom the
King placed under Themistocles' rule, greatly honoured
Leucophryenian Artemis.[254] And Plutarch tells us that down to
his time certain honours were maintained in Magnesia for the

descendants of Themistocles, which the Athenian Themistocles, Plutarch's friend and fellow-student in the school of the philosopher Ammonius, continued to enjoy.[255]

In connection with the coinage (Pls 27-29) that Themistocles himself issued in Magnesia, the following specimens must be considered:[256]

1. A solid silver didrachm of the Attic standard (8.56 grams) in the Bibliothèque Nationale, Paris. Obverse: a standing male figure, nude except for a cloak (chlamys) extending over his shoulders (probably Apollo, perhaps a representation of his statue in the Magnesian temple of Apollo Pythius); his right hand rests on his hip, his left holds a long staff (of or entwined with olive or laurel?). The inscription reads *Themistokleos* in Greek capitals to designate the coinage as 'of Themistocles'. Reverse: a bird (raven, hawk or eagle?) with outstretched wings in an incuse square. The letters M and A (to designate the coinage as of Magnesia) are inscribed on either side beneath the tail feathers (Pl. 29).

2. A solid silver didrachm of the Attic standard (8.59 grams) in the Berlin Museum. Obverse: Apollo striding left, his right hand outstretched to dispatch a bird. The inscription reads *Themis[tokle]os*. Reverse: like no. 1 above (Pl. 27).

3. A silver-plated didrachm of the Attic standard (5.83 grams) in the British Museum. Obverse: like no. 1 above. Reverse: like nos 1 and 2 above (Pl. 28).

4. A silver-plated didrachm, unpublished, but reported as belonging to a private collection in Turkey.

It is perhaps characteristic of Themistocles that he would issue Magnesian coinage of the Attic standard (which apparently was not a usual practice in Asia). Thus he remains Athenian, despite his exile, in his coinage as well as in the religious celebrations that he is said to have instituted in Magnesia. That there were tangible economic as well as patriotic motives behind his policy we can only surmise.

The solid silver didrachms (nos 1 and 2) are struck from finely-cut dies. Those for the silver-plated one (no. 3) are inferior and it is likely that it (and no. 4?) are forgeries. Yet it has been suggested that Themistocles with typical shrewdness issued plated coins to defraud his subjects!

Two other coins can be identified with less certainty as further examples of Themistocles' Magnesian issues. A quarter-obol in the Ashmolean Museum, Oxford, found at Colophon (which is about 300 miles from Magnesia), depicts an owl on the obverse, which should indicate Athens, but need not represent the owl reported to have alighted as an omen on Themistocles' ship before Salamis,[257] and the letters ΘE (THE) in ligature on the reverse could perhaps stand for Themistocles' full name. A quarter- (or half-) obol from a collection in Athens said to have been found in Asia Minor has the same letters in ligature on the reverse, whereas the obverse depicts a head with beard and crested helmet, conjectured to be a depiction of Themistocles. One can readily believe that Themistoclean coinage found easy circulation outside Magnesia, without the plausible conjecture that he kept soldiers under his personal hire. But can we rest assured that either of these coins was issued in Magnesia at all or by Themistocles himself, even if the letters THE are accepted as referring to his name?

The Magnesian coin (Pl. 30) from the period of Antoninus Pius (second century AD) bearing Themistocles' full name, to be discussed later in connection with his suicide, confirms once again the long-standing link between Themistocles and Magnesia.

The Adventures of a Hero

The meagre historical information that may be gleaned from the ancient testimony concerning Themistocles' power under the aegis of the Persian King, corroborated in particular by the numismatic evidence for his governorship of Magnesia, should not make us forget the obviously legendary nature of the tradition recorded by Diodorus and Plutarch. Their tales about Themistocles' travels in Asia Minor, his meeting with the King and his various adventures all bear the unmistakable character-istics of folk-tale, saga and romance: divinely inspired predictions, dreams portending future events, dramatic encounters and intrigues, obstacles to be overcome and rewards to be won – fictitious elaborations playing upon themes appropriate for a hero and resting upon a very few basic and indisputable facts.

CHAPTER X

THE EPISTLES OF THEMISTOCLES: A HERO'S JUSTIFICATION

The twenty-one Epistles of Themistocles have come down to us in only one manuscript, Palatinus 398, of the ninth or tenth century (Pl. 33).[258] The letters themselves cannot be genuine. Vocabulary, thematic material and style suggest the second century AD, but it is impossible to be certain. There is a problem too about authorship. Some minor inconsistencies in the narrative may imply that more than one hand has been at work, but the case for multiple authorship is not conclusive. We do not know if the collection is complete as we have it and the order of the letters in the manuscript (which I follow) is not always the most logical.

The Greek text of these Epistles is dismally corrupt and a completely satisfactory edition (if that is possible) has yet to be published. Perhaps their difficulty has been in large part responsible for their relative neglect. The fact that they have never before been translated into any language other than Latin also has contributed to their limited circulation.[259]

Yet there is much in this body of material that merits attention, particularly since our other evidence for Themistocles is in general meagre and of a dubious nature. For these letters obviously rest upon fact and tradition, much of which can be corroborated. They provide as well other information that is unique but nevertheless carries with it the stamp of historical authenticity. And most important of all, the insights and the interpretations presented are at times startling in their perception – as credible as many of the hypotheses postulated by modern historians. In the case of the letter writer at least, there is always the nagging suspicion that he has made use of other evidence, now lost, all of which need not necessarily have been bad. It is not impossible that he knew the work of Charon of Lampsacus or Hellanicus of Lesbos, contemporaries of Herodotus and Thucydides, our earliest extant literary sources for Themistocles' career.[260]

But there is also inevitably a strong element of imaginative invention in these letters. The epistolographer works very much in the manner of a good historical novelist who uses his evidence to create his drama, to weave his artistic design and to elucidate his political or philosophical points of view. He is not above creating characters and situations. The numerous names in particular reveal the nature of the problem. A few seem to be obviously fabricated; but many are verified by various sources and others, which are not, have about them the ring of truth; the corrupt text poses further difficulties, because we can not always be sure that every emendation is correct.

Above all, these letters should be enjoyed as a kind of historical novelette in epistolary form. Admittedly they provide much that is precious and sophistic, and their rhetorical artifice and bombast at times merge on the ludicrous. Yet underlying all is a sincere personal and tragic note and a dramatic thrust that is to be found nowhere else in the literature about Themistocles. It is as though we can hear at times his anguished voice as he writes of his domestic and political dilemma. In the last analysis, our hero emerges as a great, though pathetic, patriot, absolved from any guilt and driven to desperate actions because he has been betrayed by ruthless and vindictive men.

It is extremely doubtful that the epistles reflect in any way the original correspondence of Themistocles himself. Yet the evidence for his career makes it implicit that he wrote many letters – to Xerxes and Artaxerxes, to Pausanias, and to his family and friends whom he left behind in Athens – an ideal scenario for epistolary fiction. A lexicon of about the tenth century AD observes that Themistocles wrote letters teeming with spirited thought ($\phi\rho\delta\nu\eta\mu\alpha$).[261] Probably the reference is to our collection; if so, each reader may decide for himself about the meaning and validity of this description.

Here then is an English translation (in some sections free

adaptation) of the letters, interspersed with my own brief summaries and elucidation. Despite the numerous textual problems, in most cruces the general tenor of the argument is discernible, although the exact wording of the original must remain in doubt. In my treatment of the few passages that seem hopelessly corrupt, I have been bold in my ruthless attempts to offer a fair interpretation in readable form.

In the first letter, to Aeschylus (presumably the playwright), we are told that Themistocles has been ostracized. While on his way to Delphi he encounters three Argive friends (Nicias, Meleager and Eucrates) who persuade him to go to Argos; Themistocles' father Neocles had once sojourned there. In Argos Themistocles is troubled by the insistence of the Argives that he hold office or assume power (ἄρχειν).

1   To Aeschylus

Upon leaving Athens, I decided to go to Delphi and live there as the Athenians would allow. On the way I happened upon two of my Argive friends, Nicias and Meleager, and a third, Eucrates, who recently had spent some time in Athens. They pressed around me with questions and, as soon as they learned about my ostracism, they became angry and made many accusations against the Athenians. When they found out that I was bound for Delphi, they stopped accusing the Athenians and insisted that they would consider it an insult if I did not accept them as suitable friends to share the burden of my misfortune. They argued that my father Neocles had lived in Argos for the longest time and that I should be a neglectful son if I did not live up to his love for Argos and for his friends there by return-ing with them. They almost went so far as to praise the Athen-ians on the grounds that I was paying a just penalty.[262] Finally they begged me not to consider them worthy only of a chance meeting, and not to treat with insulting contempt the good fortune of our encounter;[263] once again they mentioned my father Neocles and claimed that it was fitting for me to live in the same city and home as he. And so, Aeschylus, they took hold of me and brought me to Argos. Now I have put a stop to my flight and suffer much because I do not want to assume power over the Argives. For they believe that I do them an injustice if I do not assume power, and are angry. But I am happy not to be looked upon as great not only because greatness has already brought me harm, but also because it is enough for me to accept the things that I must.

In Epistle 2 Themistocles writes to Pausanias of his dilemma in Argos and cautions the Spartan to be careful lest he suffer a similar reversal of fortune in the region of the Hellespont. Along with 14 and 16, this letter provides an epistolary sub-plot by tracing the career of Pausanias in some detail. The point is clearly made that Themistocles is completely innocent of collaboration in the criminal activity of Pausanias.

2   To Pausanias

O Pausanias, I have been ostracized by the Athenians and now I am in Argos so that the Athenians may not suffer adversity because of me; for they believed that they were going to suffer and I without any delay (as indeed it was no longer possible to delay) left Athens and freed them of their fear. The Argives welcome me much more than as a mere fugitive and wish to turn the benefit that the Athenians once had to their own advantage; and so they consider me worthy of assuming the generalship with command over all Argos; and they do a great wrong by not allowing me to be only an exile as the Athenians wish. I am ashamed to slight their enthusiasm for me but it is even more difficult to submit to what they offer; for, to be sure, if I were to pursue such ambition, I should appear to have been ostracized deservedly and it is, I believe, virtual condemnation if I who have been expelled by the Athenians, as one striving after power, flee from Argos since I am being compelled to rule.[264] But it would be most futile for me, O Pausanias, to move on and pass my time in another city, if they were to press their appeal too far; for, wherever I should flee, I should always realize that I was not in Athens.

I don't know whether I ought now to be especially concerned and troubled on your behalf, since you are having such great success; for I hear that you are in command of nearly all the Hellespont as far as the Bosporus, that you are making an attempt on Ionia, and that your name has by this time been heard of by the King; and so we who pray for what is best for you wish that you had not gone so far. O Pausanias, put a restraint upon your good fortune and do not be ignorant of the fact that success breeds utter misfortune for mankind; this has always turned out to be so for everyone and especially for those who are subject to the laws and the people. We accept command as servants of the multitude but once we have our power we become envied by those who gave it to us. Thereupon they do not reduce us to the same place in which we were before we held office but, confirming the extent of their powers and taking advantage of the surge of fortune, they eliminate their leaders by exile and death. Thus, those who wish to prosper in the state must be wary of this very prosperity most of all. Therefore, O Pausanias, see to it how you may minimize the impact of the great reversal that will overtake you as a result of your present circumstance. For because of my own experience I no longer shall pursue prosperity.

In Epistle 3 Themistocles writes to Polygnotus (the famous painter?) about his flight from Argos. He is on his way by ship to Corcyra when he is detained by a storm at Cyllene. He expresses his thanks to his friend Polygnotus for warning him in the nick of time of the necessity for immediate flight.[265]

3   To Polygnotus

I am fleeing as quickly as possible, just as you urge, O Polygnotus. I have left Argos and I am on the sea and my destination is Corcyra; when our ships were fresh we had a prosperous voyage to Cyllene but now we are detained by a storm.

And so you too will praise the messenger because of his speed. For he was sent at the time when the Athenians had dismissed the assembly not far into the evening as they say; and he was in Argos the next day before high noon. But I am afraid that if the storm continues it will render our haste useless and that I shall become slower in my flight than the messengers. If the Spartans as well learn of my flight they will pursue me, pressing the very same charges against me as those of which Pausanias thereupon will be innocent.[266] At any rate it is to you that I owe my safety, Polygnotus, nor do storm or Spartans prevent me from acknowledging my gratitude to you; indeed I admire you for informing me with such diligence about what the Spartans have done and about the efforts which Aristeides alone showed on my behalf, even though my enemy; and I admire you for telling me that if I did not flee I should be caught by a shameful sentence of death that has now been passed. God will be responsible for the outcome and will determine whether, after all, Polygnotus, I shall be able to repay you adequate recompense for your help.

Epistle 4 is to Themistocles' friend and colleague Habronichus (whose son Lysicles is betrothed or married to one of Themistocles' daughters) about his fears for his family left in Athens. It contains many shrewd observations about the Spartans and their motives against Themistocles. Themistocles seems to be still in Argos, so perhaps chronologically this letter should precede Epistle 3. There is no real conflict between Themistocles' hostile attitude towards Aristeides in this letter and the gratitude expressed in the previous epistle. As the correspondence proceeds (Epistles 8, 18, 19) we hear again about Aristeides' friendship in Themistocles' absence but we also learn more of Themistocles' bitterness because of the wrongs of the past that Aristeides committed against him.

4   To Habronichus

To suffer unjustly and unworthily in Athens, O Habronichus,

160, THE SAGA OF THEMISTOCLES

does not seem to me to be something strange (since not to suffer anything at all is itself stranger than this) but it is strange that up until now the ill-will was something short-lived and quickly regretted in my city or rather your city – for already I speak of it as no longer mine. But as the situation is now (for you see how great the hostility of these men in the city has increased against me), I have been ostracized and they have condemned me to another kind of ostracism, accomplishing the strange feat of exiling me in my exile.[267]

I know very well that you will say that they do not, by Zeus, even allow me to be an exile. For I have learned that exile seemed to them to be too little a penalty for a man who had done so many significant things for their enemy, but it seemed right to them to punish me with death. For this very purpose they send scouts after me to Argos and the Spartans follow them. I was not upset with the Athenians when the Spartans followed them, but when the Athenians follow the Spartans I do indeed feel distress.[268] The Spartan ephors punished Pausanias without putting any trust in the slanderous accusations made by the Athenians; they did not even trust the friends of Pausanias and those who were in on the whole business with him and scarcely believed the confession of Pausanias himself. But your countrymen, the Athenians, in business that is their own are not suspicious of any outsider, not even if he is an enemy. The reason for this is, I believe, that the Athenians take more pleasure in being jealous of their friends than the others do in feeling hatred for their enemies. But I do not write this in an attempt to expose and convict the Athenians (if only, dear gods, they could escape detection); but, as it stands, a defence by those who extol the Athenians is more impossible than a conviction by those who find fault with them is necessary; instead it seemed to me proper to confide my sorrows in you, dear friend of mine, and in addition to take thought about domestic matters, concerning which it is all the more appropriate to be wary, since we see the Spartans dominating the Athenians and getting passed in Athens decrees (ψηφίσματα) against their personal enemies.

You know, my friend, that their anger and its cause are

similarly directed against both me and you, because we two went as ambassadors to them and negotiated the ruse by which our city was walled. As for our colleague on the mission, since he is a just man and fittingly won among the Hellenes the name 'just' as part of his booty, he has gained forgiveness from the Spartans because of his alliance with them against me. Hail and farewell to him, for he was always malicious, hostile and vengeful and, just as Callaeschrus once said of him, he is more like a fox in his real character than is implied by his deme name ('Αλωπεκῆθεν).[269]

And so, Habronichus, take care of present circumstances and look ahead as far as possible to the future and remember to be fearful of being in great repute among the Athenians; but if you would be so, as you have been already, still keep anything excessive hidden and be content to be unnoticed. This advice, then, my dear fellow, for you and to you. As far as my affairs here go, I shall clearly be concerned that I escape the hunters and the Spartan dogs hastening from home to hunt me. And I shall not yield to becoming a sinner and polluting the Athenians with blood-guilt because of me, or to contaminating the city as someone impure for whom there is no cure and whose taint cannot be removed by bronze statues (as the gods prophesied to the Spartans for Pausanias) but whose crime instead is potent and inescapable, greater even than that of Cylon; nor will I yield to providing the Spartans with a double joy, no rather a triple joy: by taking vengeance for the hostility engendered by the embassy that I undertook with you, by charging that our prevention of their injustice was a trick on our part and by transferring their guilt in bringing down upon the heads of the Athenians a pure and effective avenging fury through their unholy murder of me, the Spartans believe that the shame incurred in the eyes of the Hellenes because Pausanias a King of Sparta[270] betrayed them will be lightened, if I a general, in like manner, am shown to be punished by the Athenians on the charge of being a traitor.

I shall see to it that none of these things happens, as I said, in so far as I can; you will learn about it all and I shall inform you of each and every happening – how I shall have guarded well against the dire pitfalls of human calculation and all the rest – when finally all turns out safe and sound.

As for matters there in Athens, I can entreat and beseech you, O best of friends, to help me without stint, in so far as you can, by not keeping the money for me and my children but by spending it opportunely and wisely on behalf of my children and their mother and by daily looking out for this one thing – how you can save the lives of Cleophantus, his sisters and his mother for me. Because of your son Lysicles, my daughter Sybaris ought to be particularly dear to you yourself and of no little concern to him, if I am to be deemed worthy of a family relationship, since she is your daughter-in-law and his wife, and, if it is not so, because it was at one time designed and expected; your good will to the rest of my family imposes itself upon you because of me.[271]

I don't believe that the Athenians themselves, even if they should suffer greatly and the envy of those who hate me were to become overbearing, would attempt to maltreat my dear wife and children; but yet if there is even a slim chance and no more than a dim suspicion that they would, may my family not remain as hostage for a moment longer but let my fears come to their aid. In what way they should be delivered and how they should effect their escape leave to the attendant of Cleophantus, who once helped me too, the fellow Sicinnus by name, whom you know. Tell him only that they must not stay in Athens; he will himself know how to do the rest.

But indeed I ought not now to hate the Athenians so much that I suspect things about them which they have never done before and which I believe will not be done by them; but if such things were to happen I have made clear to you what you must do – for it is not redundant to remind you again in these pressing circumstances – and it is evident that you will do just as I instruct.

And so it seems best for me to write you this in all urgency; I shall write more about the same matters later after subsequent developments.

In Epistle 5 Themistocles writes to his friend Temenidas in Argos about his encounter with King Admetus. Temenidas has ties with Cratesipolis and Stratolaus at the court of Admetus. Cratesipolis may be Admetus' wife, although Plutarch calls her Pythia.[272]

5   To Temenidas

At the house of Admetus I acted just as you expected.[273] When I arrived, he was not at home but he was away visiting the Chaones. I met Cratesipolis and Stratolaus there and gave them a letter for you.[274] Admetus came back shortly afterwards, within about eight or nine days; and I sat as a suppliant at his hearth (for Cratesipolis so instructed me) and I held little Arybbas[275] in one hand and a sword in the other. And so when Admetus saw me and the child, he recognized me and I know full well that he hated me but pitied the child and was afraid of the sword. He bad me stand up but he said that he was unable to keep me safe in his house because he feared the Athenians and even more the Spartans; yet he promised to send me where I should be safe and he did. I boarded a merchant vessel of Alexander of Macedon; the ship had at this point reached Pydna and from there was expected to sail for Asia.[276] Thus you have what happened to me with Admetus. Please write your news from Argos – not to Admetus himself (for he did not seem at all like one who wanted me to get away safely) but to Cratesipolis. She would welcome a letter from you and from your sister as well, for it seems to me that she thinks a lot of her but she thinks a lot of you too.[277]

In Epistle 6 Themistocles, already in Ephesus, is angry with his banker Philostephanus, whom he suspects of dishonesty. For reasons unexplained, Themistocles has agreed to pay some money to a certain Meidon and others (e.g. Pamphilus in the next letter). Tibius, one of the group, or merely an agent, has come to Themistocles at Ephesus to report that Philostephanus has claimed that, although he is willing to provide the sum requested, he owes Themistocles nothing. Themistocles knows that this is a lie, but he cannot be sure whether his banker is trying to protect or to cheat him. Epistles 6 and 7 concerning Themistocles' finances are perhaps the most fictitious and the most strained in their invention of all the letters.

6   To Philostephanus

I am distressed, O Philostephanus, about your ingratitude and utter baseness towards me and I am no less, but in fact all the more, annoyed by my own slow stupidity because I run the risk of seeming to have been a complete dunderhead from my birth until now – and why? Because I could not reach a firm judgment and correct understanding even about one individual like you – a man sitting at the crossroaas of Hellas whose character is exposed for all to recognize by the plain evidence of his conduct.

And yet, I believe that it is through me you have become the richest and most famous of bankers not only in Corinth but anywhere else. If you were not so wealthy before I had business with you, yet you were well trusted and more trustworthy than you are likely to be considered now that you have become rich because of me. And so, it is not my fault for trusting a man whose character was so manifest and open to scrutiny, but rather my misfortune that he was a person who was never untrustworthy to anyone by whom he profited but acted unjustly to me alone, through whom he gained so very much.

Where did I get my information?[278] Tibius came to Ephesus from Athens and said he had been sent by Meidon and his associates and they had to have seventy minas of silver from my friends; he was to get this amount, a mere fraction of my full forty talents, from you. For according to the last reckoning, which we made together at the Isthmus, this was the balance of my account still in your hands. According to Tibius, when you read the letters and learned of the need for the money, you replied in one vein, that was seemly and kindly, and then in another that was unfair and wrong – indeed I refrain from saying unholy. For the assertion that you wished to forward that silver without charge rather than to lend me the money and become

my creditor was civilized and worthy of your good will
towards me, but when, as Tibius says, you became sharp and
denied that you owed me anything at all, you perpetrated a
crime that outweighed your previous magnanimity. Your
generosity is worth seventy minas, but the price of your dishonesty is forty talents. But if it were not for your own gain
that you were shamelessly brazen and even untrue and unjust in
a matter of trust and integrity and if it were in my interest (as
you saw it) that you made your denials, you would not be an
evil man and you would agree that I was not foolish for feeling
the way I do about you – this could be the case, and even now,
although I am still stunned at the prospect of my hopes and
expectations being dashed in this way, yet I cannot abandon so
quickly the suspicion that somehow you are a good and just
man. But if I am right in believing that you are dishonest and
my judgment is completely confirmed in all respects by the
Athenians,[279] your crime will not escape the detection of the
gods, O Philostephanus, nor will you get away with your
injustice towards me; even if you despise me and are disdainful
of the gods, yet in the end you will not escape the Athenians.
For all in all I should take it more kindly in this as in everything
else if I were robbed by my own country than by the Corinthian
banker Philostephanus.

And so then write to me in answer who you are to me and
how you have decided to carry out the rest of this business so
that, if you are that good friend of mine and continue to be the
man you were, I may plan how my money will be saved to
allay my misfortune; but if you are not, how it may not be
lost against my better judgment.

In Epistle 7 Themistocles apologizes to Philostephanus for
jumping to the wrong conclusions. It is Tibius who is the
rogue responsible for the whole misunderstanding.

7   *To Philostephanus*

Menyllus, the helmsman from Chalcis, the one who also once

brought that great ship of grain from Gelon of Syracuse into the Piraeus, came to Ephesus, bringing me letters from you on the last day of Boedromion by the Athenian calendar, on the tenth of Panemus according to yours (for they are the same day).[280] He spoke to me in riddles which he did not understand but which I did, since I was familiar with the code that we had worked out.

Moreover he also delivered the letter in which you seemed so grieved and upset, considering yourself completely unworthy of my judgment that you would ever be untrustworthy or hostile to any person, and least of all to me. Then you informed me about my money, not denying that you have it and promising to hand it over whenever and to whomever I should so instruct; and you made it perfectly clear about Meidon and Pamphilus that they did not have the necessary information, and as for Tibius, that he was a scoundrel who was acting unfairly. I blush at the admission, O Philostephanus, that since you are so disposed I am delighted not as much about the forty talents as I am by the fact that my hopes in you have not been destroyed.

Indeed please realize this fully. Although you didn't as yet hand over my forty talents, you were ready to do so. You had not yet received them, and I considered you worthy of being entrusted not only with these talents but also an additional thirty others! For seventy it was that formed the maximum deposit I had with you. I who entrusted you with a greater sum should automatically not be in any way discredited if I should appear to entrust you with a lesser.[281]

As for my being too prone and too ready in my indignation, I ought not to have believed such charges about a dear friend and been so quick to accuse you falsely. Saying this, I should be speaking the greatest truth, O Philostephanus, since the villain Tibius made me grumble against you and my fate led me to trust him. So much for these matters. Let the silver stay with you for now; when I have deliberated and reach a firmer decision, then I shall write you.

Epistle 8 is one of the most important letters for the historian, since it deals with the prosecution of Themistocles, about which our evidence is so meagre. It is also one of the most difficult. The text is even more corrupt than usual and details of events as envisaged by the writer are unknown. Thus ambiguities remain but in general the argument runs as follows. Themistocles is angry because he has been made a scapegoat and even his friends have supported his enemies in their actions against him. Leobotes, Lysander and Pronapes have been induced to swear an oath by Aristeides, Phaedrias, Tisinicus and Alcmeonides, who have perjured themselves to incriminate Themistocles. Leager, to whom the letter is written, was also forced to comply but Themistocles still has confidence in his loyalty and that of his other friends.

Many of the names provided are textually corrupt but the emendations seem to be reasonably sound. Some support for credibility in the reality of the men who are mentioned is provided by various other sources and Leobotes is, according to Plutarch, the one who indicted Themistocles on the charge of treason.[282]

We learn for the first time that Themistocles, much to his shame, is on his way to the King of Persia, who is not named. One might assume that Xerxes is intended. In Epistle 20, we find that his actual meeting is with Artaxerxes, although even here the name does not actually appear in our text.

8   To Leager

O Leager, indeed Leobotes (Agryleus) and Lysander (Scambonides) and Pronapes (Prasieus)[283] now court the Athenian people, who never at any time before considered them so trustworthy, so just and so true to their oaths that in a matter involving such a great crime as the betrayal of all the Hellenes they allowed them to perjure themselves. And now these men think of themselves as high and mighty (even more so than others would concede), since they not only have escaped from the consequences of blasphemy of which they were guilty and even any suspicion of it but they have even emerged as pious and righteous men to be trusted. But, to be sure, my contemporary and the companion of my youth,[284] Leager, son of Glaucon, will not admire the Athenians for this (although he may respect and love them for other reasons) nor will he be proud of them on this account, but rather he will be ashamed. All you Athenians, Leager, will not be amiss in being grateful for your own salvation (which I do not share) and for my misfortune (which no one else shares), since you offered me, like some great and fat beast that had been felled, as feast enough to satisfy the Athenians and this for me (I shall be bold enough to say) was the only fortunate thing that resulted from my having fared so unspeakably badly in all other respects. For by suffering what I suffered, I helped you, my friends, in no small measure. But what man in his right senses could bear to take courage and still even more to take delight in such a salvation? Would it be because you yourselves proclaimed to the Hellenes a charge against me that was so terrible and fatal, so unjust and false, or because those who perjured themselves were Aristeides and Phaedrias and Tisinicus and Alcmeonides and you were the ones who also swore an oath? O gods and divinities, witnesses to the truth among men, didn't the statue of the goddess by which you swore, and what is more, the temple itself fall on top of the heads of those criminals at the time when they got you to swear your oath?

But do they trust you now because you were sworn in, whereas before they did not? Why then didn't they make me swear too so that they might trust me as well? Yet if they thought that I was base and you upright, why didn't they accuse you men of good standing at the same time as they accused me the villain. Either a man's character or god's oath ought to be accepted as trustworthy; if they knew that they could trust you on the basis of character, they wouldn't have put you under oath and if they knew that your oath was to be trusted, they wouldn't have been foolish enough to accuse you because of your character.

There is nothing sound in any of this; nor are things as they say they are, Leager. No, they arranged their present deal with you because of envy. The reason is that they do not yet need a successor to Themistocles and that they have had enough of me. But if, in all likelihood, their case against me were to be thwarted, then I fear for you and you ought to be frightened for yourselves lest your oath become an empty bond, and you, believing that you are trusted, are deceived by those who put their trust in you, while I, whose oath is not trustworthy, manage to escape the hunters and their nets; and you who testify that you are pious and unperjured in this business are impiously sinned against by the false testimony of witnesses.

Perhaps someone will exclaim, 'You frighten and terrify us, O Themistocles, by these words of yours.' For if I remain silent I do not scare you, but if I speak you will listen to me, even if you do not always do so. Do you not remember that, when I told all the Athenians to leave the city and board their ships, I persuaded them and moreover they listened to me. Yet I did not convince these same people to submit to my living together with them in Athens. Why do I say 'with them'? Not even in Hellas outside of Athens. But I their Pythian (for they called me this when I interpreted the oracle for them) have no place – not in Delphi or Delos and elsewhere beyond, not even in Xanthus – unless finally I were to migrate to the Hyperboreans. The Hellenes stood up for me at Olympia as I entered to view the gymnastic contest but now for this very same man there is no honour or special seat at festivals and in the theatre. But I do not even have an ordinary home in any part of Hellas, let alone the sacred refuge of a suppliant in a holy sanctuary.

Are you people not horrified at this, O Leager? Aren't you overwhelmed with astonishment? Or, after your oaths, do you think that all will go well for you? O lady Athena, would it were so! But nothing is so senseless as when prayers and hopes make no difference. 'What then ought to be done?' you will ask me. 'Are we to flee when no one is driving us out?' I am not saying that you should. But don't go to sleep; be distrustful and afraid. The circumstances of the time will tell you to leave, if you have to, or whatever you should do; only be prepared to act. But if you are slack, thinking that everything is going your way, I fear lest I, poor wretch, will lose all of Athens completely. For up until now I still retain something of Athens, which was not, by Zeus, the least significant but the very best – namely, friends, who still live there and survive. Therefore if, as I wander an exile somewhere on this earth, my enemies were to become glorious and extremely powerful and you, my companions, could not only not remain in Athens but were scattered apart, leaving behind our many orphan children surrounded by the threat of slavery and our destitute wives, both yours and mine, along with the aged men and women who are our parents (for some of them are still alive) – if all this together, as I say, were to happen, then would it not be better for me to desert, give myself up to total exile, and suffer what my enemies ordain than to see any of these things come about or hear it even mentioned that they have?

Therefore think about and ponder over these matters thus for me, O Leager, and make an effort to take the initiative in informing and arousing all our companions about them – not only those who have sworn but also those who have not, for you know them all. Show all of them the first part of this letter up until this point if you wish and read it aloud, but either erase and destroy the section that follows or cut it off and keep it and let it be known to no one except you alone.

For I am not ignorant of the fact that I am taking a gamble that is rash, bold and desperate, if not of the most extreme danger; nevertheless, I dare to take the gamble and I have made my decision to do so. Neither my comrade Leager will want to stop me from my undertaking, for he will not stop me; nor will Neocles my father or Themistocles my uncle, should they now come back to life and visit me here; but no omen, either that of a bird or an oracular response will hold me back, not even if it be from the very one who prophesied to your fellow citizens that they were protected by the wooden wall.

But wish me well, my dear fellow, and pray to the gods to preserve me, to make my journey safe and to grant the end to my undertaking for which I hope and of which I am worthy. For I have decided to leave Ephesus at once to go to the King, who is my enemy as you know, but my friend according to what the Athenians say – and O lord Zeus may their divination be correct and may they be telling the truth! I have already sent him a letter and he has given me a kindly reply by messenger; in fact his response has been such as to amaze and astound me utterly and completely, if for the only reason that I never told him or wrote to him anything that was true. But to be sure he would not deign to act like me since he is a great King and it would be no advantage to him to be false and do me harm, for he has the power to harm me if he wished even by being truthful. And so I go to him. What I shall do if I am able, I am ashamed to say, but I do admit that I wish to act if I can.

You yourself see to matters there and attend to my interests as secretly as possible, since this is to our mutual advantage. But be especially prudent in your actions, as I know full well that you will. I should prefer you to tend to my concerns openly rather than through fear to handle them carelessly. But do be cautious, if you love me, first for your own sake (you who are dearer to me than life), then too for my sake and in the interest of my affairs so that you may be of use and advantage to me for a long time. I have written to you in terms of how I believe the situation is and I shall try to make clear to you as quickly as possible how the rest will turn out for me so that you may know everything that happens.

In Epistle 9 Themistocles is angry with Callias, who has been reprimanding the people for electing unworthy magistrates like Themistocles. Callias is reputed to have obtained his great wealth from a Persian hoard of riches that he unearthed at Marathon;[285] according to this letter he was little more than a tomb robber. One is reminded by way of contrast of the anecdote according to which Themistocles proudly ignored the temptation afforded by the Persian corpses decked out in gold (19, below, pp. 218f.)

9   To Callias

O Callias, don't try to emulate Aristeides in his ill will. For he on his side said that he did not much try to emulate you in your wealth. And yet it was far better, in terms of what everyone wants for himself and his posterity, that you cultivate even Aristeides than that you emulate actions which everyone despises and considers to be abominable. Please do not reproach the Athenians or call them to order on the score that they vote rashly and choose their magistrates from unworthy candidates. But first consider that you reprove them for having elected officials who have been victorious; then consider too what sort of person you are yourself and that you who make these foolish charges have in no way been able, after many others like Themistocles, to become a conspicuous general in like manner.

For the city did not need as generals men who robbed the tombs of the Persian corpses at Marathon; but it did have need of generals like those who fought and killed the enemy mustered at Salamis and Euboea. Nor did the city require at all leaders who had obtained a great deal of wealth and were not able to say where they got it, instead of those who accomplished great and splendid achievements.

But in the capacity in which you, more than anyone else, were able, you did not help the city in the least. But in areas in which you, of all Athenians, were the most inept, you attempted to be an officious busy-body. Since you possessed as much wealth as many myriads of Persians, whose inheritor you became, and since you robbed those who fought against them and the whole city of all the spoils, I don't know how you managed to offer no service at all, either great or small, to your country. But with words, in which you are most inadequate, you attempt to chastise her, and you reprimand the Athenians for choosing one way rather than another in military actions, in which you are most ineffectual and cowardly.

Yet this is how it is, O Callias. Neither bulls nor any other great and mighty animal can withstand lions while they are alive; but when the lions are fallen and prostrate, it is not amazing if even flies crawl all over them. And so now even you enjoy yourself as you wish at my expense and walk all over me to your heart's content, since I am trampled upon by everyone. Don't be surprised, however, if god at some time will grant that I have occasion to remember this oratory of yours. He will do so – I know full well that he will. As the poets say, bad deeds do not prosper.

In keeping with the spirit of Epistle 8, Themistocles in shame obliquely alludes to his ambitions in Persia and the fact that he is on his way to the King.

10   To Habronichus

I have been bold enough to venture upon great and terrible things, O Habronichus. I sent Euxitheus to you and, when he came to talk with you directly and to reveal what I had decided, you were silent, stooped and looking to the ground as he was talking, not able to applaud, I imagine, and not wishing to impede my designs. You did well. But I go, and sitting in my carriage now I write this to you. Farewell and be of good spirits about me.

The next letter is to Ameinias, the brother of Cynegeirus, a renowned fighter at Marathon, and of Aeschylus, the dramatist. Ameinias, a captain (τριήραρχος) under Themistocles at Salamis, won a prize for valour after the war. Diodorus[286] tells us that prizes were awarded to Aegina and to Ameinias of Athens through the efforts of the Spartans, who wanted to humble the pride of the Athenians after their victory. The Spartans, however, were afraid that Themistocles would be angry at being slighted and so they honoured him with double the number of gifts that had been given to those who had won. Themistocles accepted the gifts and as a result fell out of favour in Athens. In the unique version found in this letter, Themistocles (the noble hero) does not begrudge Ameinias his prize; in fact, he had supported him for the award and, therefore, eventually incurred enmity and exile. Thus he wants Ameinias to help him now. The specific names are as usual problematical but at least most of them have a certain ring of authenticity.

11   *To Ameinias*

Even if we have not associated with one another for a long time,
yet we have been kindred spirits all our lives, and the duties
that we shared in, although short-lived, were momentous so
that the day on which we fought together in the same battles
was enough for us; for we were not an insignificant part of the
army – I, whom you and most of mankind now alive know
well enough, and you, the best ship-commander (τριήραρχος)
in the whole force. Thus we have a greater and more secure
friendship than would develop with time among men who
breakfast and dine together every day for a long time, even if
you were to allow them the extreme old age of the legendary
Tithonus.

Since you were so brave and just as a commander, I am convinced that you also have not forgotten things that you should
remember, but I believe that you see before you that critical
moment in which you were acclaimed by all because of me; I,
however, because of you came into conflict with many famous
men, not only Athenians, but other Hellenes too. How could it
be anything else but terrible that Alcibiades, Stratippus,
Lacratides, and Hermocles, all Athenians, along with Aristeides
of Aegina, Dorcon of Epidaurus, Cleon[287] from Troezen and
many other Hellenes condemned me for betrayal of my
generalship? As a result, I was deprived of the very thing that
everyone wishes for himself and his leaders, namely to dwell
in one's own country, it being enough for them that they were
hostile to me because of you.[288] They made a just decision in
awarding you the prize for valour, but they were resentful of
you and therefore, on your account, I am driven and expelled
by them and many others, since I did not value my interest or
theirs higher than yours. Will my remembrance of these wrongs
with their injustice be in every way stronger than the gratitude
that you justly owe me? Will those who wrong me unjustly
be more powerful in inflicting harm upon me than you are in
your efforts to do me some good? I do not believe this of you,
Ameinias, the son of Euphorion, a man of nobility both because

of your father and also because of your brothers, Cynegeirus, who was outstanding in the battle of Marathon, and Aeschylus, who all his life has been pre-eminent for his moderate character and his learned art. But you will be true to your character and you will act like your brothers and you will come to the aid of your admiral (ναύαρχος), Themistocles.

The best help lies in your opposition on my behalf in the assembly (*Ecclesia*); and if, in the deliberation of the people, any fresh trouble is fabricated and devised against me or my poor wife, you will do well to promise to offer me adequate help and assistance. If you do promise, you will yourself be burdened with nothing more than solicitous good will and serious concern.

In Epistle 12 Themistocles curses Aristeides and anyone else who will use the fact that he has been well received by the King of Persia against him. He makes perfectly clear that he was not a traitor and never anticipated that he would be forced to take refuge in Persia. The conclusion that his political enemies in Athens manipulated the evidence of Themistocles' flight to the Persians to discredit his actions is another of the many perceptive insights provided by these letters.

12   To Aristeides

I have made my way, O Aristeides, I have made my way to the Persians and I have experienced nothing terrible at their hands. I know that privately you will be amazed but that publicly you will pretend that for you this news was not unexpected – you will even use it as proof to the people that the slanderous accusations against me are confirmed by my hope in the Persians and their kindness towards me. Yet when you are in the process of delivering this nonsense, my fine fellow, may the trophy set up at Salamis fall down upon you; it is of stone, you know, huge and heavy. Then, I believe, you would no longer stir up the people nor envy their other benefactors, if some god in absolute justice not just because of your arrogant posture were to make that stone fall on your ungrateful and accursed head.

The great King offers me safety not as a return favour (to be sure he least of all would grant me any kindness in payment for the sufferings that he suffered) but he knew that I had been his enemy in other times and yet he marvelled at my courage (*arete*) and pitied my fate. And so you run personal risks in coming on an embassy about me. For you were unjust to me but he is ready to help me who was wronged; and you are the ones who made me pitiable by driving me out but he rightly took pity upon me, the one who had been expelled.

But indeed in my present situation I am no longer a miserable exile. And so let Aristeides, the son of Lysimachus, go hang and let everyone else go hang too, who are not pleased that I happened upon more favourable circumstances than he expected.

The next letter, one of despair, once again vindicates Themistocles by depicting him as a patriot who is driven and torn by unfortunate and unjust circumstances. He faced his immediate departure bravely but as his exile continues he becomes more and more confused and wretched.

Themistocles is still in Argos and thus this Epistle and Epistle 14 seem to be out of place.

13   *To Polygnotus*

To be sure, O Polygnotus, reflecting upon my sea-battles and my years as general, you urge me also to bear my absence from the city with noble resolution. When I was setting out and I had before my very eyes what I was leaving behind, I promised myself that I should endure my being away more resolutely and, when I also reflected upon my own sea-battles and all the rest that I had withstood, I believed that I should suffer this too with equal nobility – and you know that I did leave without too much lamentation.

Now as things are, O Polygnotus, time does not make me forget what I have left behind nor does it make me grow accustomed to exile. Exile would be a light burden if it were not prolonged but, as time passes, the things that I have lost become even more desirable and there is no consolation in the fact that I resolutely faced many other risks and fought against the Persians. But, upon reflection, this too has turned out quite contrary to my calculations. For it seems to me that I endured all these dangers in order that I might be able to enjoy Athens, and hence my disturbed thoughts multiply if many others who were not even spectators of the sea-battles at Euboea and at Salamis will be allowed to live in Athens and to throw out those whom they wish and to recall them, if they think it is right; but I alone, who assisted the Athenians in safeguarding their power (if even for only a brief time), have no share of either this power or of Athens itself. But I am named an exile, the sweetest designation for one's bitterest enemies.

I myself feel this strongly, bereft as I am of you my friends, bereft of home and the hearth at which I offered sacrifices to celebrate my victory over the Persians, a foreigner in a foreign land and city; and perhaps I shall die unrecalled and still an exile. Indeed should I have fought so bravely against the enemy, if I had any inkling that these sufferings were in store for me? Should I have so vigorously pursued a victory entailing these rewards? Should I, after the Persians had gone, have put myself in jeopardy with the Spartans in the matter of the city of Athens?[289] As it is, the Argives have received me and I must offer my prayer on behalf of the Argives and any and every city, since (as seems to be the case) I have a place everywhere else except in Athens.

But I am driven to utter these miserable words by my exile as though by a madness. For what evil, what that is not good, have the Athenians done to me? How shall I not be proven a liar in my hostility and how can it not help but be that these words of abuse will be dispelled? For, if the Persians attack Attica again, I shall not think that I should abstain from the danger because I am an exile nor shall I consider it to be a contest for those who have not suffered such a calamity as mine; but, even if I am not an admiral or general, O Polygnotus, I shall fight as an exile and I should not be any the worse at riding a horse or manoeuvring a ship because of this but I should even be more able. And so it would not be unlikely that I should prove to be a better fighter now than I was before as a result of my experience. The most base of the Athenians could make me an exile but they would never be able to turn me into a coward. Indeed in their punishment of me I must inevitably perceive the power which I myself preserved for the Athenians.

It happens that I ponder these things over and over again and I am full of a thousand arguments by which I seem to be able to combat my anxieties; but the present terrible desolation forcing itself upon my thoughts presents a counter-threat and drags me down and indeed it even dissuades me from the logic of my stronger convictions. Not even the many Argives here with me will argue that this is not desolation for me, and in the midst of their numbers the absence of friends and relatives appears all the more real.

But if your daughter, whose illness you allege to be the cause of your delay, is now recovered, come to rid me of my many sufferings. And if there are some matters that still detain you, I pray that they will be taken care of. And let us both (I by letter and you still by your presence there with him) persuade Megacles to stop his promises and come to fulfil my hopes.

In Epistle 14 Themistocles, who has railed against Fortune and bemoaned his fate, now feels that Pausanias by jeopardizing his power and success in the Hellespont because of his criminal ambitions has provided a good case for the possibility that Fortune (*Tyche*) may in the long run act with justice. This is a difficult letter because the text seems to be plagued by more than one lacuna. Yet the general sense is clear enough. Notice how the traitorous ambitions of Pausanias contrast by implication with Themistocles' subsequent innocent refuge among the Persians.

14   *To Pausanias*

You have provided a defence for the fate that Fortune brings, O Pausanias. For because of your actions through which you have been so justly unfortunate, you have eliminated even for me the grounds for continuing my accusations against Her. By attempting to become a Persian when you are a Spartan and in your efforts to add Hellas to the Persian empire, you have deprived yourself of the command that you had in the Hellespont and the power by which you undertook these ambitions. And you yourself persist and long for the opportune moment in which you might even be able to accomplish what you have planned.

And so you have been unjust to the Fortune that you had then and it was not She who was unjust to you. And yet you are still in Her good graces because undeterred you will be risking your power at its height and, even if you are going to be killed at the hands of the Spartans, you will have the consolation that you do not die unjustly. You are bound in closest alliance with Artabazus and you are anxious to become the son-in-law of the King. How can you believe that the give and take of your bargain is on an equal basis when you get a foreign wife and with her the territory of the Carians perhaps, or of the Phrygians, and in return surrender the country of Hellas and the cities of the Hellenes – and you don't even exclude Sparta in the deal? Do you hope to accomplish what you intend, poor fool? And if you fail, do you expect not to get caught because your intentions only were those of a traitor but your actions fell short of your design?

The region of Troy and Colonae, where you have been hiding and negotiating with the King to his advantage, is not so far distant that your activity there is unknown; besides, Gongylus the most vile of the Eretrians is the one who has been responsible for handling many of your negotiations with the King (if you have really employed this fellow as a trusty messenger) and rumours bring word back to Hellas; and you have treated Mnastoridas arrogantly, a man who is a Spartan and wishes to remain so and who continually has tried to warn you about the law in Sparta. But stop and consider, poor wretch, if Artabazus or the daughter of the King, who is now ripe for marriage, will be any help to you at all. And let these reproaches that I have written be all the more severe to you, since they come from me, who am an exile myself.

In Epistle 15 Themistocles wants a true account of the situation
in Athens. He feels that Athenian prosperity in his absence has
resulted from the soundness of his leadership.

15   *To Autolycus*

I should much prefer, O Autolycus, that you tell me the truth
rather than offer me consolation. But when you write that the
Athenians are now very repentant about my exile, it seems to
me that you are consoling me rather than speaking the truth.
For those who offer their slanderous accusations to the multitude
because of me are still strong and no opportunity presents itself
for rendering these evil men powerless in the city, at the same
time making it apparent that they succeeded in throwing out
better men than they are. But now they cloud and obscure their
lack of worth in the people's sense of well-being. I should not
find fault with their cover-up, provided that the city prosper.
For I should be very happy at Athens' good fortune, even though
it come by hearsay, even if I do not seem to be responsible for
or to benefit by this good fortune of hers since I have been an
exile. For actually perhaps this too follows upon my years in
power and what was well established then proceeds well now.
Perhaps too I should blame myself justly for having opened up
such a broad path of progress that leadership is no longer
required.

But, O Autolycus, write to me not how you yourself wish
the Athenians to repent but how they really are disposed. Their
disposition, I believe, is turned by the whim of the men who
continually come before them and whose wickedness would be
all the more manifest, if I had not been driven out.

In Epistle 16 Themistocles argues that he is much luckier than
Pausanias and provides a lengthy outline of Pausanias' ambitious
career and tragic end to prove his point. In the process he clears
himself from any guilty association with Pausanias and reveals
that he is far different in character from the traitorous and
hubristic Spartan.

16 To Alcetas

You were accustomed, O Alcetas, to count the fate of Pausanias as a blessing, while bemoaning my exile, and you have often written that the goddess of fate abandoned me and attached herself to Pausanias. That man, I hope you realize, Alcetas, is gone with her. Gone is his great command in the Hellespont, gone are the wealth and a name and reputation that had reached the King; and there wasn't even proper burial prepared for him when he died. Those who most of all marvelled at Pausanias now refrain from mentioning even his name, as though it would contaminate those who heard it with great evil.

And so it is no longer the time for you to deem Pausanias fortunate because of his greatness or to bewail the final catastrophe that has befallen him. Indeed he suffered just deserts and I approve of his punishment. But if you are astounded when you think of how drastic his reversal was, I shall rid you of your astonishment by telling you what a helot who came to see me told me to rid me of mine. Think differently about his fate and marvel at the fact that a man like that survived and once was fortunate and enjoyed for a long time the fruits of his betrayal.

Pausanias was for selling out Hellas to the King, consistently showed himself a Persophile and kept on imitating the Persians, and was distressed that he was a Hellene and not one of those who came against Hellas. When he seemed to have proved by his achievement at Plataea that he was not an evil man, he was entrusted with command in the Hellespont. Immediately, while he held power there, he offered to the Persians the defence that he had not been a willing patriot at Plataea; and he betrayed Hellas to them as payment for his actions in that battle. He entered into an agreement with Artabazus, who was the King's satrap over the people on the coast, and he informed the King of his actions. He himself was now a Persian both in how he thought and how he lived. Even his dress made him a Hellene no longer.

At first, as you know yourself, little news of all this reached Sparta and, even though their information was scanty, they were disturbed but nothing more. But when he was recalled, Pausanias paid a penalty, was removed from office and became a private citizen. Immediately he went to Asia. Angry and anxious for vengeance because of the loss of his command, he pursued his ambitions with great vehemence. Still he acted secretly, not in shame of being found out but in fear of failure if his plans became known. Only after he had worked out the whole plot for his betrayal was he going to go over to the King openly.

Therefore he devised a scheme for secretly dispatching a message to the King. It was by the very nature of this scheme in particular that he was saved for some time and then destroyed. Each messenger who was sent by Pausanias was killed by Artabazus. For Pausanias, being scrupulous about every detail in his plot for betrayal, ordered the messengers to be killed so that no account would be preserved of what he had done. The trick succeeded for him up until the murder of three and four messengers; but in the case of the fifth, it was exposed. For the fear that gripped the servants of Pausanias was increased by the even more frightening realization by those who had not yet been dispatched that not a single one of those already sent had returned.

Pausanias was recalled a second time and returned to Sparta. When he faced charges and sent messengers to the King, the last of those dispatched was all the more afraid. Reflecting on the possibility of being murdered and not wanting to submit to this terrible prospect until he knew for sure, he copied the seal of Pausanias so that he might be able to use it if he were wrong. He opened the letter and read the many details concerning the enslavement of the Hellenes and at the very end learned about his own death. He brought the letter to the ephors and showed it to them.

The ephors had acquired both in writing and in words proof against Pausanias and still they contrived even further to lay bare the truth. They brought the messenger to Taenarus as a suppliant, sending in secret along with him some of their own men. When Pausanias came to him and asked for what reason, he, the man whom he had sent as a messenger to Asia, had become a suppliant, the fellow immediately called upon Pausanias as a witness to confirm his testimony that he had never done anything worthy of death and confronted him with the fact that he had been sent to his destruction. He maintained that the enslavement of the Hellenes was of little consequence to him (for he was not even secure in his freedom now) and he asked that before all else he be granted his release. Pausanias gave his assurance that he would not be killed and asked that he keep quiet about what he knew. Then he raised up the suppliant and returned to Sparta and the men who had listened to his every word followed him.

As soon as it was clear that, when all the ephors had learned about the conversation, they were going to arrest him, Pausanias anticipated their action by rushing into the temple of Athena of the Brazen House and sat as a suppliant in one of the rooms of the sacred precinct. But they walled up the entrance and removed the roof and left him, a suppliant, to die of starvation. And when they knew he was almost dead, they brought him, still breathing, out of the sacred precinct and they deliberated whether they should grant him burial or not.

This was how the good fortune of Pausanias ended and I have passed on to you the entire account of the helot. Don't bewail my exile any longer; I am thrice blessed since I was a match for the measure of envy that was meted out to me. But I must blame my virtues (*arete*) for my present circumstance and the termination of my good service in the democracy that I have faced. Yet, if somehow they feel pity and regret for my suffering, instead of envious hostility, and you learn about it, let me know, O Alcetas, and perhaps then I should believe even Autolycus, who writes that this is the case.

In Epistle 17, which is out of order chronologically, Themistocles tells his Argive friends about his voyage to Corcyra and his inhospitable reception there.

17   To Nicias and Meleager

I have come to Corcyra, just as I had decided to do when I set sail. My voyage was an easy one and greatly compensated for the time that I was detained at Cyllene. Also I sent back the ship to you at once and most of the slaves so that I should not make any heavier a demand on you than I believe fitting for an exile like me.

I don't know with what disposition the Corcyraeans evade their responsibility towards me. For they acknowledge that they remember my good service and never deny that they owe me thanks, but they say that it is not a good and opportune moment to demand payment; for they are weaker than my pursuers. They do not think it is right that they all be forced to face destruction because of a return favour to one man and they ask that they not be annihilated as a result of repayment of their debt for my good service.

And so they send me away with nice arguments and I am afraid that this is the beginning of a longer flight.

In the next epistle we learn once again (cf. Epistle 3) that Aristeides is now working on behalf of Themistocles, and Themistocles writes to him to express his deepest gratitude and to explain why he chose to run away. Some significant observations are made about the nature of the pan-Hellenic court before which Themistocles was to be tried.

18   To Aristeides

The disparity in our fortunes had already dissolved our enmity and it was an indication of weakness on your part to remain hostile to an exile;[290] but you have even gone further in your support than this, O Aristeides. You have undertaken to help me in my misfortune in a way that I never expected; in fact you have even supported me to a point beyond my wildest dreams. My gratitude to you for this has not been dissipated, even though you were not strong enough to set things aright for me; nevertheless I feel more grateful about your enthusiasm on my behalf than I would have inevitably felt if you had actually saved me, because you fought against the Athenians who were so ill-disposed towards me.[291]

As for my present flight, which I chose as a lesser evil, how could the same decision not seem right to you too? Polygnotus also wrote to me more than once; for he too recommended this very course,[292] namely to flee as quicky as possible, as though from a verdict of punishment that was already passed. I don't think that he was wrong in assuming that I should have been punished if I lingered.

For the Athenians intended to bring me before the common court of the Hellenes,[293] where the Dorian element is greater than the Ionian. And the majority was opposed to me and the minority was powerless to help me; in fact the whole situation was fraught with hostility. And so it seemed likely to me that every other race of men, whether foreign or Hellenic, would take me in, among whom the charges for which I am pursued will be able to work to my advantage.

Themistocles next accuses his friends, Antagoras and Autolycus, of betraying him. In keeping with the spirit of the previous letter, Themistocles feels that Aristeides is more of a friend to him than those who are supposed to be his friends.

19   To Antagoras

O Antagoras, both you and Autolycus often have promised me that you would easily release me from my ostracism. For you said that you would fight against my enemy Aristeides, that you would bring the people around to oppose him and that already he was considered of lesser consequence for not wishing to give up his enmity.

But Aristeides has turned out to be for me both Antagoras and Autolycus! I should have encountered none of these evils (both those to come and those already experienced), if you, my three or four friends in Athens, had chosen to be as devoted to

me as my single enemy Aristeides, and, what is more, if you
had even listened to this enemy of mine. But as the case stands,
am I in flight because of some others or because of you? Is it
due to my enemies or my friends that I do not receive a summons to return home?²⁹⁴ No, you have won, my friends, and
in my exile I do not blame anyone in any way, even if I shall
suffer most pitiably.

The next lengthy, important epistle tells of Themistocles'
various experiences after he has left Argos and of his successful
career in Persia. When Themistocles arrives in Ionia, Xerxes is
still alive. His encounter, however, is with Artaxerxes, who is
not named directly.²⁹⁵ This letter records Themistocles' encounter with Admetus rather differently from Epistle 5.

20   To Polygnotus

Here, O Polygnotus, are the things that happened to me after
my flight from Argos, and I write to you about them just as
you have urged me to. When the messenger arrived in haste –
the one whom you sent to tell me among other things to flee –
I immediately set out from Argos; my friends Nicias and
Meleager went with me and I came to Cyllene, the port of the
Eleans. There, because of a storm, I was in danger of being
caught by my pursuers. For I was on my way to Corcyra with
all speed (I had previously done the Corcyraeans a good turn),
when I was delayed thus for three whole days, and it did not
seem that my flight would be undetected by the Spartans any
longer. But on the fourth day we had very good weather and
were able to set sail. I thanked my friends for their devotion
(for they still wanted to accompany me even farther) but let
them go, and, having set out on the ship which they provided
for me, I had an easy voyage to Corcyra.

The Corcyraeans, however, preferred to be safe rather than
grateful and, when they were asked for a favour in recompense
for the good service that I had done them, they requested me
not to terminate my flight in Corcyra – and so I was at a loss

about what to do. For I had already sent the ship back to my Argive friends and I had left with me fewer slaves than I had dismissed. When the Corcyraeans now began to speak out even more harshly and seemed much more likely to hand me over than to fight on my behalf, I decided to sail to Gelon in Sicily. For at that time indeed Gelon was sole ruler of the Syracusans and he had close ties with me and he was not likely to listen to the Athenians. I found a ship of Leucadians, who on the following day were going to embark for Italian waters (the Ausonian Sea). But the arrival of news made me change my course. Gelon had already died and Hieron, his brother who had recently succeeded to the supreme power, was embroiled in much trouble. In the same ship as I intended, I sailed to Epirus; and after disembarking I came to the Molossians and sat as a suppliant at the hearth of Admetus.

The Molossian people were then under the rule of Admetus; he thought that his royal position would be particularly enhanced by an act of piety and it was clear that he would not ignore me who was his suppliant.

The Athenians and the Spartans, sent to surround me and take me by force, had set sail and arrived among the Molossians on the next day; they were happy to have caught me there and proclaimed that they would take me away, and approaching Admetus they spoke as follows to him:

'You are unaware, O Admetus, that you have accepted a traitor to your home and to your hearth, and, if he had been successful, we, O Admetus, would have been suppliants at the hearth of the Medes, and this fellow perhaps would have been King of the Thesprotians in your place. And so now were we then unjust towards Pausanias, since he has already paid the penalty because of the very same designs? Themistocles expects to be saved and makes you an accomplice in his crime, but not even Athena who dwells in the Brazen House came to the aid of Pausanias. So order this man to rise and stop his deceit and his pollution of your hearth and let the Athenians and the Spartans stand as your friends in the place of this one man – a traitor and a fugitive!'

When they had said these things I was about to reply with words by which they would be shamed and rejected, but Admetus spoke first.

'This critical moment alone, O Athenians and Spartans, will provide the bases for a decision about Themistocles' suppliancy. And if I were to pass judgment on his betrayal (it is a good thing that I am neither an Athenian nor a Spartan)[296] I should acquit Themistocles: it would seem that the sea-battles at Artemisium and at Salamis demand this verdict; and the betrayal of Pausanias, which you charge, will always be the responsibility of Pausanias alone, even if you would like to give Themistocles a share in it. You thought that I was ignorant of these things and I pass judgment on the question of suppliancy as though I were in fact ignorant of them. A man clinging to my hearth, in fear of men but with trust in the gods of Epirus, I protect and keep safe since he is a suppliant; I cannot deny that I fear the gods, even if it means that I incur the hostility of some men, and I believe that the protection of a suppliant is a greater favour to god than any sacrifice.'

Thus amazed and downcast, my pursuers left the Molossians; and I was sent by Admetus to Macedonia. I came to Alexander, ruler of the Macedonians, in Pydna and I was sent by Alexander to the sea there; I happened upon a ship sailing to Ionia, boarded it, and was taken to Ionia. For there to be sure I should most easily find out if I should suffer justice, especially since the King knew what evils I had perpetrated against him. We had been induced by fair weather to put out to sea but our voyage did not continue to be propitious and we encountered a violent storm. Yet the storm did not distress me so much as the fact that we were swept towards Naxos. The Athenians at that very time were laying siege to Naxos and we were borne down towards their squadron. I felt extremely helpless and I now thought that my actions as a suppliant were of no avail and I had engaged upon a flight that was disastrous. For I was about to be easily caught by the Athenians, the fugitive running right into the hands of his pursuers. Yet, since I seemed to be unknown to those on my ship and I was frightened of being discovered by the Athenians in their camp, I did not leave the vessel. But my fellow-travellers were suspicious and it seemed to them that I had become something unpropitious and evil for their voyage; and so they wanted to evict me from the ship. In the midst of this danger, Diopeithes, a native of [the city of] Bargylia [on the Carian coast], one of my shipmates who had often watched me before like a man full of wonder, then scrutinized me even more closely; and he was now convinced that I was the person whom he believed me to be. He approached me alone and getting as near as possible spoke in a whisper:

'Divine fate insults you ingloriously, O Themistocles, if your preservation depends solely upon not being recognized as Themistocles. But I know who you are and by this recognition (a disaster which you fear most of all) I shall perhaps be able to save you. For I am the one whom you saved when I, a merchant who had sailed to Artemisium, was deemed worthy of death because of a personal enemy, a man from Hestiaea, on the charge that I was sent by the King. But you, despite the situation, did not believe my accusers and reproached them for their charge, and you had never received any benefit from me before nor did you ever expect that you would, for you were the leader in opposition to the King and you did good services to others, and I did not even want or hope to repay Themistocles for this favour, for I had no desire or expectation that you would be in such circumstances that you would need me to.'

'But, my fine fellow', I said, 'what has befallen me is not a misfortune, if the situation works to my advantage and by it I have come to receive a return favour from you. Rejoice with me; it will indeed be good fortune if you have such power as to save Themistocles.'

Then he brought to me the captain of the ship, who was a friend of his; he let him know the facts and asked him to flee from Naxos as quickly as possible. But the captain was disturbed and anxious to go at once and inform the Athenians. I did not plead with him at all but resorted to the threat that I should tell the Athenians that he delivered me from Hellas, with full knowledge of who I was and under the influence of a bribe.

The man was afraid and, changing his mind, he demanded a reward for his assistance. I promised him one; and during the night we set sail and I was taken to Ephesus.

There I encountered some Persians, who were stationed by Artabazus as sentinels in Caria, and now I was not afraid that Xerxes be told who I was and I revealed my name and how I had come to give great aid to the house of the King; they brought the report of what I said to Artabazus and then they led me to the Phrygians, for Artabazus was in Phrygia. When he learned the full story from me and that I was determined to go to the King, he expressed his approval and straightway sent me off; and he gave me the gift of two horses, the same number of slaves, and sent along in addition thirteen other Persians who were to attend to the journey and the necessary supplies; they made use of camels. On the way I passed small mountains, shallow valleys and low brushwood and I saw and traversed plains that were vast and completely flat. They were for the most part cultivated and inhabited, but the desert nourished wild beasts and herds of other animals. And I sailed over many rivers and encountered all sorts of peoples. And now from these associations I also began to get some grasp of the Persian language and the road no longer appeared difficult and trying because of my growing familiarity.

My journey came to an end and I had reached my goal, the court of the King. When the message was brought to him that the Athenian Themistocles was at his doors, I was led into his presence; and after I was brought right up to his throne I stood there fearlessly. But he was disturbed and looking me up and down spoke as follows:

'O Athenian guest, there has already been much talk about you in my house and you along with the disaster that befell the Medes at Salamis have been on everyone's tongue. Would you tell me how you have the audacity to be seen in my sight and to listen to my voice? Have you come here, you that Themistocles who the Medes say are responsible for keeping both me and my father from ruling the Hellenes? Yet it was better for me to have the Hellenes than to exact retribution from you;

but you have offered me the latter alternative instead of the former – and so, having sounded your praises, I shall punish you.'

When he had spoken these words, it occurred to me, under the pressure of necessity, that by extolling my trickery I might in this crisis turn it to my own good. Using this strategy I spoke as follows:

'O King, I flee punishment and I have come to you as your ally for the Hellenes were going to punish me in retaliation for the good service towards your father because, out of friendship to you, I sent the message that he should sail to Salamis quickly, telling him that the Hellenic force was then divided and confused, on the verge of fleeing to the Peloponnesus and offering the best opportunity for attack; and I prevented those who wanted to from breaking the yoke that bridged the Hellespont; because of this most of all the Medes returned home out of Europe for you, but for these reasons I was being led to punishment. Yet I anticipated my accusers by resorting to flight so that I might help you in some way and find justice for myself. The avenging Fury, Erinys, promises to accomplish these goals, and with her aid I shall wreak more evils upon the Greeks than I seemed with them to wreak upon the Persians.'[297]

And he replied, 'When you hand over Hellas to me (for I was deprived of Hellas, I believe, because of you), you may rejoice for you will be blessed with every good. We shall put your words to the test of action.'

As a result, O Polygnotus, I have been staying in the royal palace, receiving honour and giving instructions about Hellenic matters. The King himself, since I have been conversing with him now in the Persian language about many things, has given me as a gift a Persian sword of gold and a Persian garment woven of gold; and immediately following his example those around the King also presented me with gifts.

Now he considers Artabazus to be less trustworthy than I am and he has sent me down to the sea to the area of Artabazus' command. Now he no longer favours me with gold or clothes but instead with cities and much territory. He has taken Myus,

Lampsacus and Magnesia on the Maeander from his own
kingdom and given them to me. I freed Lampsacus and remitted
all its great burden of tax and I reap the fruits of Myus in
Magnesia and Magnesia itself. But I do not feel any pleasure
from power and money, yet I consider that I have enough
resources as long as they are sufficient to keep my exile active
and productive, for as it is you my friends do not even enjoy
my present prosperity. As Hellenes, how could prerogative of
their kind ever content us? And so I look upon the present circumstances as treacherous and necessary rather than as good fortune.
Now to be sure I am overtaken by an even greater disaster: the
King is in a rage and presses his campaign against the Hellenes;
and this news has already been brought to me a second time.
Indeed he puts me forward as leader of the army and he will
place Medes under Themistocles' command and I shall lead an
army against Athens and I shall fight with the admiral of the
Athenians. Many other things will happen, but this never!

This last dramatic outburst, which may be intended to forbode
Themistocles' suicide, would have provided an appropriately
climactic ending for the collection. But instead there follows
a short and obscure appeal to Temenidas, who is presumably
still in Argos, for some treasured possessions which apparently
will help serve Themistocles' ambitions among the Persians.
Some if not all of these prizes may belong to Temenidas himself.
At any rate 'the iron breast-plates from Admetus' remind us
of Temenidas' possible ties with Admetus suggested in Epistle
5. Themistocles' distrust of the Corinthians reflects his conflict
with them at the peak of his career. Perhaps we are also to remember Themistocles' misunderstanding with his Corinthian
banker in Epistles 6 and 7. The letter writer seems to be particularly well informed in his reference to the Old Assyrian
letters (i.e. the Aramaic script) as distinct from the letters recently
written or prescribed by Darius (i.e. the Achaemenian cuneiform
script).[298]

21   *To Temenidas*

Send me the four biggest of the silver kraters and gold censers
that are inscribed in Old Assyrian letters and not in the script
recently used [or prescribed] by Darius, father of Xerxes, for
the Persians and send me half the number of iron breast-plates
from Admetus that you showed me. Do not, however, be slow
and careless and do not ship them from Corinth; but dispatch
them as quickly as possible, setting them in the safest hands you
can find and putting those in whose care they are on a boat
sailing from anywhere rather than Cenchreae, the port of
Corinth. Farewell.

CHAPTER XI

THE DEATHS OF A HERO

Thucydides tells us about Themistocles' death and burial and his account is generally accepted:

Themistocles ended his life after an illness. But some say that he died of his own volition by means of a poisonous drug (φαρμάκῳ) when he realized that it was impossible to carry out what he had promised the King. There is a monument (memorial, or tomb μνημεῖον) of him in Magnesia in Asia in the market-place, for he was in charge of this district. . . . They say that relatives, at his bidding, brought his bones home and they were buried in Attica, without the knowledge of the Athenians; for it was forbidden to bury him because he was a fugitive charged with treason.[299]

Cicero (like most historians) believes Thucydides' verdict about Themistocles' death and attempts to explain the reasons why the suicide must be fiction:

Clitarchus and Stratocles tell an invented story about Themistocles' death. Thucydides, on the other hand, who was an Athenian of the highest birth and greatest distinction and only a little later in time than Themistocles, simply wrote that he died naturally and was secretly buried in Attica, adding that there was a suspicion that he committed suicide by poison; Clitarchus and Stratocles, however, say that, when Themistocles had slaughtered a bull, he drew off the blood into a bowl (patera), drank it and died. By this version they were able to elaborate rhetorically and tragically about his suicide, whereas an ordinary death offered no material for such elaboration.[300]

Themistocles' suicide by bull's blood is not merely an invention of fourth-century historiography, whatever Cicero believes and however much embellishment later writers may have provided. Thucydides' mention of death by poison suggests that he probably knew at least the basic elements of the story even though he does not specify bull's blood (perhaps deliberately);[301] and a reference found in Aristophanes' *Knights*, produced in 424, seems to prove that it was already current by at least the last quarter of the fifth century. In this comedy, as two slaves contemplating suicide wonder how it can be done most heroically (ἀνδρικώτατα), one of them exclaims:

> It is best for us to drink bull's blood
> For the death of Themistocles is most preferable.[302]

The rhetorical and tragic elaborations of Themistocles' suicide referred to by Cicero in the passage above can be readily detected in the version offered by Diodorus, who presumably is following Ephorus:

Now Themistocles was freed from his fear of retribution at the hands of the Hellenes – a man who had, contrary to every expectation, been driven into exile by those who had benefited most from his good services and in turn had received great benefits himself from the very ones upon whom he had inflicted the most terrible sufferings. He spent his life in Magnesia, Myus and Lampsacus, well provided with good things for his pleasure. And he died in Magnesia where he was given a notable burial (funeral or tomb? ταφή) and a monument (μνημεῖον) which still stands today. Some writers say that Xerxes was anxious to raise another army against Hellas and summoned Themistocles to be the commander for the war; Themistocles agreed and obtained from Xerxes trustworthy oaths that he would not campaign against the Greeks without Themistocles. After a bull had been sacrificed and oaths taken, Themistocles filled a wine-cup with blood, drank it and died on the spot. Xerxes abandoned his plan and Themistocles by his own suicide left behind the finest testament to the fact that he was a good citizen in his actions pertaining to Hellenic affairs.[303]

In Diodorus' account we have all the dramatic and ethical ingredients inherent in the story. The patriotic hero of Salamis confronts his former enemy Xerxes and vindicates himself from all wrong.

Plutarch retains the version of the suicide but chooses a more credible chronological and historical setting, thereby diluting to some extent the dramatic, if not the moral, impact. It is under Artaxerxes (not Xerxes) that Themistocles drinks bull's blood and the revolt of Egypt from the great King becomes the specific catalyst for the tragedy. The theatrical juxtaposition of Themistocles and his bitter rival Cimon is on the face of it

dubious, but it is interesting how in Plutarch Themistocles
emerges as more the calculating pragmatist than altruistic
patriot:

Egypt had revolted from the King with the help of the Athenians and
Hellenic triremes were sailing up to Cyprus and Cilicia; thus Cimon's
control of the sea now compelled the King to oppose the Hellenes and
prevent the growth of their power against him. Forces were already
being moved and generals dispatched when messages were sent to
Themistocles (in Magnesia) to the effect that the King ordered him to
abide by his promises and turn his attention to this Hellenic crisis.
Themistocles was neither provoked by any feeling of anger against his
fellow Athenians nor elated by the great honour and power afforded
him by the war; but perhaps he did not think that this undertaking
was even possible since now Hellas had other great generals, especially
Cimon who was so extraordinarily successful in his campaigns. Most
of all, however, he was concerned about the reputation that he should
win both for his actions now and also especially for his past victorious
achievements. Thus he decided that it was best to put an end to his life
that was fitting. He sacrificed to the gods and clasped in farewell the
hands of his friends whom he had summoned together. Then he drank
bull's blood, as the most prevalent account goes; but some say that he
took a quick poison. And so Themistocles died in Magnesia after having
lived for sixty-five years, most of which he had spent in politics and
leadership. And they say that, when the King learned the cause and the
manner of his death, he admired the man still more and persisted in
treating his friends and relatives kindly.[304]

Plutarch seems to be thinking of the revolt of Inarus in Egypt
(460/59) as the instigation for Themistocles' suicide. If so, he
is wrong to imagine Cimon, who had been ostracized previously, as still in command of the Greek forces; yet his appreciation of Cimon's successful aggression against the Persians is
in general accurate.

In his biography of Cimon, Plutarch again dramatically
brings Themistocles into conflict with his former enemy. In this
context, however, the emphasis on motivations is inevitably
different and the chronological setting becomes Cimon's last
expedition against Cyprus and Egypt in 450. According to
Plutarch here, Cimon's intention was the complete destruction
of the Persian King's supremacy, especially because he learned

that Themistocles had acquired great power and esteem and had promised the King he would himself take command in a war against Hellas. It was said, Plutarch goes on, that one of the chief reasons why Themistocles committed suicide was his despair about any Hellenic undertakings because he might not be able to surpass Cimon's valour and success.[305]

SUICIDE BY BULL'S BLOOD?

It has often been pointed out that bull's blood is not in itself poisonous. But since the ancients believed that it was, perhaps we might suspect that for them the drinking of bull's blood implied connotations (lost to us) of a deadly potion, with bull's blood only one of the ingredients, possibly drunk in ritual form after a sacrifice. Characters both legendary and historical were said to have died from the blood of bulls, among them Psammenitus, King of Egypt, whose death Herodotus reports with no apparent disbelief.[306]

I have consulted a toxicological expert on the subject, Emmerich von Haam, MD, and his comments reveal that death by bull's blood itself need not be completely preposterous; but we should have to adjust details in the dramatic scene of Themistocles' suicide to insure a lethal draught:[307]

I have searched my entire toxicological library and I couldn't find anything concerning poisoning by bull's blood. The only possible connection which could be construed would be contamination of bull's blood with anaerobic bacilli which would produce the symptoms of botulism. In order to do this, you have to let clotted or unclotted blood be exposed to the air for several days. The bacilli action will also work on the blood clots so that the bull's blood would have the appearance of dark red wine. This toxin is so potent that the victim would die within a few hours.

Fresh and uncontaminated blood is eaten by many individuals, including Germans with their famous blood sausage.

Another piece of evidence must be brought to bear on the question of the suicide. A bronze coin from Magnesia of the second century AD has been found, which may be described as follows, although details are worn and difficult to perceive from a photograph (Pl. 30):[308]

Obverse: Head of Antoninus Pius with the inscription of his name (Caesar Antoninus) in Greek capitals.

Reverse: Male nude figure, bearded with a wreath, fillet or crown in his hair, grasping a sheathed sword in his left hand and holding in his right a bowl (*patera*) over a lighted altar, at the foot of which lies a slain animal. The name Themistocles is inscribed in Greek capitals and also the year, designated by the name of the Secretary (to the Council), Dioscourides Gratus of the Metropolis of the Magnesians.

This scene cannot help but call to mind the dramatic accounts quoted above concerning Themistocles' suicide; and the most compelling interpretation is that we have commemorated on this coin in the second century AD the glorious moment before his death – a scene which had become crystallized and commonplace in a literary tradition reaching as far back as the fifth century BC. Stylized elements found elsewhere in numismatie depictions of a hero (or a god) would thus appropriately appear for obvious reasons. Yet some have been sceptical about such a simple and immediate interpretation.

Our ancient sources agree, as we have seen, that there was some kind of monument of Themistocles in Magnesia; but Nepos alone specifically describes it as statues or a statue (*statuae*, emend. *statua*) in the forum there.[309] It has been argued that the depiction on the coin was inspired by this very monument. It was not inappropriate, on this assumption, to depict Themistocles' honourable suicide on his tomb or cenotaph; but one wonders how soon after his death the memorial was erected and whether at the time the suicide was imagined as fact or fiction? It has also been suggested that, although the coin copies the statuary of the Magnesian memorial, the scene is not one of suicide but merely the stylized depiction of Themistocles as civic hero, to whom sacrificial offerings have been brought; and that 'stupid people' readily interpreted the scene to mean that Themistocles' death was self-inflicted. Thus the myth arose and thus the details of literary versions which seem to describe the coin (i.e. the monument).[310] But why should one see in the statuary group a representation of Themistocles' suicide unless some oral or literary version about his death was already extant? We do not know that the scene was any kind of artistic stereotype for suicide, and although the lethal drinking of bull's blood by others does appear, as I have mentioned, in literary tradition, we have no assurance that it was common knowledge. And so such conjectures about the Themistoclean monument and coin, imaginative and interesting though they may be, lack the support, as yet, of sufficient evidence.

Conclusions

It is a pity to reject the stirring account of a vindicated Themistocles driven to suicide because of his loyalty to Athens. Yet the serious historian must feel compelled to do so, if only because the motives for invention appear so transparent. Besides, Thucydides himself says that Themistocles died from an illness, and he in the last analysis stands as our final authority. Yet it would be most interesting to know the reason for Thucydides' verdict. Did he have a reliable source or is he merely applying the same rational and analytical principles to be found elsewhere in his treatment of other material that smacks of legend? If so, it is just possible that he may be wrong!

Finally, a few words about the date of Themistocles' death. It should be apparent how extremely unlikely is the tradition that Themistocles died under Xerxes, despite Diodorus (quoted above) and others who link the suicide with the Greek campaign against the Persians at Eurymedon, although admittedly the year of this battle cannot be established securely. The chronographic tradition of Eusebius (and Apollodorus?) dated Themistocles' death by bull's blood in 468/7 or 467/6.[311] Plutarch, as we have seen, associates Themistocles' death with the revolt of Egypt (460), but he is chronologically confused in his suspiciously dramatic contrast between the exiled Themistocles and triumphant Cimon, who by 460 was in ostracism; and in a different context he sets Themistocles' death in the time of Cimon's last expedition to Egypt (450).

In conclusion, the best we can do, assuming the sixty-five years attested by Plutarch for Themistocles' life to be correct, is to conjecture that Themistocles died *c.* 459; *c.* 449, although not impossible, seems too late in terms of his earlier career, and any date before 465 (the death of Xerxes) is also improbable.[312]

CHAPTER XII

THE TOMBS: A HERO'S
MONUMENTS

IN MAGNESIA

Themistocles died in Magnesia, but, as we have seen in the last
chapter, Thucydides calls the monument in the market-place
there a memorial and does not identify a tomb as such, thus
leaving the question open whether or not he was ever buried
in Magnesia at all. For Thucydides also reports and does not
refute the tradition that Themistocles' relatives, at his own
bidding, buried his bones in Attica, without the Athenians'
knowledge. If this is true, one may very well wonder about the
nature of the whole proceedings. Were any of the Magnesians
aware of Themistocles' request? Is it politically feasible that the
removal of his remains, after, say, an elaborate state funeral,
could have, at least originally, been public knowledge in
Magnesia, however secret his subsequent burial in Attica may
have had to be?

On the other hand, Diodorus, also quoted in the previous
chapter, may be making a distinction between the monument
in Magnesia and his actual tomb there, although this is not the
most natural interpretation of the text. For Diodorus, the monument and the tomb are probably one and the same, whether
or not he means to tell us (a logical inference on his or our
part) that Themistocles' funeral was a splendid one.

Only Nepos appears to distinguish clearly between two
monuments to Themistocles, both in Magnesia, one of which
was his actual burial place:

Two monuments (*monumenta*) to Themistocles have endured up until
our time: a sepulchre (*sepulchrum*) near the town, in which he is buried;
statues (or a statue) in the forum of Magnesia.[313]

Nepos goes on to prefer Thucydides' version, which for

Nepos is that Themistocles died a natural death in Magnesia and
his bones were secretly buried in Attica by friends. I cannot help
but wonder then if his text quoted above has not suffered corruption and should be construed to have originally meant that
there was a monument outside a town in Attica (e.g. on a
promontory in the Piraeus) where he was buried and another in
the forum of Magnesia. As we shall soon see, a memorial in the
Piraeus was by Nepos' time well known as the supposed tomb
of Themistocles. At any rate Nepos, in the last analysis, can
shed no significant light on the problem.[314]

There exist five sepulchral epigrams from Book 7 of the
Greek Anthology. All are literary compositions of the Augustan
Age that confirm the ambiguity of the tradition. Was the
monument in Magnesia a tomb or a cenotaph? Here are literal
translations, which do not attempt to render the elegiac couplets
of the Greek originals in English verse:[315]

73 Instead of a plain tomb, put Hellas on my grave and on Hellas
ships to signify the Persian wrecks. Around the base delineate Xerxes
and his Persian hordes. With this monument bury Themistocles. And
the stele set above will be Salamis to proclaim my deeds. Why cover
the great man with little?

74 For Themistocles the people of Magnesia have erected this foreign
[or empty] tomb when after saving his fatherland from the Persians
he was buried under alien earth and stone. Indeed thus envy wished and
won, for virtue wins a lesser prize.

235 Do not measure the greatness of Themistocles' name by this
Magnesian tomb. And do not be forgetful of his deeds. Judge the
patriot by Salamis and the ships and from these you will know him
to be greater than Cecrops' Athens.

236 Not of Themistocles am I, this Magnesian tomb, but I stand as a
memorial of the jealous and evil judgment of the Hellenes.

237 Depict on my tomb above, mountains and sea and in the midst
of both Apollo the sun as a witness and the deep streams of the ever-
flowing rivers, whose waters once were not enough for the might of
Xerxes' thousands of ships. Also depict Salamis here where the Magnesian people extol the tomb of the dead Themistocles.

Of course these epitaphs prove nothing about the nature and

architectural design of any tomb or memorial of Themistocles anywhere. Nos 74 and 236, for example, may or may not imply that his Magnesian monument was a cenotaph; nos 73 and 237 may or may not reflect the decoration and design of an original, perhaps commonly known in antiquity. But it is rash to assume that these literary conceits are inspired by anything more than themes which had become commonplace: Themistocles' glorious achievement with the fleet at Salamis against the mighty power of Xerxes; the exile of this great Athenian patriot inspired by jealous hostility.

The best that we can conclude, then, is that there was a memorial to Themistocles in the forum of Magnesia, erected at some time after his death, which may have never been his actual tomb. We do not know for sure if he was ever buried in Magnesia at all.

In Attica

His bones therefore could have been buried secretly in Attica. But only in later accounts (and not in Thucydides) are we explicitly told that Themistocles' remains were dug up and transferred, as in a dubious variation offered by a scholiast to Aristophanes:

The god [Apollo] directed the Athenians, who were suffering from a plague, to bring back the bones of Themistocles; when the Magnesians objected, they claimed the right to sacrifice at the tomb after 30 days; they encamped about the place, and having dug up the bones carried them off secretly.[316]

The need to recover the remains of a hero is a recurrent legendary theme, for example the recovery of the body of Orestes by the Spartan, Lichas, and that of Theseus by Cimon.

Although Plutarch is extremely doubtful about stories that elaborated upon the transfer of Themistocles' remains to Attica, his arguments are difficult to assess, and therefore cannot carry much weight. After specifically mentioning the splendid tomb (τάφος) of Themistocles in Magnesia, he goes on to refer sceptically to the testimony of works by Andocides and Phylarchus (lost to us) in an oblique and ambiguous manner. It seems that for political and dramatic reasons these authors wrote that Themistocles' remains were stolen by Athenians either in Magnesia or Attica or both and desecrated with some kind of participation by his sons in the whole proceedings. Nor is Plutarch any more convinced by the precise identification of a tomb of Themistocles in the Piraeus.[317]

Concerning Themistocles' remains Andocides, in his *Address to His Associates*, is not worthy of attention when he says that the Athenians, having stolen the remains [or, perhaps better, having searched for the stolen remains] scattered them indiscriminately, for he is lying to instigate the oligarchs against the people. Anyone would know that what Phylarchus writes is fiction because, just as in tragedy, he all but introduces stage machinery and brings on Neocles [who died when a boy] and Demopolis [a fictitious character?] as sons of Themistocles, in his desire to arouse pathos. And the account of Diodorus the Topographer in his work *On Tombs* is based upon conjecture rather than knowledge – namely that near the large harbour of the Piraeus a kind of elbow extends from the promontory of [or opposite] Alcimus and as one rounds this where the sea is calm there is a foundation of good size supporting an altar-like structure which is the tomb of Themistocles. Furthermore, Diodorus believes that the following lines by Plato the Comic poet offer proof for his identification:

> This your tomb raised up on a beautiful site all around
> will be a proclamation for merchants to proclaim.
> It will survey those sailing out and sailing in
> and witness whenever a contest of the ships occurs.

The last lines may refer to official boat-races held in the Piraeus, to ships in battle or merely vying in their course. Pausanias too reports that there was a grave of Themistocles beside the largest harbour of the Piraeus – perhaps the same structure as that identified by Diodorus.[318]

It is not clear to us from Diodorus (as quoted by Plutarch above) whether the monument that he describes as Themistocles' tomb belongs inside or outside of the main entrance to the Piraeus. The Alcimus which he mentions cannot be identified with certainty; it may very well be the point just opposite the tongue of land on the northern shore, called Eetioneia, but perhaps it is to be located elsewhere, e.g. further south.

Remains at various sites have been singled out in modern times as Themistocles' tomb.[319] Two of these are of particular significance (see Map I). One is located on Kavos Krakari on the north side of the harbour's entrance. Here, in 1897, the drums of two columns could be seen and a circular foundation, in the exact centre of which a hole had been dug in the rock. Inside this hole were found a marble burial cask and a little bone dust in the soil, indicating, significantly enough, that the burial was intended not for an entire corpse, but only for bones.

But perhaps the most likely site for the tomb is indicated by remains of a sepulchre on the opposite side of the entrance to the Piraeus, on the shore of the Acte peninsula near a bay just to the south (Pl. 34). This area today belongs to the Greek Naval Command, and access is difficult. In the last century A. Milch-höfer provided a description and it was not until the 1970s that Paul W. Wallace provided reports of his re-examination of the ruins.

Milchhöfer identified an area about 19 feet square levelled in the rock, within which were two small graves and a large one, and, just outside the enclosure, a large sepulchre hewn in the rock. The outer margin of the square was finished to a width of $2\frac{1}{2}$ feet, perhaps as a bed for a wall, part of an original sub-structure that could have been described by Diodorus as 'altar-like.'

When Wallace visited the tomb he found considerable modifications, due in large part to recent restoration. Of the graves mentioned by Milchhöfer only the large one within the structure (which was filled with water) could be seen. The tomb itself is now lined with two or three courses of ashlar blocks (some of which may be ancient?) and a modern inscription in Greek capitals records the name of Themistocles with his patronymic (misspelled) and his deme. To the south of the tomb there stands an unfluted column $c.$ 9 feet high, reconstructed in 1952 from seven column drums, presumably ancient.

It is tempting then to see here the remains of the structure (assuming there was only one) identified in antiquity, rightly or wrongly, as the tomb of Themistocles.[320] Certainly the site is

imposing and appropriate, looking as it does over the straits of
Salamis and Psyttaleia, the scene of his greatest triumph. The
structure would probably not have been built before 424, the
date of Thucydides' exile, since he does not mention the tomb;
perhaps in 395, when Conon rebuilt the walls of the Piraeus, the
time was ripe to erect a memorial to the great man. Certainly
by then his family and his reputation had been firmly reinstated
in Athens. Whether this tomb or any other in Attica bears any
relationship to the burial of tradition (secret at least originally)
must remain in doubt to all but the romantics.

It is fitting to conclude with the lines of Lord Byron which
were inspired by the sight of the ruins of this tomb, since they
so beautifully capture the heroic aura of the saga that very early
surrounded Themistocles and his achievement:[321]

> No breath of air to break the wave
> That rolls below the Athenian's grave,
> That tomb which, gleaming o'er the cliff,
> First greets the homeward-veering skiff,
> High o'er the land he saved in vain;
> Where shall such hero live again?

CHAPTER XIII

THE PORTRAITS OF A HERO[322]

By this time the character and actions of Themistocles will have become only too evident. His individuality and genius appear clearly enough in our sources but at the same time historical and mythological themes tended to make them become generic; and so both Themistocles the man and Themistocles the hero often were delineated as larger than life, with thematic elements of the supernatural, incredible and fantastic imaginatively invented as his legend grew. One has only to read Plutarch's biography of Themistocles to realize what a hodge-podge of fact and fiction eventually emerged to make up what may justifiably be called the Themistoclean saga. Because of his duplicity, versatility and ingenuity Themistocles appears both legitimately and imaginatively as a veritable Odysseus, with an Odyssey all his own on both sea and land, replete with real and fanciful dangers and itineraries.

I have concluded in Chapter IV that Herodotus' depiction is fundamental and penetrating. He gives Themistocles full credit for creating a significant Athenian navy, interpreting the 'wooden wall' of the oracle as a reference to the ships, and so on; at the same time he is extremely frank and critical of the more dubious side of Themistocles' nature – his lack of principles and greedy ambition. Herodotus interrupts his account of Xerxes' invasion to pay a sincere tribute to the Athenians. The context is as follows: The expedition of King Xerxes was nominally directed against Athens but in reality all the Hellenes were threatened. Some gave the required tokens of earth and water to the Persians and felt secure; others who did not comply were afraid because the number of Hellenic ships was inadequate and too many states, unwilling to participate in the war, were going over to the Persians (i.e. Medizing). It is here that Herodotus offers the following perceptive comments:[323]

At this point I am compelled to interject an opinion which will arouse the hostile jealousy of many; nevertheless, since it appears to me to be true, I shall not hold it back. If the Athenians, in fear of the approaching danger, had abandoned their country or if they had stayed and surrendered to Xerxes, no one would have attempted to oppose the King on the sea. Thus, if no one opposed Xerxes on the sea, the following would have happened on land. Even if the Peloponnesians built many lines of defence-walls across the Isthmus, the Spartans would have been abandoned by their allies, not of their own accord but of necessity, once city after city was captured by the Persian fleet. Thus the Spartans would have stood alone and in so doing would have displayed great deeds of valour and died nobly. Either they would have suffered so or before reaching such an extremity, as they saw the other Hellenes going over to the Persians, they would have made an agreement with Xerxes. Thus in either case Hellas would have fallen to the Persians. For I am unable to ascertain what the advantage would have been in building walls across the Isthmus, when the King had control of the sea. Now then, anyone who would say that the Athenians became the saviours of Hellas would not fall short of the truth; for they held the balance and whichever way they decided was bound to prevail. Having determined that Hellas was to remain free, they themselves were the ones who roused all the rest of the Hellenic world that had not Medized and they were the ones who were ultimately responsible, after the gods, for repulsing the King. Not even the frightening oracles that came from Delphi to strike terror in their hearts persuaded them to abandon Hellas, but they endured and stood firm to oppose the invader of their country.

In his account of Salamis that follows, Herodotus is perfectly aware of Themistocles' vital role, and if he may obscure or distort it in any way through error or prejudice, in the last analysis he does give him the credit that is his due. Thus, when he pays this honest tribute to the Athenians as the saviours of Hellas, he is also honouring the glorious achievement of Themistocles himself even though he does not name him directly in this context; I cannot believe that he is unaware of this fact.

It was the historian Thucydides who generically expressed the full implications of this obvious but inevitable conclusion with reference to Themistocles in particular: Themistocles by his intuitive genius was the saviour of not only Athens but all Hellas and with his naval programme initiated the potential for power that was to be fully exploited by Pericles and the Athenian maritime empire. Thucydides' assessment is to me particularly reminiscent of Herodotus who, after explaining that Themistocles had given the preferable interpretation of the oracle concerning the ships and Salamis, goes on to remark that 'on a previous occasion another opinion of Themistocles proved to be best at a critical moment', i.e. his naval proposal for the funds from Laurium. And so Thucydides, then, in a famous passage provides the most generic summary of the special qualities that made Themistocles a great statesman and victorious general:[324]

Themistocles was, in fact, one who gave the clearest and most positive evidence for the strength of his natural genius and in this respect above all he was more worthy of admiration than anyone else. For because of his native intelligence, without the help of previous or subsequent study, he was the keenest judge of an immediate situation after the briefest deliberation, and the best prophet of what would happen in the future in each particular event. He was able to communicate to others whatever he had in hand and he was no less successful in adequately sizing up anything that he had not yet experienced or undertaken. Most especially he foresaw in what was as yet unclear the better and the worse. To sum up, in the power of his natural genius and in the scant preparation that he required, he was the best at accomplishing intuitively what was necessary.

Lysias puts it most succinctly: 'Themistocles was brilliant in speech, perception and action' (ἱκανώτατον εἰπεῖν καὶ γνῶναι καὶ πρᾶξαι).[325]

Themistocles is very important for Thucydides' thematic manipulation of his material not only in Book 1 but throughout his *History*. For Thucydides, Themistocles is the precursor of Pericles and the greatness of the Athenian empire in both his policies and his statesmanship; thus Themistocles is given full credit for the creation of a significant Athenian navy and the victory at Salamis. Thucydides[326] makes the Athenians themselves explain to the Spartans the importance of Themistocles: when the safety of the Hellenes lay in their ships at Salamis they, the Athenians, contributed the largest number of vessels, the

most astute general and the keenest zeal; Themistocles as commander was the one most responsible for the battle being fought
in the straits and this strategy was their greatest salvation; for
this reason the Spartans themselves bestowed greater honours
on him than on any other visitor.

We have seen too how Thucydides appreciates Themistocles'
fortification of the Piraeus. All these policies, then, provided
the foundation for Periclean financial prosperity and imperialistic power. Thucydides perceives Themistocles as the fore-
runner of Pericles in his attributes of statesmanship. But in his
summary of Pericles' outstanding virtues in Book 2, 65.8 there
is one striking quality that is attributed to Pericles but noticeably
and rightfully absent in his assessment of Themistocles. Pericles
was exceptionally incorruptible and unsusceptible to bribery
(χρημάτων τε διαφανῶς ἀδωρότατος). This moral integrity of
Pericles was obviously important to Thucydides but he could
scarcely say the same about Themistocles, regardless of his
other virtues.

The excursuses on Themistocles and Pausanias in Book 1 also
afford rich and potent leitmotifs for Thucydides' *History*.[327]
Just as Athens and Sparta provide the basic duality and antithesis
upon which the structure of his work is built, so Themistocles
and Pausanias exemplify fundamental traits of their city-states
on an individual and personal level. Certainly Themistocles'
travels dramatically and vividly characterize a dynamic ingenuity, versatility and daring that belong both to him and to
Athens.

It is startling and impressive to realize to what extent Themistoclean motifs are among the most vital elements of Thucydidean thematic material. Themistocles' interest in the West,[328]
his antagonism to Corinth and his flight to the Corcyraeans as
their benefactor relate beautifully to the immediate issues in
Book 1 concerning the outbreak of the great Peloponnesian
War in 431. Thucydides' depiction of Themistocles, then, is
rich and complex; but in the last analysis I see his portrait as
complementary to that of Herodotus. They both really tell us
very much the same things. Thucydides, however, emphasizes

the generic and universal; Herodotus stresses specific and vital personal characteristics.

In the tradition later than the fifth century, Diodorus pretty well typifies by his portrait of Themistocles what is to become a standardized paean of adulation; after recounting Themistocles' flight and death he provides the following tribute:[329]

We have reached the death of a man who was the greatest of the Hellenes. Many are in dispute about him – whether he wronged his native Athens and the other Hellenes and fled to the Persians or whether on the contrary, both his city and all the Hellenes, having received great benefits because of him, forgot their debt of gratitude and unjustly drove their benefactor into the extremities of danger. But if anyone minutely scrutinizes, without envy, both the nature of the man and his deeds, he will find that Themistocles deserves, on both scores, to be placed first among all of whom we have record. Therefore one should rightfully be amazed if the Hellenes wished to deprive themselves of the natural genius of such a man.

What other person by his own actions deprived Sparta of that glory that was hers since she was superior in strength and a Spartan, Eurybiades, held supreme command of the fleet? What other person in history has by a single action made himself the superior of commanders, his Athens the superior of Hellenic cities and the Hellenes the superiors of the Persians? In whose generalship have resources ever been less or the dangers greater? Who else has conquered when stationed in defence of a city in exile against an entire power from Asia? Who by comparable actions in time of peace has made his native city so powerful? Who has saved his country when it was engulfed by the greatest of wars and through the single ruse involving the bridges of the Hellespont reduced the land force of the enemy by one half, with the result that they were easily conquered by the Hellenes? Therefore when we look at the magnitude of his deeds and examine each of them individually we find that he was dishonoured by his city when it was exalted because of his actions and in all fairness we must conclude that Athens, despite its great reputation for wisdom and justice, was most unreasonable and harsh in its actions against him. And so even if we have digressed at too great length about the virtues (arete) of Themistocles, it has been because, in our judgment, they are not worthy of being passed over in silence.

THE OSTIA PORTRAIT[330] (Pl. 35)

A portrait bust (or herm) inscribed with Themistocles' name

was discovered in 1939 near the ancient theatre at Ostia. Although the possibility always exists that the identification is erroneous, the consensus is that this likeness is intended, however faithfully, to represent Themistocles himself. Beyond this there is little or no general agreement among scholars. Many believe that it is a Roman copy from a Greek original, but the date of both the original and the extant bust and the accuracy of the depiction of the real Themistocles are very much in dispute. For some the Ostia portrait represents virtually a literal reproduction of a likeness of Themistocles made in his own lifetime. Stylistic elements of the rendering have been identified as characteristic of the period 480–450. Yet others are disturbed by the individuality of the features, which seems unusual and uncharacteristic for the idealized sculpture from this period as we know it; thus in adherence to a doctrine that claims such realism is anachronistic for the first half of the fifth century, they would place the original in the fourth century BC or the first century AD. Yet the style of the bust itself (with its inscription) has been said to belong in the second century AD; and the claim has even been made that it is in fact an original creation executed in the third century AD. Thus, on the authority of the specialists, the most that we can assert is that the Ostia portrait is probably late Roman, perhaps a copy of an original that goes back to the time of Themistocles. The question remains: does it represent in any way an authentic depiction from life?

Our ancient sources actually do mention likenesses of Themistocles known in antiquity:[331] a small portrait statue (εἰκόνιον) stood in the temple of Artemis Aristoboule, which depicted him as heroic in spirit and appearance; a monument or tomb in Magnesia was decorated with statues, or a statue, which may have represented Themistocles himself; a painting in the Parthenon, dedicated by his sons, included Themistocles; a painting is mentioned, which showed Themistocles speaking before the Persians; statues of Miltiades and Themistocles stood in the theatre of Dionysus at Athens, each with a captive Persian; and there were statues in the Athenian Prytaneion of Miltiades and Themistocles which had been renamed to designate a Roman and a Thracian. This latter reference lends dubious support to those who see in the Ostia portrait evidence of foreign traits that Themistocles is imagined to have inherited from his mother. But we can have no assurance that these (or any other depictions, however contemporary) provided the model for the extant bust.

Virtually every facet of Themistocles' personality has been discerned in this portrait by one viewer or another. It is said to convey admirably both specific and general characteristics – to sum up as it were both the individual and essential nature of the man as revealed by the tradition: his headstrong ambition, unscrupulous aggression, energetic strength, brutal determination, and so on. Perhaps all this and more are there, if one is determined to find them. Certainly it would be difficult to deny the striking individuality of the bust with its startling (and perhaps disturbing) lack of idealization. Let us believe, then, that it does in truth represent a faithful portrait of the essential Themistocles. Inspired by the ancient testimony – a splendid concatenation of fact and fiction in its recreation of the personality, character, life and career of a real man and legendary hero – each of us, in the last analysis, upon careful perusal of the features, expression and feeling of the Ostia bust, will interpret what he sees in the light of his own personal and individual response.

CHAPTER XIV

THE ANECDOTES: A HERO'S WIT

Themistocles' character and personality, as crystallized in the tradition, are perhaps most vividly illustrated by the numerous anecdotes that grew up around him. Plutarch, in a chapter of his *Life of Themistocles*, brings together many of them and in the *Moralia* he devotes a section to Themistocles in his collection of the *Sayings of Kings and Commanders*.[332] But these stories crop up everywhere in various contexts and they are important for the image of Themistocles that was developed. They afford as well a disconcerting reminder of the mythical tone inherent in our sources from the very beginning. Some are patently false but others, which appear early, may in essence be true. At any rate they confirm in general what we should suspect about Themistocles on the basis of other evidence: he possessed a sharp and ready tongue and a shrewd wit. Plutarch observes: 'Indeed Themistocles was by nature most enamoured of honour and distinction, if one may infer as much from his memorabilia.[333] Here then is a composite collection of typical Themistocleana, illustrating his many qualities and especially his perspicacity and humour; wherever necessary, I add my own explanatory comments.

1. Once when Themistocles was still a boy and he was returning from school, Peisistratus came towards him. Themistocles' tutor told the lad to step a little aside out of the road of the tyrant as he approached. Themistocles retorted with independent spirit: 'Isn't the road wide enough for him?' So even from childhood he revealed his nobility and spirit.[334] Since Peisistratus died in 528/7, this anecdote assumes Themistocles was born before 524.

2. When he was still a young man, Themistocles devoted himself to wine and pleasure; but after Miltiades as general won his victory at Marathon, one could never again find Themistocles

misbehaving. He became introspective and sleepless and refused to go to drinking parties. To those who were amazed at the change, Themistocles said: 'Miltiades' trophy of victory does not allow me to sleep or to be idle.'[335]

3. Themistocles was intemperate and unstable in the first flush of youth and gave vent to his natural impulses without any control. He later admitted this, claiming that the wildest colts become the best horses when they receive the proper training and discipline.[336]

4. Themistocles, who was, according to some, himself the son of a prostitute, in the wildness of his youth drove with a chariot full of prostitutes into the city one morning when there were crowds of people. The prostitutes' names were Lamia, Scione, Satyra and Nannion.[337]

5. Themistocles had to give up his extravagance when he was disinherited by his father, and his mother committed suicide because of his reputation. He abandoned his love-affairs and developed a different passion – one for Athenian politics. He feverishly campaigned for public offices and was most eager to gain first place for himself. As he explained to his acquaintances, he realized that he was worthless until he became great and famous: 'What would you give for a man like me who is not yet the object of envy?'[338] The sentiment that a man who seeks glory in reality courts envy, Aelian tells us, is reminiscent of a quotation from Euripides.

6. Themistocles fell in love with Antiphates, once a handsome youth who fled from his advances and treated him disdainfully in earlier days but who later, when Themistocles had acquired great reputation and power, courted and fawned upon him. 'My boy,' Themistocles said, 'it is late to be sure, but we have both finally come to our senses.'[339]

7. When he was chosen to be admiral (*nauarchos*) by the city, Themistocles did not carry out every item of his private and public affairs one at a time but he used to put off each duty as it

came along until the very day on which he was about to sail
so that, by doing many things at the same time and meeting
with all sorts of people, he might seem to be great and most
powerful.[340]

8.   Some maintained that Themistocles was eager to make
money because he needed a generous income to indulge his
fondness for lavish entertainment. Others, instead, accused him
of great stinginess, saying that he would even sell provisions
sent to him as gifts. Once a horse-breeder named Philides was
asked by Themistocles for a colt. Philides refused and Themistocles threatened to turn his home into a wooden horse, darkly
intimating by this that he would stir up accusations and lawsuits
between Philides and his relatives.[341]

9.   When Simonides or someone else promised to teach him
the art of remembering, Themistocles replied: 'I should prefer
the art of forgetting, for I remember even what I do not want
to remember, but I am unable to forget what I want to forget.'[342]

10.   Themistocles once jokingly said to Simonides that it was
senselessly inconsistent of him to malign the Corinthians, who
inhabited a great city, while he had portrait statues made of
himself, who was so ugly.[343] The reference is to a comment
made by Simonides in one of his poems (no longer extant),
which was interpreted by the Corinthians as an insult.

11.   Indeed Themistocles got along well with the people
because he could address from memory each of the citizens by
name and because he offered himself as a dependable arbitrator
in disputes concerning private contracts. Once when Themistocles was general he told Simonides of Ceos who had asked as
a favour for something that was not proper, that just as Simonides
would not be a good poet if he sang contrary to the rules of
poetry, so he (Themistocles) would not be a useful official if he
granted his request contrary to law.[344]

12.   Plutarch records the preceding anecdote in his *Life of
Themistocles*. Yet in his *Life of Aristeides*, despite the contradiction,

he tells the following story in order to pit an unscrupulous Themistocles and his party against Aristeides the Just, who followed a private path of virtuous statesmanship: When Themistocles joined a political group of friends he acquired considerable security and power. And so when someone remarked that he would govern the Athenians well, provided he were fair and impartial to everyone, Themistocles retorted: 'May I never sit on a tribunal where my friends will receive from me no advantage at all over complete strangers.'[345]

13. At the conference in which Themistocles urged that the Greeks ought to remain at Salamis and face the Persians he was so eager that he broke into a long, passionate speech as soon as the meeting took place, even before the Spartan commander-in-chief of all the forces, Eurybiades, could announce its purpose. Themistocles was finally interrupted by Adeimantus, the son of Ocytus, commander of the Corinthian contingent (or, according to some, by Eurybiades himself), who said: 'Themistocles, in the games, those who start too soon get whipped.' 'Yes,' Themistocles retorted in self-defence, 'but those who start too late are not crowned as winners.'[346]

14. After the exchange related above Eurybiades raised his staff to strike Themistocles, who exclaimed: 'Go ahead and strike but listen me!' Eurybiades was amazed at Themistocles' control and ordered him to speak.[347]

15. The Corinthian general Adeimantus again attacked Themistocles as he argued for battle at Salamis and this time Themistocles was more vehement in his response. Adeimantus commanded Themistocles, as one who had no city, to be silent and he forbade Eurybiades to put a question raised by a man without a country to the vote; for he ordered Themistocles to name the city that he represented before he offered any opinion. Adeimantus made these jibes because the city of Athens had been captured and was being held by the enemy. Thereupon Themistocles did indeed pour out many bitter abuses upon both Adeimantus and the Corinthians and he made it quite clear that

the Athenians, as long as they possessed two hundred ships fully manned, had a city and a country greater than theirs and none of the Hellenes could withstand their attack.[348]

16.   In his eloquent plea that the Hellenes should remain at Salamis and fight there because of the many advantages in such a course of action and because an oracle promised victory, Themistocles observed: 'Success is generally sure to follow those who make the proper plans; but not even god is on the side of those who do not.'[349]

17.   Again at this same conference, when an Eretrian attempted to offer some argument against him, Themistocles remarked in jest: 'Indeed, what argument can you Eretrians offer about war, who like cuttle-fish have a pouch or a sword but no heart.'[350] This retort, obscure to us, seems to refer to the greed and lack of patriotism of the Eretrians, some of whom betrayed their city to the Persians in 490. The 'bone' or funnel-like pouch of the cuttle-fish, which was called a 'sword', was believed to take the place of an embryonic heart; the cuttle- or ink-fish was easily thought of as all 'sword-funnel' and no heart.

18.   After their victory against the Persians, the Athenians established the custom of having a public cock-fight in the theatre for one day each year as a memorial and incentive to grave actions. When Themistocles led out the forces of the city against the Persians he noticed some cocks fighting. He paused over the sight and brought his soldiers to a halt and said to them: 'These cocks suffer and fight not for fatherland or national gods or ancestral tombs or reputations or freedom or children but so that each may not be beaten or one give in to the other.' With these words he gave the Athenians courage.[351]

19.   After the battle, as he was looking at the corpses of the Persians cast up along the sea, Themistocles noticed that they wore gold on their arms and around their necks. He himself passed them by but pointed them out to a friend who was following and said: 'Go ahead and help yourself; after all, you are not Themistocles.'[352] This anecdote is told to illustrate

Themistocles' haughty pride or his thoughtfulness in helping less fortunate friends.

20.   After Salamis, the Spartans bestowed extraordinary honours upon Themistocles. When he returned to Athens, Timodemus, a fellow Athenian from Aphidna(e), who was not among the famous and was insanely jealous, taunted Themistocles about his visit to Sparta and claimed that he received such honours from the Spartans because of Athens and not because of himself. Since Timodemus was endless in his abuse, Themistocles replied: 'You are right; if I were from the little island of Belbina I should not have been honoured so by the Spartans nor would you, my fellow, even though you are, like me, an Athenian.' Later writers change the double edge of this Herodotean version of the anecdote (Themistocles and Timodemus are both Athenian) by having Themistocles' assailant come from Seriphus, as follows: When a man from Seriphus told Themistocles that he had acquired his fame not because of himself but because of his city, Themistocles replied: 'What you say is true but, if I were from Seriphus, I should not have become famous nor would you, if you were an Athenian.'[353]

21.   Themistocles is said to have ridiculed Aristeides about the praise he was receiving for his able assessment of the tribute – i.e. income from the members of the Delian Confederacy. 'Such praise,' Themistocles jeered, 'is more fitting for a money-bag than for a man.'[354]

22.   At the next Olympic festival celebrated after the great honours that the Spartans had conferred on Themistocles, the following incident is said to have taken place: When Themistocles came into the stadium the audience looked at him the whole day and paid no attention to the contestants, while pointing him out to strangers with both admiration and applause. And so he also was pleased and admitted to friends that he was reaping in full the fruit of his labours on behalf of Hellas. When someone once asked Themistocles what pleased him most in his life, he replied: 'Seeing the audience at the

Olympic games turning to look at me as I entered the stadium.'[355]

23.   When the Sicilian tyrant Hieron sent horses to compete at Olympia and constructed quarters of some kind that were expensively decked out, Themistocles delivered a speech among the Hellenes telling them they must detroy the quarters of the tyrant and stop his horses from competing. He explained that a man like Hieron, who had not helped the Hellenes against the Persians and participated in the greatest of their crises, should not be allowed to take part in their national festivals.[356]

24.   When Themistocles fell into disfavour with the Athenians he once said to those who were hostile to him because he was compelled to keep reminding the people of his own achievements: 'Why do you grow weary of being benefitted again and again by the same men?'[357]

25.   A fellow general of Themistocles or certain generals who were successful after him thought that they had conferred some benefit upon the city and boldly compared their services to those of Themistocles himself. And so he told this story: The Day-After had a quarrel with the Festival-Day, claiming that the Festival-Day was full of wearisome occupations but on the Day-After everyone could enjoy at his leisure what had been prepared. To this the Festival-Day replied: 'You speak the truth but, if I had not come first, you would not have come at all.' 'And so,' Themistocles concluded, 'if I had not first saved the city against the Persians, where or of what service would you generals be now?'[358]

26.   Once when the Athenians impeached him and then called him back to power Themistocles exclaimed: 'I do not admire the sort of men who use the same vessel as a chamber pot and a wine-pitcher.'[359]

27.   Themistocles said that the Athenians did not really honour or admire him but used him as they would a wide-spreading plane-tree, under which they ran for protection in the danger of a storm but at which they tore and plucked as they went by, when the weather was fair.[360]

28. Themistocles was accustomed to remark: 'If someone were to show me two roads, one leading to Hades and the other to the speaker's platform, I should rather take the one straight to Hades.'[361]

29. When Themistocles was taunted by those reputed to be educated for his limitations in refined and polite accomplishments, he felt compelled to defend himself rather brazenly as follows: Although he did not know how to sing or tune a lyre or play the harp, he could take hold of a small and inglorious city and make it great and glorious and rich.[362]

30. When Themistocles first had an audience with the great King after he arrived in Persia, he did not know the Persian language and was dependent upon interpreters. Because he wished to communicate with the King directly, Themistocles asked for time to learn Persian, explaining that speech was similar to embroideries with their patterns, for, like them, it too revealed its figures only when fully extended, but when rolled up or compressed its intricacies were hidden or lost. The King granted his appeal.[363]

31. While he was in exile, Themistocles became great and rich because of the generosity of the King of Persia and he was courted by many. Once, when a magnificent table was set out for him, he said to his children: 'If we had not been ruined, my children, we should indeed have been ruined.'[364] Exile had, as it were, turned out to be their salvation.

32. After Themistocles had built a very beautiful dining room (τρίκλινον) with three couches which would accommodate only nine persons, he exclaimed, 'I should be very happy indeed if I could fill it with friends.'[365] It is not clear whether or not this incident is supposed to belong to his period of residence as an exile in Magnesia.

33. About his son, who manipulated his mother and through her himself, he jokingly remarked that, of all the Hellenes, the boy held the greatest power; for the Athenians ruled the Hellenes, Themistocles himself ruled the Athenians and was

ruled by the boy's mother, who in turn was ruled by the boy.[366]

34.   Of the suitors for the hand of his daughter, he chose the man of promise over the man of wealth, saying: 'Indeed I prefer a man without money rather than money without a man.'[367]

35.   Wishing to be an individualist in everything, when he put up a plot of his land for sale he ordered it to be announced that an excellent neighbour came along with it.[368]

36.   When someone asked Themistocles whether he would rather have been Achilles or Homer, he replied: 'How about yourself? Who would you rather be, the victor or the herald of the victors at the Olympic games?'[369]

37.   They say that the most renowned Athenian Themistocles, when asked whose voice he listened to with the most pleasure, answered: 'The voice of the one who best celebrates my excellence (*virtus*).'[370]

CHRONOLOGICAL FRAMEWORK FOR
THEMISTOCLES' CAREER

561/0	Peisistratus' First Tyranny
528/7	Death of Peisistratus
*c.***524**	Birth of Themistocles
514/13	Murder of Hipparchus
521	Accession of Darius
511/10	Expulsion of Hippias
508/7	Cleisthenes' initiation of democratic reforms
499	Outbreak of the Ionian Revolt
496/5	Archonship of Hipparchus
494	Fall of Miletus
493/2	Archonship of Themistocles
490	Battle of Marathon; generalship of Miltiades
489/8	Archonship of Aristeides
488/7	Ostracism of Hipparchus
487/6	Ostracism of Megacles; reform of the archonship
486/5	Ostracism of Callias (?); accession of Xerxes
485/4	Ostracism of Xanthippus
483/2	Themistocles' Naval Bill; ostracism of Aristeides
480	Battles of Thermopylae, Artemisium and Salamis; generalship of Themistocles
479	Battles of Plataea and Mycale
478/7	The fortification of Athens; organization of the Delian Confederacy
477/6	Completion of the fortification of the Piraeus
476	Phrynichus, *The Phoenician Women, Persians, Sack of Miletus* (?); Themistocles *choregos*
*c.***476/5**	Themistocles' first trial?
474–471/0	Themistocles' ostracism
472	Aeschylus, *Persians*; Pericles *choregos*
471/0–465	Death of Pausanias; flight of Themistocles; siege of Naxos
465/4	Siege of Thasos; accession of Artaxerxes
*c.***463**	Themistocles' encounter with Artaxerxes
*c.***459**	Death of Themistocles

NOTES

CHAPTER I

1 E. Badian ('Archons and *Strategoi*', *Antichthon* 5 [1971], pp. 1–34) quite rightly cautions against the hazards of historical reconstruction based upon meagre and problematical evidence. But undaunted (like us all) he proceeds to construct his own reasoned hypotheses.

2 Aristotle *Poetics* 9 (1451a.36–1451b).

3 Cf. the discussion by C. Hignett, *Xerxes' Invasion of Greece* (Oxford, 1963), 'Prolegomena,' especially p. 25.

4 The critical survey of the evidence by Podlecki (*Themistocles*) bears ample testimony to the obvious and subtle fiction inherent in the tradition. For the characteristics of the various facets of mythological invention see Mark P. O. Morford and Robert J. Lenardon, *Classical Mythology* (New York, 2nd ed. 1977), pp. 1–17 and 283–6.

CHAPTER II

5 Plutarch *Them.* 1.1. For discussion of Themistocles' family with full bibliography see J. Kirchner, *Prosopographia Attica*, 6669 (Berlin, 1901), pp. 431–5; Bauer (rev. Frost), *Themistokles*, pp. 123–34; Davies, *Propertied Families*, pp. 217–20; Podlecki, *Themistocles*, pp. 1–3, 205–7.

6 Cf. Plutarch *Them.* 25.3 and *Arist. and Cato* 1.4: Themistocles' family was not illustrious (λαμπρός) and of moderate possessions (he was said to have been worth three or at most five talents when he first entered politics). I take this to confirm the political obscurity of the family, which was well enough off, if not among the richest, or among the very highest social élite (καλοί). See also Aelian *V.H.* 10.17, quoting Critias.

7 Plutarch *Them.* 1.3. The reconstruction of the chapel may be merely a political move by Themistocles to link his name to that of the Lycomidae but in the face of all the evidence we must assume Plutarch's inference to be correct.

8 Pausanias 1.22.7 and 4.1.5–7. Also inscriptional evidence from the second century B C seems to indicate that descendants of Themistocles were related to the Kerykes, one of the priestly families at Eleusis.

9 Plutarch *Them.* 22.2 and below, p. 101.

10 See Frank J. Frost, 'Themistocles' Place in Athenian Politics', *California Studies in Classical Antiquity* 1 (1968), pp. 105–24; e.g. Themistocles' family interests were perhaps mining or agriculture and he kept a home in Athens to escape the remoteness of his isolated deme of Phrearrhioi.

11 Epistle 1, below, p. 156; Nepos *Them.* 1.2. I doubt that we can deduce anything historical from the fact that Neocles means 'New Fame'.

12 Plutarch *Them.* 1.1. Athenaeus 13 (p. 576C), quoting Amphicrates, and the *Palatine Anthology* 7.306 provide variations of this invented epitaph for Abrotonon or Habrotonon.

13 Nepos *Them.* 1.2. I suppose this is what *uxorem Acarnanam civem duxit* must mean. The similarity between Carian, Halicarnassian, and Acarnanian suggests corruption of a single, original tradition; see Davies, *Propertied Families*, p. 213. If, in Nepos' text we should perhaps read 'Acharnian' for 'Acarnanian', Themistocles' mother would indeed be Athenian.

14 Athenaeus, *loc. cit.*; Plutarch *Amat.* 9 (*Moralia* 753D); Menander *Epitrepontes* and *Perikeiromene*.

15 Plutarch *Them.* 1.2. Suidas, *s.v.* Κυνόσαργες, says that those who were true aliens (νόθοι, i.e. both their parents were non-Athenians) exercised at Cynosarges. See S. C. Humphreys, The *Nothoi* of Kynosarges, *Journal of Hellenic Studies* 94 (1974), pp. 88–95.

16 See below, p. 36.

17 Plutarch *Paral. Graec. et Rom.* (*Moralia* 305D–E).

18 Plutarch *Them.* 2 and 5.

19 Herodotus 8.57 translated below, p. 72; Plutarch *Them.* 2.4 links Mnesiphilus to Solon and comments on the difference between them and the later Sophists who turned to forensic techniques and language; see also *Sept. Sap. Conviv.* (*Moralia* 154C and 156B).

20 Plutarch, *An Seni* (*Moralia* 795G); Frank J. Frost, 'Themistocles and Mnesiphilus', *Historia* 20 (1971), pp. 20–5.

21 Plutarch *Them.* 5.1–2; in this context we find the anecdote about Philides the horse-breeder, no. 8, below, p. 216.

22 Plutarch *Them.* 5.2.

23 The basic information for Themistocles' wives and children comes from Plutarch *Them.* 32.1–2. Important persons are identified from the deme Alopeke, including Alcmaeonid nobles, and it has been conjectured that Themistocles' marriage indicates financial, political and social improvement; Frost, *op. cit.* (note 10 above), p. 113 and P. J. Bicknell, *Studies in Athenian Politics and Genealogy* (*Historia*, Einzelschriften 19, 1972), p. 62.

24 Diodorus 11.57; see below, p. 146.

25 See below, p. 149.

26 Suidas, *s.v.* θεμιστοκλέους παῖδες; see also Plutarch *Them.* 32.3 and below, p. 204. Pausanias 1.37.1 mentions a Poliarchus, who may be yet another son of Themistocles, or his son-in-law; see Davies, *Propertied Families*, p. 218.

27 Plutarch *Them.* 30 and below, p. 147.

28 E. Badian ('Archons and Strategoi', *Antichthon* 5 [1971], p. 34) has suggested that the archon for 460/59 Phrasicles or Phrasicleides was Themistocles' nephew; and that the archon for 483/2 was Nicomedes, Themistocles' son-in-law; but that archon's name may have been Nicodemus, not Nicomedes. See Podlecki, *Themistocles*, p. 206.

29 One of Themistocles' daughters (perhaps Italia?) is referred to as a foreigner or alien: Suidas, *s.v.* Athenaias; Podlecki, *Themistocles*, pp. 55–6 quoting Ion (F11) with Jacoby's comments. In Epistle 4 a daughter of Themistocles is betrothed to Lysicles, son of Habronichus; see below, p. 162 with note 271. As in the case of Themistocles' marriages, the evidence permits no certainty about the dates of the births of his children. Davies (*Propertied Families*, pp. 217–18) suggests for his daughters that: Mnesiptolema was born very soon after 480; Nicomache and Asia after 475; and Italia and Sybaris need not be born *c.* 480 merely because of Themistocles' threat to deport the Athenians to Siris (Herodotus 3.62, translated below, p. 74).

30 For the evidence and the problems see Robert J. Lenardon, 'The Archonship of Themistocles, 493/2', *Historia* 5 (1956), pp. 413–15; Davies, *Propertied Families*, p. 214; and below, p. 200.

31 Margaret Thompson, *The New Style Silver Coinage of Athens* (New York, 1961), pp. 221–6, 568, 604 and plates 62–3; Bauer (rev. Frost), *Themistokles*, p. 134 and plate 6.

32 Plutarch *Them.* 32.5, *Quaest. Conviv.* 1.9 (*Moralia* 626E).

CHAPTER III

33 For a more thorough survey see any of the general histories of Greece listed in the bibliography. C. Hignett, *A History of the Athenian Constitution* (Oxford, 1952) offers a scholarly analysis of the innumerable problems; amidst the fragmented and obscure evidence, Aristotle's account of the Athenian constitution (*Ath. Pol.*) is basic. My object is to isolate information vital for understanding my detailed study of Themistocles' life.

34 See below, pp. 120f.

35 For the evidence and fuller discussion see Eugene Vanderpool, *Ostracism at Athens, Lectures in Memory of Louise Taft Semple* (Cincinnati, 1970) and Podlecki, *Themistocles*, pp. 185–94.

36 Aristotle *Ath. Pol.* 22.4.

37 Plutarch *Arist.* 7.5.

38 Herodotus is our major source for the growth of the Persian Empire, the Ionian Revolt and the wars between the Persians and the Hellenes. Any of the histories of Greece and the Persian Wars listed in the bibliography will provide more lengthy treatment.

39 Dionysius of Halicarnassus, *Ant. Rom.* 6.34.1. For a lengthy discussion of the problematical evidence see Robert J. Lenardon, 'The Archonship of Themistocles', *Historia* 5 (1956), pp. 402–19. I still believe that Thucydides 1.93.3 (translated below p. 89 with note 128), when he tells us in the context of the building of the walls after Salamis about Themistocles' earlier beginning of the fortification, is most likely referring to the archonship, whether or not he had a specific date in mind. But the Greek is ambiguous.

40 See Alden A. Mosshammer, 'Themistocles' Archonship in the Chronographic Tradition', *Hermes* 103 (1975), pp. 222–34, who argues convincingly that the archon date 493/2 for Themistocles, with the notice of the beginning of the fortification of the Piraeus, goes back to Hellanicus. But there is no compulsion to believe that Hellanicus was necessarily in error and that Thucydides' reference (see note 39 above) was intended to correct Hellanicus. When Herodotus, 6.116 (cf. 8.66), mentions the Persian fleet off Phalerum in 490, he states: 'At that time this was the port of the Athenians.'

41 N. G. L. Hammond, 'Studies in Greek Chronology of the Sixth and Fifth Centuries BC', *Historia* 4 (1955), pp. 406–11, distinguishes three chronological phases in the war between Athens and Aegina: 505; 491–490; and 483/2–482/1.

42 Herodotus 6.104.

43 Plutarch *Them.* 4. I follow the cogent suggestions of Erich S. Gruen, 'Stesimbrotus on Miltiades and Themistocles', *California Studies in Classical Antiquity* 3 (1970), pp. 91–8. My reconstruction of a temporary alliance between Themistocles and Miltiades in 493/2 (Lenardon, *op. cit.*, p. 411) I now consider extremely hypothetical. Miltiades, however, will have his own naval policy after Marathon. It is possible that the contrast between a hoplite Miltiades and a naval Themistocles at any time is artificial and erroneous.

44 See Herodotus 6.21 and below, pp. 105f. The dating of *The Sack of Miletus* in the period of Themistocles' archonship has by its general acceptance almost become a 'fact'. But E. Badian, for example, suggests the early years of the Delian league: 'Archons and Strategoi', *Antichthon* 5 (1971), pp. 15–16 with note 44.

45 A. Diamantopoulos, 'The Danaid Tetralogy of Aeschylus', *Journal of Hellenic Studies* 77 (1957), pp. 220–9. Phrynichus also is said to have written a *Δαναίδες*!

46 For the numerous theories see A. F. Garvie, *Aeschylus' Suppliants: Play and Trilogy* (Cambridge, 1969), especially pp. 1–28 and 141–62, and A. J. Podlecki, *The Political Background of Aeschylean Tragedy* (Ann Arbor, 1966), pp. 42–62.

47 Plutarch (*Them.* 6.2–3) tells us that, when the King of Persia sent envoys to Athens to demand earth and water, Themistocles had the interpreter of the group arrested and put to death; also through Themistocles' effort, Arthmius of Zeleia with his family was proscribed because of pro-Persian dealings. There is a question about whether or not the Persian King was Xerxes (as Plutarch's context implies) or Darius (as other evidence indicates); thus these events may belong in the 490s before Marathon, perhaps in the very year of Themistocles' archonship, rather than in the 480s before Salamis. See Lenardon, *op. cit.*, pp. 410–11.

48 See anecdotes 11 (with note 344) and 12, below, p. 216.

49 See below, pp. 147f.

50 See below, pp. 128–131; Nepos (*Them.* 2.1–3) relates that the first step in Themistocles' career was his election by the people to carry on a war with Corcyra; he persuaded the Athenians to build a fleet with revenues from the mines, subdued the Corcyraeans and then made the sea safe from pirates! But Nepos must be in error; the context suggests the reference should be to the war with Aegina, despite the credulity of Peter Green, *Xerxes at Salamis* (New York, 1970) = *The Year of Salamis 480–479 BC* (London, 1970), note on pp. 25–6.

51 Herodotus (7.32 and 133) specifi-

cally states that Xerxes sent no heralds to Athens and Sparta because those sent by Darius had been murdered. Cf. note 47 above.

52 Herodotus 6.95.

53 See A. R. Burn, *Persia and the Greeks* (New York, 1962), p. 241.

54 Herodotus 6.102–15.

55 Herodotus 6.117.

56 Herodotus 6.121.

57 Plutarch *Arist.* 5.3.

58 Plutarch *Arist.* 5.1–3.

59 Herodotus 6.132–6.

CHAPTER IV

60 Plutarch *Them.* 3–4.1. See also anecdote 5, below, p. 215.

61 Aristotle *Ath. Pol.* 22.4–7.

62 For the evidence of the *ostraka* with fuller bibliography and discussion see Eugene Vanderpool, *Ostracism at Athens, Lectures in Memory of Louise Taft Semple* (Cincinnati, 1970) and Podlecki, *Themistocles*, pp. 185–94.

63 See Podlecki, *Themistocles*, pp. 187–8 with notes 13 and 14. I offer the most reasonable and generally accepted chronological interpretation of Aristotle's difficult text. It is possible, however, that Hipparchus' ostracism belongs in 487/6 and that of Aristeides, discussed below, in 484/3.

64 Podlecki, *Themistocles*, p. 194.

65 A few *ostraka* belong to another Hippocrates, the son of Anaxileos, who also may be an Alcmaeonid.

66 The deme of Myronides Phlyeus, who is named on the *ostraka*, suggests that he may have belonged to a branch of the Lycomid family of Themistocles.

67 For a stimulating and iconoclastic review of various theories about the reform, this period, and Themistocles' career see E. Badian, 'Archons and Strategoi', *Antichthon* 5 (1971), pp. 1–34.

68 Aristotle *Ath. Pol.* 22.2.

69 Herodotus (6.109) in his account

of Marathon must be in error when he maintains that Callimachus was appointed Polemarch by lot.

70 For an exhaustive study of this topic see Jules Labarbe, *La Loi Navale de Thémistocle* (Paris, 1957); cf. also Podlecki, *Themistocles*, pp. 201–4.

71 Herodotus 7.143.

72 Herodotus 7.144. See also How and Wells, *Commentary* 1, pp. 185–6.

73 Thucydides 1.14.3.

74 Aristotle *Ath. Pol.* 22.7.

75 Plutarch *Them.* 4.1–2. It is perhaps a question whether the first sentence could mean 'when the Athenians were disposed to distribute the revenue' (πρόσοδον ἔθος...ἐχόντων ᾽Αθηναίων διανέμεσθαι); then subsequently Themistocles' proposal was that 'they must give up [their intention of] the distribution of this money'. But Nepos (*Them.* 2.1–3 and 8) probably reflects the same tradition as Plutarch, when he maintains that the public funds which came in were distributed annually at the time Themistocles made his proposal. Yet Nepos mistakenly has the new fleet used against Corcyra and pirates (instead of against Aegina). He goes on to add that one hundred more triremes were built once Themistocles convinced the Athenians in 480 that they should take to their ships. Thus the discrepancy between whether one or two hundred vessels were constructed becomes reconciled.

76 Actually Darius was succeeded by Xerxes in 486/5.

77 The other sources essentially reflect the versions of Herodotus, Thucydides, Aristotle and Plutarch, which I have quoted. For a collection of all the testimony pertinent to Themistocles' naval bill see Labarbe, *op. cit.*, pp. 10–17.

78 I do not think it likely that Herodotus implies that the dole had been going on for some time when he says that 'On this occasion Themistocles persuaded the Athenians to stop this distribution of money.'

79 Doubt has been cast on the curious details recorded by Aristotle in his version of the secrecy involved in Themistocles' suggestion to the assembly that one talent be lent to each of a hundred most wealthy Athenians. But we do not know the intricacies of the workings of Cleisthenic democracy; and the aristocratic dominance that Themistocles' move reflects need not be anachronistic. The nobles may have actually been the ones to realize most fully the dangers about which Themistocles warned and thus have been willing to co-operate. Cf. Podlecki, *Themistocles*, p. 202, who is suspicious and lists other parallels for the motif of secrecy, among them Diodorus' account (11.42) of Themistocles' intrigue concerning the fortification of the Piraeus; see below, pp. 93f.

80 P. E. Legrand in his text of Herodotus (Paris, 1952) goes so far as to insert ἐς before the numeral.

81 Labarbe, *op. cit.*, pp. 21–52.

82 As we have noted in the last chapter, Herodotus (6.132) says that the Athenians provided Cimon with a squadron of seventy ships.

83 Some scholars conjecture that Themistocles reformed the 'naucraries' that are believed on the basis of a fragment of Cleidemus to have been instituted by Cleisthenes; see Podlecki, *Themistocles*, p. 203 with n. 14.

84 Plutarch (*Arist.* 25.7) actually states that it was through Themistocles that Aristeides was ostracized.

85 Plutarch *Arist.* 2–4; see also anecdote 12, below, pp. 216f.

86 We cannot be sure what office or what year is intended. The whole story that follows smacks of fiction.

87 More exhaustive treatments will

be found in the Histories of Greece and the Persian Wars listed in the Bibliography. In general I follow Herodotus' account.

88 Herodotus 7.184–5.

89 Herodotus 7.173.2. Diodorus 11.2.5 names Synetus, not Evaenetus, as the Spartan commander.

90 Herodotus 8.1–2 and 14. A reinforcement of 53 Athenian ships arrived later; of the Athenian vessels, 127 were manned by Athenians and Plataeans, 20 by Chalcidians.

91 Plutarch *Them.* 6.1; cf. also *Reg. et Imp. Apoth. Them.* (*Moralia* 185A).

92 Herodotus 8.4–6. Plutarch (*Them.* 7.4) provides a dubious addition: according to Phanias, the Athenians also wanted to leave, but Themistocles forced the captain, Achiteles, to accept money to pay the crews and induce them to stay.

93 Herodotus 8.21–2.

94 Themistocles previously had called the captains together on the sea-shore of Euboea and disclosed to them only that he had a plan whereby he could win over worthy allies from the King. He suggested that in the meantime they should slaughter as many of the cattle of the Euboeans as they desired, since it was better that their own men rather than the enemy should have them; Herodotus 8.19–20.

95 Herodotus 7.140–1.

96 Herodotus 7.142–4.

97 The rampart may have been a wall of olive wood or a thorn hedge.

98 Herodotus 8.40 and 42.8.

99 Herodotus 8.41.

100 Plutarch *Them.* 10.1–4. The concluding sections (5 and 6) of this chapter describe in pitiful detail the evacuation of Athens with tearful farewells to loved ones and the sad abandonment of the aged.

101 A correction γενεάς by Madvig for γονέας, 'parents'.

102 Themistocles as an ex-archon would be a member of the Areopagus. Plutarch (*Them.* 10.4) quoting Cleidemus adds questionable details: Themistocles was responsible for the funds given to the naval force. As the Athenians were going down to the Piraeus, the Gorgon's head was missing from the statue of the goddess; Themistocles pretended to look for it and discovered an abundance of money hidden away that was used to provide for the crews.

103 I follow the text of A. Geoffrey Woodhead (*Supplementum Epigraphicum Graecum* 22 [1967], pp. 84–9; see also 18 [1962], pp. 56–8 and 245–7; and 25 [1971], p. 117). For a review of basic arguments and theories, see Podlecki, *Themistocles*, pp. 147–67. Bibliographies also may be found in M. Chambers, 'The Significance of the Themistocles Decree', *Philologus* 111 (1967), pp. 157–69 and L. Braccesi, *Il problema del Decreto di Temistocle*, Saggi di antichità (Bologna, 1968). In addition to Herodotus and Plutarch, Aelius Aristeides in the second century AD (Orations 13 and 46, ed. G. Dindorf [Leipzig, 1829], vol. 1, pp. 225–6 and vol. 2, p. 256) also offers parallels to the wording of the inscription. The earliest definite reference to a decree of Themistocles is given by Demosthenes, *On the False Embassy* (Oration 19.303), in the year 343. Arguments for or against the decree have thus far been inconclusive. The prescript, for example, offers no designation of date, in the manner of later inscriptions (e.g. the name of the eponymous archon or the tribe in prytany with its secretary and president); but it appears that epigraphical headings were not necessarily formalized until later in the century. Arguments about words or expressions that to some appear suspicious and anachronistic (e.g. the

epithet Almighty [*Pankrates*] for Zeus)
are equally tenuous because of the
limitations in our knowledge of contemporary religious terminology and
practice. The specific and detailed
instructions for embarkation have also
been questioned; but they need not be
too complex for the structure of the
early (rather than the later) Athenian
democracy. Difficult questions also are
concerned with when and under what
circumstances the decree was first
committed to stone and how and where
it was preserved; and, if it is not
authentic, the motive and context for
the forgery are also problematical.
Finally, as my discussion readily dis-
closes, the discrepancies between the
text of the decree and our literary
sources, especially Herodotus, have to
be accounted for; and it must be
admitted that any reconciliation must
remain hypothetical.

104 Who are meant by the *hyperesiai*
is uncertain; trained sailors or rowers,
petty officers and slaves have been
suggested.

105 See above, note 90.

106 See above, note 74.

107 Herodotus 8.56–63.

108 Plutarch (*Them.* 12.1) in his
account of these events relates that an
owl was said by some to have flown
through the fleet from the right and
alighted on the rigging of Themistocles'
ship. As a result of this omen, Themistocles' arguments became all the more
convincing.

109 Herodotus 8.74–5.

110 Plutarch (*Them.* 12.3–4) says that
Sicinnus was a Persian prisoner of war,
devoted to Themistocles and pedagogue of his children; and he adds that
Xerxes accepted the message with
delight since he took it as delivered
out of good will towards him.

111 Herodotus 8.78–82.

112 Herodotus 8.83.

113 Herodotus 8.92. Polycritus seems
to refer to accusations of Medism made
in 491 against the Aeginetans and his
own father Crius (Herodotus 6.49–50,
73 and 85); if his reproach then is
directed at Themistocles personally, it
may perhaps provide further evidence
for Themistocles' career in the 490s.

114 Plutarch *Them.* 14.2–3. It has
been observed that the sea-breeze
would not rise until late forenoon; but
the battle would have begun at daybreak. See Perrin, *Plut. Them. and
Arist.*, p. 212.

115 Plutarch *Them.* 13.2, *Arist.* 9.0
and *Pelopidas* 21.

116 Diodorus (11.12, 15–18 *passim*)
in his account of Themistocles' role in
the second Persian War provides
nothing of value to add to Herodotus
and Plutarch. Cf. Podlecki, *Themistocles*, p. 94.

117 The identification of Psyttaleia,
for example, has been keenly disputed;
I should think that it is the island,
Lipsokoutali, at the entrance of the
straits, rather than St George, within
the narrows. There can be no doubt
that the Persian fleet far outnumbered
the Hellenic, and the special capabilities
of each were different. Thus the
Hellenic strategy (for which Themistocles seems to have been primarily
responsible) was to employ their
smaller number of ships to the best
advantage. Hellenic triremes were low
and heavy, and they were particularly
able to ram an enemy ship broadside;
whereupon, heavily armed marines
would be ready to board and fight
with sword and spear. The Persians'
vessels, on the other hand, were
generally larger and faster, and would
bear down on a Hellenic ship and
shower arrows and javelins from their
higher decks.

118 Herodotus 8.108–12.

119 Pausanias (10.14.5–6) tells a

questionable story about how Themistocles came to Delphi to dedicate
some of the Persian spoils to Apollo,
and the Priestess refused to accept his
offerings. One of the reasons given is
that Apollo, knowing that Themistocles
would some day seek refuge with the
Persians, did not wish to jeopardize his
future position.
120 Herodotus 8.123–4.
121 See anecdote 20, below, p. 219.
A trophy of Themistocles was set up on
Salamis in honour of the battle; Plato
Menexenus 245a; Pausanias 1.36.1 and
I.G. II² 1035, 1.33. For the identification of the site of this trophy see Paul
W. Wallace, 'Psyttaleia and the
Trophies of Salamis', *American Journal
of Archaeology* 73 (1969), pp. 299–302.
122 See below, pp. 137–191; Nepos
Them. 9.3 (following Thucydides?)
also makes no mention of this first
message in the letter to Artaxerxes.
123 Plutarch *Them.* 16 and *Arist.* 9.3.
124 Podlecki (*Themistocles*, pp. 67–72)
represents the consensus of opinion.

CHAPTER V

125 Thucydides 1.89.3–93.2.
126 Namely Salamis, Aegina and
Troezen (Herodotus 8.41.1).
127 For Themistocles' great reception
at Sparta about a year before see above,
p. 82.
128 Thucydides may refer to Themistocles' archonship, generalship, or
some other office, or more generally
to the period of his earlier political
dominance.
129 A much discussed sentence,
which some believe to be a later
insertion in the text; the meaning
seems to be that the wall was wide
enough for the passage of two chariots.
I follow Gomme, *Commentary* I, p. 263.
130 Diodorus 11.39.1–40.4 and 41.1–
43.3.

131 Cf. Gomme, *Commentary* I, p.
258; Podlecki, *Themistocles*, pp. 95–6
and 202. The motif of secrecy appears
elsewhere, e.g. in Aristotle's version
(*Ath. Pol.* 22.7) of Themistocles' proposal for the building of a fleet.
132 Plutarch *Them.* 19.
133 Andocides 3.38 in a speech delivered in 393 also suggests bribery
when he says that the Athenians built
their walls without the knowledge of
the Spartans and bought from them
immunity from punishment.
134 Aristophanes *Knights* 814ff.; cf.
Plato *Laws* 4.706.
135 Compare the story of Polycritus
the Aeginetan who encountered Themistocles at the battle of Salamis (Herodotus 8.92, above, p. 77). But should
one go so far as to emend Plutarch's
Polyarchus to Polycritus?
136 See below, pp. 159, 161, 184ff.
137 Plutarch *Reg. et Imp. Apoth.
Arist.* 3 (*Moralia* 186B) and *Praec. Reip.
Ger.* 14 (*Moralia* 809B); Suidas *s.v.*
Aristeides; Polyaenus, *Strat.* 1.31. Cf.
also Herodotus 8.79 and Plutarch
Arist. 8.3.
138 See Travlos, *Pictorial Dictionary*,
pp. 158–63; Gomme, *Commentary* I,
pp. 261–9; and Podlecki, *Themistocles*,
pp. 179–83.
139 The dedicatory epigram for the
building of the walls in the Piraeus
preserved by Harpocration (*s.v.* πρὸς
τῇ πυλίδι Ἑρμῆς) affords no help in
dating the construction or Themistocles' archonship.

CHAPTER VI

140 See Podlecki, *Themistocles*, p. 35.
141 See Robert J. Lenardon, 'The
Chronology of Themistocles' Ostracism and Exile', *Historia* 8 (1959), pp.
23–48.
142 Herodotus 8.123–225 and above,
p. 81.

143 Plutarch *Them.* 21.1.

144 Anecdote 20, below, p. 219.

145 Diodorus 11.26.2–3.

146 See below, pp. 174f. Some later accounts have Athens and Themistocles winning the prizes for valour, e.g. Aelius Aristeides *Panathenaicus* sec. 18.

147 Plutarch *Them.* 20.3–4.

148 Plutarch *Them.* 20.1–2; *Arist.* 22.2; Cicero, *De Off.* 3.11.49 presents a dubious variation: Themistocles proposed to burn the Spartan fleet at Gytheum.

149 E.g. A. J. Podlecki, 'Cimon, Skyros, and "Theseus' Bones",' *Journal of Hellenic Studies* 91 (1971), pp. 141–3.

150 Plutarch *Them.* 1.3 and above, p. 18.

151 Plutarch *Them.* 22.1–2 and *De Hdt. Mal.* 27 (Moralia 869D).

152 Travlos, *Pictorial Dictionary*, p. 121.

153 See Podlecki, *Themistocles*, pp. 173–7 and 179, n. 27, who suspects that Themistocles was especially devoted to Artemis; Themistocles is also credited with setting up after Salamis a sanctuary of Aphrodite in the Piraeus.

154 See C. M. Bowra, *Greek Lyric Poetry*, 2nd ed. (Oxford, 1961), pp. 308–72 and Podlecki, *Themistocles*, pp. 49–54.

155 Anecdotes nos 9, 10, 11, below, p. 216.

156 Plutarch *Them.* 15.2.

157 See below, p. 111.

158 Plutarch *Them.* 21.2. Simonides uses the Doric form Lato (for Leto) in his verses.

159 See notes 142 and 143 above.

160 Plutarch *Them.* 21.4.

161 The word κόλουρις, 'stump-tailed', may mean one who has lost his tail (i.e. was exiled), or it is a synonym for fox.

162 Athenaeus 10.416A quoting Thrasymachus of Chalcedon.

163 Plutarch *Them.* 5.4.

164 Herodotus 6.21 and above, p. 38; Phrynichus was fined one thousand drachs and no one was to perform the play again.

165 Suidas, *s.v.* 'Phrynichus'; cf. also *Tragicorum Graecorum Fragmenta* 1, edited by Bruno Snell (Göttingen, 1971), pp. 74–7.

166 For the evidence and the problems see Lenardon, *op. cit.*

167 Anecdote no. 22, below, pp. 219f.

168 Anecdote no. 24, below, p. 220.

CHAPTER VII

169 Thucydides 1.95 and 128.3–135; in my close paraphrase of Thucydides, I have combined both passages in order to present a continuous and chronological account of Pausanias' career. See also Gomme, *Commentary* 1, pp. 431–7; and Epistles 2, 14 and 16, translated below, pp. 157f., 178ff., 181ff.

170 It is cause for wonder that Xerxes ignores Pausanias' proposal of marriage to his daughter and that, according to Herodotus (5.32), Pausanias was engaged to Megabates' daughter, 'if the story is true'.

171 The outcome, as we have seen, was the formation of the Delian Confederacy in the spring of 477 under the command of the Athenian Cimon, vehemently pro-Spartan and anti-Persian in his sentiment.

172 This golden tripod was set upon a bronze pillar of three intertwined snakes; this pillar (the famous serpent column) stands today in Istanbul; see *ATL* 3, pp. 95–100. According to Pausanias (3.8.2) the offensive, deleted epigram was composed by Simonides.

173 Diodorus (11.45.6) offers a dubious variation illustrating the traditional character of Spartan motherhood: Pausanias dies within the temple and the Spartans block up the entrance following the example of Pausanias' mother, who stoically sets the first brick in place.

174 E.g. P. J. Rhodes, 'Thucydides on Pausanias and Themistocles', *Historia* 19 (1970), pp. 387–400 and J. F. Lazenby, 'Pausanias, Son of Kleombrotos', *Hermes* 103 (1975), pp. 235–51 review various theories and provide ready access to earlier literature.

175 For a perceptive study of the narrative of Pausanias and Themistocles and its role in Thucydides' *History* see Brent Malcolm Froberg, *The Dramatic Excursuses in Thucydides' History* (unpub. diss., The Ohio State University, 1971).

176 Diodorus 11.54–5.

177 Plutarch *Them.* 22.3–24.1.

178 Leobates, variant in Plutarch, *De Exsil.* 15 (*Moralia* 605E). For the identification of Leobotes see P. J. Bicknell, 'Leobotes Alkmeonos and Alkmeon Aristonymou' in *Studies in Athenian Politics and Genealogy* (*Historia, Einzelschriften* 19, 1972), pp. 54–63.

179 There is no good exhaustive treatment of the problems that I know of. See M. de Koutorga, 'Mémoire sur le Parti Persan dans la Grèce Ancienne et le Procès de Thémistocle', *Académie des Inscriptions et des Belles-Lettres* 1ᵉ sér. 16 (Paris, 1860), pp. 361–90; G. L. Cawkwell, 'The Fall of Themistocles' (*Auckland Classical Essays*, London, 1970), pp. 39–58.

180 Longinus *Peri Heureseos* (C. Walz, *Rhetores Graeci* 9 [Stuttgart, 1832], pp. 548–9. For similar late rhetorical treatments of critical episodes in Themistocles' life see Podlecki, *Themistocles*, pp. 124–6.

181 See below, p. 202.

182 It has been conjectured that Argos after 494 became more democratic and that *c.* 470 the open hostility of Argive anti-Spartan policy is reflected in their acceptance of Them-

istocles; the flight of Themistocles *c.* 467 and the collapse of the Argive democracy are thus to be connected; see W. G. Forrest, 'Themistocles and Argos', *Classical Quarterly* 10 (1960), pp. 221–41.

183 The indictment may have been preserved by Craterus, who in the late fourth century compiled a collection of decrees; he is quoted by Plutarch elsewhere (*Arist.* 26.1 and *Cim.* 13.5).

184 Plutarch *Arist.* 25.7; cf. Epistles 3, 8 and 18; Lucian *On Slander* 27.

185 R. J. Lenardon, 'Charon, Thucydides and "Themistocles",' *Historia* 15 (1961), pp. 20–32.

186 W. R. Connor, 'Lycomedes Against Themistocles? A Note on Intragenos Rivalry', *Historia* 21 (1972), pp. 569–74.

187 See P. J. Rhodes, *The Athenian Boule* (Oxford, 1972), pp. 62ff.; cf. A. R. W. Harrison, *The Law of Athens, Procedure* (Oxford, 1971), pp. 50–9.

188 See note 174 above and Robert J. Lenardon, 'The Chronology of Themistocles' Ostracism and Exile', *Historia* 8 (1959), pp. 30–2.

189 *Ath. Pol.* 25; if this treatise is not by Aristotle, the error concerning Themistocles may perhaps be more readily comprehensible.

190 Aristotle *Politics* 2.12.

191 For differences between the accounts of Aeschylus and Herodotus see A. J. Podlecki, *The Political Background of Aeschylean Tragedy* (Ann Arbor, 1966), pp. 131–41.

192 Aeschylus *The Persians* 353–432.

193 Aeschylus *The Persians* 447–71.

194 Podlecki (*Themistocles*, pp. 37 and 198) suggests that Aeschylus wrote *The Persians* in support of Themistocles and that at the time of its performance in March, 472, Themistocles was an unsuccessful 'candidate' for ostracism and was actually ostracized in the spring of 471.

195 I have argued that the play was written on Themistocles' behalf (Lenardon, *op. cit.*, pp. 29–30 with note 34); but I am no longer confident about my hypothesis.

196 I.G. II² 2318.

197 See Aeschylus *The Persians*, translated with commentary by A. J. Podlecki (Englewood Cliffs, N.J., 1970), pp. 19–20.

CHAPTER VIII

198 Thucydides 1.136.1. Nepos *Them.* 8.3 explains that the Corcyraeans were afraid that the Spartans and Athenians would declare war. Cf. also Epistles 17 and 20 below, pp. 184, 186f.

199 Plutarch *Them.* 20.3. Cf. also Herodotus 8.112, 168 as a possible inspiration for or confirmation of these later elaborations.

200 Plutarch *Them.* 24.1 and POxy 1012C(fr. 9), 11, 22.23–34; the common source may be Theophrastus and ultimately an Atthis. See L. Piccirilli, 'Temistocle εὐεργέτης dei Corciresi', *Annali della scuola normale superiore di Pisa*, Classe di Lettere e Filosofia, Serie 3, vol. 3.2 (Pisa, 1973), pp. 317–55. Themistocles' interest in the West, his friendship with Corcyra, and his opposition to Corinth anticipate events preliminary to the outbreak of the Peloponnesian War in 431, when Athens joined with Corcyra against Corinth. Thus Themistocles' association with the Corcyraeans is pertinent to the thematic material in book 1 of Thucydides.

201 Or by reading ἀσθενέστερος for ἀσθενεστέρου 'Indeed in the present circumstances, he would be a victim who was much weaker than Admetus and the noble thing to do . . .' See Gomme, *Commentary* 1, p. 439.

202 Thucydides 1.136.2.

203 *Acharnians* (425 BC), 326ff. and *Thesmophoriazusae* (411 BC), 689ff.

204 Homer *Odyssey* 7.133–81.

205 Plutarch *Them.* 24.2.

206 It is characteristic of Diodorus, as we have seen, to omit the role of the Athenians altogether in the pursuit of Themistocles.

207 Diodorus 11.56. Notice how in Thucydides we have the appeal of Themistocles; in Diodorus the speech of the Spartans; and in Epistle 20 a full-blown rhetorical exchange between the Spartans and Admetus.

208 Contingent upon the dual tradition is whether or not Admetus was away upon Themistocles' arrival and the role of Admetus' wife (or others) in the whole affair.

209 Nepos *Them.* 8.4 says that Themistocles seized Admetus' daughter; but is is easy to emend *filiam* (daughter) to *filium* (son). Nepos' statement (8.3) that Themistocles took refuge with Admetus, with whom he had a bond of guest-friendship, may also be emended by inserting a negative; but Nepos may merely be anticipating the scene of suppliancy which follows. Piccirilli, *op. cit.*, pp. 351–5, sees Ephorus as the source for both Nepos and Diodorus, who writes that at first the King received Themistocles kindly. It is just possible that the omission of Admetus' hostility may be due to the remnants of the hostile tradition that depicted Themistocles as a traitor who had been in league with the Persians. Thus the logic of his flight was determined by a systematic recourse to those who were his friends, i.e. the Corcyraeans, Admetus and Xerxes.

210 See my comments against the extreme scepticism of critics, R. J. Lenardon, 'The Chronology of Themistokles' Ostracism and Exile', *Historia* 8 (1959), p. 36, n. 68. But we must be critical, even of Thucydides!

211 Schol. Thucydides 1.136.2; Schol. Aelius Aristeides 46.233.17. Piccirilli, *op. cit.*, pp. 348–51, suggests Porphyry's Commentary on Book 1 of Thucydides as the source. We cannot date Themistocles' service to the Corcyraeans or the appeal of Admetus precisely, assuming that they are historical. Perhaps they both belong shortly after Salamis.

212 Plutarch *Them.* 24.2–25.1. The story, as told by Plutarch, is suspect on other grounds; cf. Herodotus 7.158 where Gelon would join the Hellenic forces against Xerxes, if he were given supreme command.

213 If, somewhere in this confused tradition, it is supposed to be news of Hieron's death (*c.* 467) that deters Themistocles, we have another indication for the chronology of the flight.

214 Diodorus 11.56.2.

215 Nepos *Them.* 9.1.

216 Thucydides 1.137.2.

217 Plutarch *Them.* 25.3.

218 Nepos *Them.* 8.6.

219 Plutarch *Them.* 25.2, 26.1.

220 I have discussed these problems at length elsewhere: Lenardon, *op. cit.*, pp. 23–48.

221 E.g. Pausanias 1.1.2: Themistocles' sons returned from exile since they dedicated in the Parthenon a portrait in which Themistocles appeared. Cf. also Pausanias 1.26.4 (below, p. 150).

222 See Davies, *Propertied Families*, pp. 215 and 217–18; Podlecki, *Themistocles*, pp. 206–7.

223 Cf. Philip Deane, *Thucydides' Dates, 465–431 BC* (Don Mills, Ontario, 1972), who challenges the more traditional chronology of Gomme, *Commentary* I, pp. 389–413 and *ATL* 3, pp. 158–80.

224 Yet I wonder if the confusion between Naxos and Thasos merely represents textual corruption in either Thucydides or Plutarch rather than any real conflict between two genuine historical traditions.

225 I have argued for the following chronology (Lenardon, *op. cit.*): ostracism *c.* 474/3; 471/0 condemnation and flight; 465/4 letter to Artaxerxes. Cf. Podlecki, *Themistocles*, pp. 195–9, who also attempts to be precise; spring 471 ostracism; late 470 or 469 condemnation and flight. But we cannot be sure.

CHAPTER IX

226 Thucydides 1.137.3.

227 Thucydides may mean 'proceeding up to Susa' (ἄνω) and his Persian escort could be from Sardis (κάτω); see *ATL* 3, p. 201 with notes 40 and 41.

228 For the difficulties of this reference to Themistocles' message or messages to Xerxes see above, p. 83 and Gomme, *Commentary* I, pp. 440–1. I have deliberately tried to convey the ambiguity of the Greek in my literal translation. Thucydides may mean that Themistocles wrote to Xerxes (in one rather than two messages) to flee and that the bridges were safe or perhaps (and this to me seems less likely) Thucydides refers first to the message about the impending Greek retreat from Salamis and secondly to the message about the preservation of the bridges.

229 The Greek διάνοια may here refer specifically to Themistocles' plans or ambitions, although it may also generally connote his character and wits, i.e. political intellectualism.

230 Plutarch *Them.* 27.1. Nepos *Them.* 9 and 10, follows Thucydides closely and believes Themistocles met Artaxerxes, not Xerxes.

231 E.g. *ATL* 3, p. 201.

232 The following narrative of

Themistocles' travels represents a fairly close paraphrase of Diodorus 11.56.4–8.

233 Herodotus 7.27, mentions a Lydian named Pythius, son of Atys (the son of Croesus?), who entertained Xerxes and his army at Celaenae in the time of the Persian Wars.

234 Are Lysitheides and Nicogenes supposed to be one and the same man or have two distinct friends of Themistocles become confused in the tradition?

235 Plutarch *Them.* 27; Nepos (*Conon*, 3) tells a story about the Athenian admiral Conon that bears some similarities to this interview between Artabanus and Themistocles. Artabanus was the man who murdered Xerxes and helped Artaxerxes win the throne.

236 Plutarch *Them.* 28.

237 Plutarch *Them.* 29.

238 In this context Plutarch records the anecdote about the nature of language, no. 30 below, p. 221.

239 In this context dealing with Themistocles' affluence or power, Plutarch quotes Themistocles' remark to his children; see anecdote no. 31 below, p. 221.

240 This is the Demaratus who accompanies Xerxes to Greece in 480. The story may be a fiction to bring these two great exiles (Spartan and Athenian) together but Themistocles, as far as we know, could have encountered Demaratus.

241 Athenaeus 1.54 (28f–30a); cf. 12–49 (535e). Demaratus like Themistocles was given certain cities by the Persian King.

242 Diodorus 11.57; it has been suggested that romantic details came from a *Persika*, used by Ephorus; Podlecki, *Themistocles*, pp. 93–8, following Jacoby.

243 Plutarch *Them.* 30 and 31.

244 I have been free in my interpretation of the section of the story to avoid the ambiguity and confusion of a literal translation.

245 Strabo 14.C647 preserves another tradition: Themistocles' wife served as priestess.

246 According to Perrin (*Plut. Them. and Arist.*, p. 254) it is 'probably an invention' but the inspirations that he suggests for the fiction are by no means compelling.

247 Although we have no other evidence for this office of water-commissioner (ὑδάτων ἐπιστάτης) in the fifth century, such a post for Athens is in itself not incredible. Perhaps these duties were part of some other office that Themistocles held. The office ἐπιμελητὴς τῶν κρηνῶν is attested in the fourth century.

248 Thucydides 1.138.5; Diodorus 11.57.7.

249 Plutarch *Them.* 29.7; Athenaeus 1.54 (29F–30A).

250 Gomme, *Commentary* 1, p. 292 with n. 4.

251 *ATL* 3, pp. 111–13. The second half of the pertinent lines is restored but the names of Themistocles and Cleophantus appear on the stone.

252 The authors of *ATL* 3, p. 112 suggest the following: the hostility against Themistocles ceased after the Peace of Callias in 449; then the festival was instituted, after Cleophantus was recalled to Athens; Cleophantus probably was present at the celebration dedicating honours to him and his descendants but his residence was in Athens rather than Lampsacus. I do not believe that the reference in Plato's *Meno* (93D) to Cleophantus compels us to believe that he waived his title in Lampsacus.

253 Athenaeus 12.45 (533D–E); a crowned magistracy for Themistocles may be an anachronism; Podlecki, *Themistocles*, p. 42, suggests he was *prytanis.* See also anecdotes nos 31 and 32, below, p. 221.

254 Pausanias 1.26.4, with notes by J. G. Frazer, *Pausanias' Description of Greece* 2 (London, 1898), pp. 328–9. There was a magnificent temple of Artemis Leucophryenian ('White-browed') at Magnesia. See also Podlecki, *Themistocles*, p. 177.

255 Plutarch *Them.* 32.5.

256 Concerning the coinage see the following for discussion and fuller bibliography: Gisela M. A. Richter, *The Portraits of the Greeks* (London, 1965), pp. 98–9; Bauer (rev. Frost), *Themistokles*, pp. 135–8; Podlecki, *Themistocles*, pp. 169–72.

257 Plutarch *Them.* 12.1.

CHAPTER X

258 For the contents and history of Palatinus 398 see A. Diller, *The Tradition of the Minor Greek Geographers*, Philol. Monographs of the American Philol. Assoc. 14 (1952), pp. 3–10.

259 I have used the text with a Latin translation in R. Hercher, *Epistolographi Graeci* (Paris, 1873), pp. 741–62, with *adnotatio critica*, pp. lxxix–lxxxij. I follow most of the emendations suggested by J. Jackson, 'The Text of the Epistle of Themistokles', *Classical Quarterly* 19 (1925), pp. 167–76; 20 (1926), pp. 27–35.

260 For a discussion of the nature of the epistles, their problems and their historicity, including the identification of names, see R. J. Lenardon, 'Charon, Thucydides, and "Themistocles",' *Phoenix* 15 (1961), pp. 28–40 and Carl Nylander, 'ΑΣΣΥΡΙΑ ΓΡΑΜ-ΜΑΤΑ Remarks on the 21st "Letter of Themistokles",' *Opuscula Atheniensia* 8 (1968), pp. 119–36. Podlecki, *Themistocles*, pp. 129–33, offers a brief survey.

261 Suidas, *s.v.* 'Themistokles'.

262 His penalty is just because he is so stubborn or because he can now fulfil his obligations to the Argives.

263 Another possible interpretation is: 'Finally they begged me not only to treat them as though they were responsible for what had befallen me but also not to treat with insulting contempt the good fortune of our encounter.'

264 The text is difficult and probably deliberately ambiguous; Themistocles is condemned by the irony of his situation—whether he accept or reject the Argive offer he will appear guilty to those who do not know the real situation. Also it might appear reprehensible to run away from the opportunity for power.

265 Jackson's emendation of the first sentence is most plausible; it allows for a delay at Cyllene in keeping with what is implied later in this same letter and stated explicitly in Epistles 17 and 20. Thus one of the arguments that adduce conflicting testimony in the letters as an argument for multiple authorship is eliminated.

266 This argument is elaborated in Epistle 5, where Themistocles maintains that the Spartans are anxious to transfer their guilt and the guilt of Pausanias to the Athenians and Themistocles.

267 A precious bit of oratory typical of this epistle and difficult to render in English. The height of the various manifestations of the strange behaviour of the Athenians is the fact that, after ostracizing him and thereby imposing flight or exile, now they force a second kind of flight or exile upon him; thus the play on words.

268 Another flight of rhetoric involving the difference between the Athenian and Spartan character and the question of who is following whom in their witch hunt.

269 Aristeides was from the deme Alopeke; the Greek word for fox is ἀλώπηξ, εκος.

270 Pausanias, the son of King Cleombrotus, was regent and not king of Sparta.

271 Jackson's restoration of the name Sybaris (see Plutarch *Them.* 32) makes good sense; Hercher's text leaves the daughter unnamed. But Plutarch says that Sybaris married the Athenian Nicomedes.

272 Plutarch *Them.* 23.41.

273 Perhaps this clause should be negative as the Latin translation suggests: 'I acted in a way that you would not have expected.'

274 I follow Jackson's emendation; Hercher's text reads: I met your Cratesipolis and Stratolaus (your messengers? friends? relatives?) there and gave them a letter.

275 The manuscript reads Arybdas.

276 The Greek here at best is ambiguous. It may mean: 'I boarded a merchant vessel of Alexander of Macedon; its current destination was Pydna, but it was expected to sail from there to Asia.' Whether or not the implication is that Themistocles had boarded the ship before it stopped at Pydna, I see no serious conflict with Epistle 20 in the treatment of this episode.

277 This last section may mean: 'Please write news both from you and your sister not to Admetus himself . . . but to Cratesipolis, since she appears to care about me no less than the two of you.'

278 The text reads τισιννέον (?).

279 The text of this clause is corrupt and suggested emendations are extremely tenuous.

280 The date would be in October.

281 This is the best I can do with a difficult text and absurd argument.

282 Plutarch *Them.* 23.

283 Agryleus, Scambonides and Prasieus are deme-names.

284 Leager is described as *synephebos*, which may also imply that he served with Themistocles in their early education.

285 See Plutarch *Arist.* 5.

286 Diodorus 11.27.2.

287 Cleon is suggested by Jackson for Molon, the emendation in Hercher's text.

288 A particularly troublesome sentence, possibly because of a lacuna. I have provided a free interpretation.

289 The reference is presumably to the rebuilding of the walls.

290 Or with Hercher: 'The disparity in our fortunes and the weakness that is the affliction of exiles have already dissolved our enmity.'

291 Possibly the gist of another very corrupt sentence.

292 See Epistle 3.

293 τὸ κοινὸν δικαστήριον τῶν Ἑλλήνων

294 Another baffling sentence.

295 The name Artaxerxes does not appear in this letter as we have it. Is the omission deliberate or has the name been obliterated by a corrupt text? Notice how the initial stages of the conversation between the King and Themistocles do not make it clear whether Xerxes or Artaxerxes is intended.

296 Or following Hercher's text: 'not gratifying either the Athenians or the Spartans'.

297 Or following Jackson's emendations: 'My soul promises to accomplish these goals, if backed by your strength, with which I shall wreak. . . .'

298 Nylander, *op. cit.*, pp. 123–4.

CHAPTER XI

299 Thucydides 1.138.4–6.

300 Cicero *Brutus* 11.

301 Plutarch *Them.* 31.5 (translated below) makes a distinction between those who said bull's blood and poison.
302 Aristophanes *Knights* 83–4. Unfortunately I do not know how we can be sure that a jocular exchange such as this is not a later insertion.
303 Diodorus 11.58.1–3.
304 Plutarch *Them.* 31.3–5. Late accounts add that Themistocles was sacrificing to Artemis at the time of his suicide; see Podlecki, *Themistocles*, pp. 114 and 177.
305 Plutarch *Cimon* 18.4–6. In his biography of Cimon, Plutarch feels compelled to provide a contrast that is pejorative to Themistocles.
306 Herodotus 3.15. Percy Gardner, 'A Themistoclean Myth', *Classical Review* 12 (1898), p. 21 also lists Jason, Midas, Smerdis (Cambyses' brother) and finally Hannibal imitating Themistocles.
307 I am indebted to K. M. Abbott for obtaining this excerpt from a letter by Dr von Haam. Pliny's observation (*N.H.* 11.222, cf. 28.147) quoted by Gardner, *op. cit.*, p. 22 seems to substantiate to some extent von Haam's observations: 'The blood of bulls very quickly coalesces and congeals and therefore becomes very noxious (*pestifer*) to drink.' Gardner observes that heated bull's blood, although not lethal, will make one ill.
308 For discussion and bibliography see: Perrin, *Plut. Them. and Arist.*, pp. xvi and 256–8; Bauer (rev. Frost), *Themistokles*, pp. 137–8; Podlecki, *Themistocles*, p. 171.
309 Nepos *Them.* 10.4. For the text and its problems, see below, pp. 201f.
310 See Gardner, *op. cit.*, pp. 21–3.
311 See Alden A. Mosshammer, 'Themistocles' Archonship in the Chronographic Tradition', *Hermes* 103 (1975), pp. 227–9.
312 I have analysed the confused and

conflicting evidence at length elsewhere: Robert J. Lenardon, 'The Archonship of Themistokles, 493/2', *Historia* 5 (1956), pp. 413–16.

CHAPTER XII

313 Nepos *Them.* 10.3–4; some read *statua* for *statuae* in Nepos' text.
314 It is impossible to know how one should relate the evidence, especially of Nepos, to the fact that the Magnesians, *c.* 400, transferred their original settlement slightly inland from the coast of Ionia. The ambiguity of a tomb or cenotaph in the forum of (old?) Magnesia probably developed early, unless Thucydides' account was written after the foundation of the new town. See Podlecki, *Themistocles*, p. 177.
315 *The Greek Anthology*, ed. and trans. W. R. Paton (Loeb Classical Library, vol. 2). See also Podlecki, *Themistocles*, pp. 133–4. No. 73 is attributed to Tullius Geminus, nos 74 and 235 to Diodorus (of Sardis, or Tarsus or Zonas), no. 236 to Antipater of Thessalonica, and no. 237 to Alpheius of Mytilene.
316 Schol. Aristophanes *Knights* 84b.
317 Plutarch *Them.* 32.2–3.
318 Pausanias 1.1.2. Aristotle *History of Animals* 599b9, mentions a Themistokleion in a sheltered and marshy place, which may designate the tomb or some other structure. Davies, *Propertied Families*, pp. 215–16, thinks that he detects a reference to the tomb in a late inscription.
319 See Paul W. Wallace, 'The Tomb of Themistokles in the Peiraieus', *Hesperia* 41 (1972), pp. 451–62. Cf. also J. G. Frazer's note to Pausanias, 1.1.2, *Pausanias's Description of Greece* 2 (London, 1898), pp. 21–2 and Podlecki, *Themistocles*, pp. 177–8.
320 On the basis of a very corrupt

fragment of Hermippus, Gomme (*Commentary* 1, p. 446, note 1) conjectures that first there was a promontory of Themistocles, later to be called his tomb.

321 Byron, *The Giaour*, 11.1–6, quoted by Wallace, *op. cit.*, p. 458, n. 12.

CHAPTER XIII

322 Cf. Podlecki (*Themistocles*), who presents a thorough survey of the sources; see also W. den Boer, 'Themistocles in Fifth-Century Historiography', *Mnemosyne*, 4th ser. 15 (1962), pp. 225–77.

323 Herodotus 7.139.

324 Thucydides 1.138.3.

325 Lysias 2.42.

326 Thucydides 1.74.1.

327 Some believe that, because of their Herodotean flavour, the excursuses on Pausanias and Themistocles were written early; for others they are so uncharacteristic of Thucydides that they must have been composed by someone else!

328 Themistocles' interest in the West is indicated not only by his flight; he offers the curious threat at Salamis of Athenian withdrawal to Siris in Italy. In addition, there are the names of his daughters, Italia and Sybaris, which some take very seriously; see G. E. M. de Ste Croix, *The Origins of the Peloponnesian War* (Ithaca, 1972), pp. 378–9.

329 Diodorus 11.58–9.

330 For further discussion and bibliography of this and other possible but more doubtful depictions of Themistocles see Gisela M. A. Richter, *The Portraits of the Greeks* (London, 1965), pp. 97–9; also Bauer (rev. Frost), *Themistokles*, pp, 135–8 and Podlecki, *Themistocles*, pp. 143–6.

331 Some of this evidence has already been discussed: Plutarch *Them.* 22.1–2; 32.3; Thuc. 1.138.5; Diodorus 11.58.1; Nepos *Them.* 10.3; Pausanias 1.18.3; Philostratus the Elder (*Imag. Themistokles* 433, ed. Kayser); and Aelius Aristeides *Oration* 14.161.13 with scholion (ed. Dindorf, vol. 2, p. 215 and vol. 3, pp. 535–6).

CHAPTER XIV

332 Plutarch *Them.* 18; *Reg. et Imp. Apoph. Them.* (*Moralia* 184F–185). I have omitted here two episodes listed in the latter work since they seem incongruous in the present context: no. 3 on the bribery of Epicydes and no. 6 on Themistocles' messages to Xerxes.

333 Plutarch *Them.* 18.1.

334 Aelian *V.H.* 3.21.

335 Plutarch *Them.* 3.3–4; *Thes.* 6.9; *Reg. et Imp. Apoph. Them.* 1 (*Moralia* 184F–185A); *De Prof. in Virt.* 14 (*Moralia* 84C); *De Cap. ex Inim. Ut.* 6 (*Moralia* 89F). Cicero *Tusc.* 4.19.44. Valerius Maximus 8.14 ext. 1. Libanius *Declam.* 9.12.

336 Plutarch *Them.* 2.5.

337 Athenaeus 12.45 (533D) and 13.37 (576C), quoting Idomeneus, who did not make it clear whether Themistocles harnessed the prostitutes to his chariot like horses or whether they rode with him in his four-horsed chariot. Themistocles allegedly drove through the Ceramicus into the agora.

338 Aelian *V.H.* 2.12. Plutarch *Them.* 2.6. Nepos *Them.* 1.2. For the sentiment cf. Epicharmis frag. 285.

339 Plutarch *Them.* 18.2; *Reg. et Imp. Apoph. Them.* 8 (*Moralia* 185C).

340 Plutarch *Them.* 18.1. We cannot be sure if Plutarch is referring to the generalship of Themistocles, or the archonship or some other office.

341 Plutarch *Them.* 5.1–21.

342 Cicero *De Fin.* 2.32.104; *De Orat.* 2.299 and 351; *Acad.* 2.1.2.

343 Plutarch *Them.* 5.5; Perrin, *Plut. Them. and Arist.*, pp. 190–1.

344 Plutarch *Them.* 5.4; once again one cannot be certain about the designation of Themistocles' office. He is an arbitrator (κριτής) in disputes. As general (στρατηγοῦντος) he tries to be a good official (ἄρχων) despite Simonides. See also Plutarch *Reg. et Imp. Apoph. Them.* 9 (*Moralia* 185D); *De Vitios. Pud.* 15 (*Moralia* 534E); and *Reip. Ger. Praec.* 13 (*Moralia* 807B). Actually the anecdote involves a pun on the Greek words μέλος and νόμος.

345 Plutarch *Arist.* 2.4.

346 In Herodotus (8.59) and Plutarch (*Reg. et Imp. Apoph. Them.* 4, *Moralia* 185B) the verbal exchange is between Themistocles and Adeimantus. But in *Themistocles* 11.2, Plutarch replaces Adeimantus with Eurybiades, perhaps to lead more naturally into the following anecdote in which Eurybiades is about to strike Themistocles.

347 Plutarch *Them.* 11.3; *Reg. et Imp. Apoph. Them.* 5 (*Moralia* 185B). Aelian *V.H.* 13.40. Diogenes Laertius 6.21. Aelius Aristeides 46, *Pro Quattuor* (ed. Dindorf, Leipzig, 1829, vol. 2, p. 258) and Schol. *ad. loc.* 613.

348 Herodotus 8, 61. This sentiment with variations was proverbial; cf. Thucydides 7.77.7 among many others.

349 Herodotus 8.60.

350 Plutarch *Them.* 11.5; *Reg. et Imp. Apoph. Them.* 14 (*Moralia* 185E). Aristotle *H.A.* 4.1 (524b.23). The cuttle-fish was a distinctive motif on contemporary coinage of Eretria, examples of which survive. See Holden, *Plut. Them.*, pp. 100 and 208; also Perrin, *Plut. Them. and Arist.*, pp. 203–4.

351 Aelian *V.H.* 2.28.

352 Plutarch *Them.* 18.2; *Reip. Ger. Praec.* 13 (*Moralia* 808F). Ammianus

Marcellinus 30, 8.8. The battle referred to is presumably Salamis, although it could be Marathon.

353 Herodotus 8.125; How and Wells, *Commentary* 2, p. 276. Belbina, a small island about ten miles south of Sunium, is chosen, like Seriphus, to exemplify a completely insignificant place. Plato *Rep.* 1.4 (329E). Plutarch *Them.* 18.3; *Reg. et Imp. Apoph. Them.* 7 (*Moralia* 185C). Cicero *De Sen.* 3.8. Origen *Cels.* 1.29 (347E).

354 Plutarch *Arist.* 24.4.

355 Plutarch *Them.* 17.2. Aelian *V.H.* 13.43. Pausanias 8.50.3. Themistocles *Epistle* 8.

356 Plutarch *Them.* 25.1. Aelian *V.H.* 9.5.

357 Plutarch *Them.* 22.1; *Reg. et Imp. Apoph. Them.* 13 (*Moralia* 185E); *Reip. Ger. Praed.* 15 (*Moralia* 812B). Johannes Damascenus (ed. Meineke, in Stobaeus, vol. 3, Leipzig, 1856, p. 186).

358 Plutarch *Them.* 18.4; *Quaest. Rom.* 25 (*Moralia* 270B–C); *De Fort. Rom.* 8 (*Moralia* 320F).

359 Aelian *V.H.* 13.40. The verb that I have translated as impeached (ἐτίμασαν) may refer to his removal from office (the generalship?) and perhaps a trial.

360 Plutarch *Reg. et Imp. Apoph. Them.* 13 (*Moralia* 185E): *De Se Ips. Ctr. Inv. Laud.* 6 (*Moralia* 541E). Aelian *V.H.* 9.18.

361 Aelian *V.H.* 9.18.

362 Plutarch *Them.* 2.3; *Cim.* 9.1 (quoting Ion of Chios). Cicero *Tusc.* 1.2.4 Procopius *De Aed.* 1.1.7.

363 Plutarch *Them.* 29.3; *Reg. et Imp. Apoph. Them.* 15 (*Moralia* 185E–F).

364 Plutarch *Them.* 29.7; *Reg. et Imp. Apoph. Them.* 17 (*Moralia* 185F); *De Fort. Alex.* 1.5 (*Moralia* 328E); *De Exil.* 7 (*Moralia* 602A). Aelius Aristeides 21, *Palinod. Smyrn.* (ed. Dindorf, Leipzig, 1829, vol. 1, p. 433). Stobaeus 40.8 (ed. Meineke, vol. 2, Leipzig, 1856, p. 65).

365 Athenaeus 12.45 (533D–E) quoting from Clearchus' treatise *On Friendship* 1.
366 Plutarch *Them.* 18.5; *De Lib. Ed.* 2 (*Moralia* 1C); here the claim is voiced by the boy Cleophantus himself; *Reg. et Imp. Them.* 10 (*Moralia* 185D); *Cat. Ma.* 8. See Perrin, *Plut. Them. and Arist.*, p. 229, who notes how the story, as well as others, is given a different turn in different contexts.
367 Plutarch *Them.* 18.5; *Reg. et Imp. Apoph. Them.* 11 (*Moralia* 185E). Cicero *De Off.* 2, 20.71. Valerius Maximus 7.2 ext. 9. Stobaeus 85.11 (ed. Meineke, vol. 3, Leipzig, 1856, p. 138); elsewhere Stobaeus attributes a similar remark to Pericles (70.17) and to a Spartan, on the authority of Serenus (72.15). A variation is offered by Diodorus Siculus

10.32 (fragment, Loeb Classical Library, vol. 4): Themistocles gave this advice (i.e. to look for a man lacking in money rather than money lacking a man) to the wealthy Euryptolemus, son of Megacles, who wanted a rich son-in-law. Euryptolemus agreed with Themistocles, who furthermore suggested that he marry off his daughter to Cimon; as a result Cimon became wealthy.
368 Plutarch *Them.* 18.5; *Reg. et Imp. Apoph. Them.* 12 (*Moralia* 185E). Stobaeus 37.30 (ed. Meineke, vol. 2, Leipzig, 1856, p. 45).
369 Plutarch *Reg. et Imp. Apoph. Them.* 2 (*Moralia* 185A). Dio Chrysostom *Oration* 2 (22M, 79R) attributes this remark to Alexander.
370 Cicero *Pro Archia* 9.20.

BIBLIOGRAPHY

Subsidiary and specialized books and articles will be found in the notes. The following list includes works (with abbreviations used) of general interest or referred to frequently.

HISTORIES OF GREECE AND THE PERSIAN WAR

Bengtson, Hermann, *Griechische Geschichte von den Anfängen bis in die römische Kaiserzeit*, 4th edition (Munich, 1969).
Burn, A. R., *Persia and the Greeks: The Defence of the West, c. 546–478 B C* (New York, 1962).
Bury, J. B., and Meiggs, Russell, *A History of Greece to the Death of Alexander the Great*, 4th edition (New York, 1975).
Ehrenberg, Victor, *From Solon to Socrates: Greek History and Civilization During the Sixth and Fifth Centuries B C* (London, 1968).
Green, Peter, *Xerxes at Salamis* (New York, 1970); *The Year of Salamis 480–479 B C* (London, 1970)
Hammond, N. G. L., *A History of Greece to 322 B C*, 2nd edition (Oxford, 1967).
Hignett, C., *Xerxes' Invasion of Greece* (Oxford, 1963).

BIOGRAPHIES OF THEMISTOCLES AND CRITICAL STUDIES OF THE EVIDENCE

Bauer, Adolf, editor, *Plutarchs Themistokles für quellenkritische Übungen*, 2nd edition augmented and revised by Frank J. Frost, *Themistokles: Literary, Epigraphical and Archaeological Testimonia* (Chicago, 1967). Abbr. Bauer (rev. Frost), *Themistokles*.

Flacelière, Robert, editor, *Plutarque Vie de Thémistocle* (Paris, 1972).

Flacelière, Robert, Chambry, Emile, and Juneaux, Marcel, editors, *Plutarque Vies*, vol. 2 (Paris, 1961).

Holden, Hubert A., editor, *Plutarch's Life of Themistokles*, 3rd edition (London, 1892). Abbr. Holden, *Plut. Them.*

Levi, Mario Attilio, *Plutarco e il V secolo*, Biblioteca Storica Universitaria, vol. 5 (Milan, 1955).

Papastavros, J., *ΘΕΜΙΣΤΟΚΛΗΣ ΦΡΕΑΡΡΙΟΣ* (Athens, 1970).

Perrin, Bernadotte, translator and editor, *Plutarch's Themistocles and Aristeides* (New York, 1901). Abbr. Perrin, *Plut. Them. and Arist.*

Podlecki, A. J., *The Life of Themistocles: A Critical Survey of the Literary and Archaeological Evidence* (Montreal and London, 1975). Abbr. Podlecki, *Themistocles*.

Walsh, Jill Paton, *Farewell Great King* (New York, 1972). A biographical novel of Themistocles for young adults.

OTHER WORKS CITED

Davies, J. K., *Athenian Propertied Families, 600–300 B C* (Oxford, 1971). Abbr. Davies, *Propertied Families*.

Gomme, A.W., *A Historical Commentary on Thucydides*, vol. 1 (Oxford, 1945). Abbr. Gomme, *Commentary* 1.

How, W. W. and Wells, J., *A Commentary on Herodotus*, 2 vols (Oxford, 1912); reprinted with corrections 1928. Abbr. How and Wells, *Commentary*.

Meritt, Benjamin Dean, Wade-Gery, H. T., and McGregor, Malcolm Francis, *The Athenian Tribute Lists*, vol. 3 (Princeton, 1950). Abbr. *ATL* 3.

Travlos, John, *Pictorial Dictionary of Ancient Athens* (New York and London, 1971). Abbr. Travlos, *Pictorial Dictionary*.

SOURCES OF ILLUSTRATIONS

American School of Classical Studies at Athens 1–14; Alison Frantz 15; J. S. Morrison and R. T. Williams, *Greek Oared Ships 900–322 B.C.*, 1968, Cambridge University Press 18; Trustees of the British Museum, London 19, 28a, b; Hirmer Fotoarchiv 20; German Archaeological Institute, Athens 22, 23; Third Archaeological District of Athens 24; Drawing by J. Travlos 25; J. Threpsiades 26; Staatliche Museen zu Berlin 27a, b; Bibliothèque Nationale, Paris 29a, b; G. M. A. Richter, *The Portraits of the Greeks*, Vol. 1, 1965. By permission of Phaidon Press Ltd 30; Courtesy of the Oriental Institute, University of Chicago 31; Antonello Perissinotto 32; University Library, Heidelberg 33; German Archaeological Institute, Rome 35

INDEX

A. Index of ancient authors quoted in the text and those mentioned only in the notes, with approximate dates (centuries) and references to *FGrH* (= Felix Jacoby, ed., *Die Fragmente der griechischen Historiker*, Leiden, 1926).

B. General Index